Woodstock at 50

Woodstock at 50

Anatomy of a Revolution

AIDAN PREWETT

Library and Archives Canada Cataloguing in Publication available upon request.

Political Animal Press
www.politicalanimalpress.com

Distributed by the University of Toronto Press

ISBN: 978-1-895131-38-3 (Paperback)

978-1-895131-39-0 (eBook)

Cover design by Klassic Designs

Printed and bound in Canada

CONTENTS

PART THREE

PART FOUR

PART FIVE

for Felix and Parker, my flower children

There's a time when the operation of the machine becomes so odious, makes you so sick at heart, that you can't take part; you can't even tacitly take part. And you've got to put your bodies upon the gears and upon the wheels, upon all the apparatus and you've got to make it stop.

—Mario Savio, Free Speech Movement leader, Berkeley 1964

Preface

In 2014, I completed a feature documentary called *A Venue for the End of the World.* For three years, it enjoyed a wave of interest during the lead-up to and fallout from the American election. The timing was perfect — the film set out a blueprint for taking command of a large audience.

In 2016, the film was picked up for North American distribution, just as the Trump/Clinton campaigns were kicking into high gear. Central themes included propaganda and the audience/performer relationship, both of which came into sharp focus in the 2016 political sphere.

Now, just three short years later, these themes have become even more relevant to our political landscape. Pop communication has become a primary mouthpiece for many of our most highly regarded institutions and organizations. Political systems around the world are taking America's lead. The line between the political and popular spheres has all but disappeared.

A Venue for the End of the World featured Woodstock as the prime example of an audience that defied the political structures of the wider society — quite the opposite of the organized mass gatherings that were key elements of fascist movements just a few decades earlier. Woodstock became a touchstone for the film. The festival represents so much more than just its *prima facie* hippie image. In its own time, Woodstock was the ultimate symbol of personal freedom in the face of oppressive adversity. The stories that emerged from that long weekend in 1969 center around people coming together, helping each other, and experiencing a collective spirit. It was about a new form of music, but it was also about gathering the members of a new form of culture. They came to be known as the Woodstock Nation, and on August 15, 1969, the world realized just how prevalent this culture had become.

As my documentary developed, more and more Woodstock participants signed on to be a part of it. I knew we were onto something special. I also knew I was going to record many more Woodstock moments than I would ever be able to fit into the film. The interview subjects were telling fascinating stories and painting them with incredible detail. I would never dream of cutting these conversations short. As the cameras rolled, I began to realize that this oral history would one day find its own place to exist. This book is it.

With all the excitement and re-imagined chaos of Woodstock 50 — amid this charged new political era — now is the perfect time to present these interviews in their purest form. Thanks for joining me as we take a trip back to Woodstock, exploring some of the most remarkable viewpoints of the sixties, and appreciating their profound relevance in today's bizarre political landscape.

Introduction

I

Part of the beauty of Woodstock was that it was *dangerous*. This internationally newsworthy gathering was truly frightening to the political establishment that was forced to watch as a new social movement gained traction and pushed for anti-war, non-conformism, and critical thinking. Woodstock was the ultimate act of defiance; it stared down the establishment in a public rebuke of outdated ideology and provided validation for the idea of unity among human beings. The festival was, of course, somewhat less dangerous for the half-a-million mud-soaked attendees. On Max Yasgur's farm in upstate New York, the youth of America stood up and made themselves heard.

In the years that followed, the festival came to occupy its own corner of twentieth century history. It became a kind of folklore fairytale, complete with giants, gods, miracles, and a magic bus. It was almost *too big* to be of human origin. As the myth-making took over, the public perception of Woodstock homogenized. It became safe. The reductive narratives created something marketable. Corporations started to take advantage of the outdoor festival brand and began to build a new empire. Lollapalooza, Coachella, Burning Man, Glastonbury: these festivals now spearhead their own multi-billion-dollar industry, and they do so by existing within a clearly defined space that challenges little of the social order.

Woodstock, on the other hand, was a power unto itself. Woodstock questioned authority. And in that very spirit, we can't simply accept the story of Woodstock as it's been handed to us. To honor the festival, we must challenge its mythology.

This book is an exploration of Woodstock and its place in history, through my interviews with performers, crew, and filmmakers who found themselves at the very heart of it. These are interviews with the people who occupied major roles onstage, backstage, and amongst the crowd itself. Later, these unique voices are joined by a number of other sixties icons who provide an illustration of the era in which Woodstock existed — from Bob Dylan's "Judas" moment, to the inner workings of the Kennedy White House. We're taken to the Paris riots, and we discover what it feels like to be featured on *Richard Nixon's Enemies List*. This brings us to the present day, where we explore modern audience concepts and Woodstock parallels with some of today's new music stars. We are then joined by theorists, professionals, and scholars who provide further insight into the psychology of crowds, defiance/obedience, and the Freudian aspects of mass gatherings.

What happened at Woodstock is truly fascinating and we explore the events of the festival here in detail, but our chief aim is to get to the crux of *why* Woodstock happened in the way that it did. What chain of events occurred that led half a million kids to converge on a farm in upstate New York, and to remain peaceful for a mud-soaked three-day period without sufficient food, water, amenities, or personal space? The answers are often surprising.

We explore the festival through the lens of music as a tool of the revolution. We look at the origins of and variety of influences upon large-scale performances and dissect the underlying systems that facilitate them. Why do crowds go one way or another? Can techniques and processes devised by nefarious forces also be harnessed for good?

This book has been separated into five parts, arranged largely in historical order: Woodstock, Post-Woodstock, Present Day, Psychology, and Conclusions. Each part follows a central thread as we delve into the labyrinth of twentieth century music and pop history. These conversations have been carefully curated to provide unique insight into the intersection between politics and music.

Spiritually, this book is a child of the film *A Venue for the End of the World*. This can be seen in the way that interviews are conducted and arranged, sometimes in a non-linear form. This book, however, quickly grew into something more distinct and bigger than its parent. This is an independent document, breaking away from the rigidity of the previous generation. Here, we are provided a much more complete treatment of the subject, with key points outlined by relevant experts. Bookending each chapter, further detail is provided to create a sense of historical context, and some startling revelations.

II

The era in which Woodstock existed encompassed some of the most disturbing political events of any decade post-World War Two. The sixties themselves seem to be a chain of events that set the world on a new and unfamiliar course: John F. Kennedy is elected in 1960. The early decade sees the Bay of Pigs invasion and the Cuban Missile Crisis. The U.S. military presence in Vietnam escalates. Then Dallas happens.

If Kennedy had lived, the world of today might have ended up a very different place. The Vietnam war may have ended much sooner. We might still have Bobby and Dr. Martin Luther King, Jr. — alive and in their nineties. But after that first assassination, Lyndon Johnson escalates the conflict in Vietnam. By 1968, student riots against this post-World War II establishment are erupting in Paris and soon spread around the world. The Chicago Democratic National Convention is interrupted by fervent protests and police brutality. Nixon is elected. By early 1969, the My Lai massacre comes to light. The subsequent trial of an American officer for 109 Vietnamese civilian deaths pushes the anti-war movement into the global spotlight. The moon landing in July. Then the Manson family murders occur, just seven days prior to Woodstock.

And then — three days of *peace* and music. When it comes to mythmaking, the real miracle of Woodstock was not simply that 456,000 people descended on a small town in upstate New York. The miracle was that in a climate that had been so recently saturated with extreme violence, almost none occurred at the festival.

Violence did occur at the Altamont Speedway Free Concert later that year. What had been marketed as a kind of Woodstock for the West Coast quickly turned ugly and resulted in four deaths — one, a stabbing in front of the Rolling Stones' stage. The concert became a kind of *Twilight Zone* version of Woodstock; a flashpoint for societal tensions just as Woodstock was a release of those tensions. The malevolent nature of Altamont was captured in the Maysles brothers' documentary *Gimme Shelter*. It is a difficult film to stomach. Several of our interview subjects were present for both Woodstock and Altamont. Their insight into these counterpoint festivals, and into the audiences' exhibited behavior, is startling to say the least.

We also speak with those who held key creative roles in the Oscar-winning documentary *Woodstock*, which exudes all the positive energy that exemplifies the spirit of the festival and continues to entrance viewers today.

Post-Altamont, the hippie movement began to come unstuck. The same tools which were seen to promote their peaceful message at Woodstock were so easily bent to other ends. For reasons we'll come to understand, the crowd went its own way. After the precedent of Woodstock, how could the same sort of festival go horribly wrong? Was the hippie dream a delusion, or was Altamont just badly orchestrated? Why did these festivals turn out so differently? Why did the crowd turn?

Crowd behavior, it turns out, is a topic of note for many performers. Of particular interest is the way that crowds might exhibit a kind of collective consciousness or become a singular entity. As we find out, many performers will reference the Nüremburg rallies when asked about the power of the stage. The idea of a crowd as a seething mass, an entity unto itself, made up of individuals who are merely cells, draws us back to another documentary: Leni Riefenstahl's *Triumph of the Will*. In this 1935 propaganda film, we see Hitler greeted as a god by throngs of worshippers under designer Albert Speer's Tower of Lights. The audience is depicted by turns as ordered, obedient, and in a state of ecstasy. Speer developed a multitude of systems for influencing audience reaction, many of which can still be found in performances and political rallies today.

Of all our subjects, we ask about their experience of *the crowd*. What does it feel like to hold sway over thousands of people? What does it take to command an audience? What is the psychology of all of this? We follow these threads, where we realize that mass gathering events tend to follow designs set out by some of the more nefarious forces of history. Could the modes and orders of Woodstock be rooted in something more frightening? Is there an inhuman monster at the heart of this intricate labyrinth?

III

The parents of the Woodstock generation were all affected by war: by rationing, by conscription, by propaganda and by loss of family and friends. The war was a major part of the collective consciousness.

Also in the American collective consciousness were images shown in theatres across the country. Frank Capra's documentary series *Prelude to War*, produced by the United States Department of War (now called the Department of Defense), was screened everywhere with patriotic fervor. The film won the 1943 Academy Award for Best Documentary, and six sequels were produced between 1943 and 1945.

Present throughout this series of films was persistent imagery of crowds. Hitler's crowds, Mussolini's crowds, Stalin's crowds, Hirohito's crowds. The film painted the crowds in these countries as brain-washed followers of evil cults. The films depicted masses of seething bodies; no longer individual people, but a diseased, unrecognizable, inhuman throng.

> From *Prelude to War (1942)*:
>
> Voiceover: *Taking advantage of their fanatical worship of the God Emperor, it was no great trick to take away what little freedom they had ever known.*
>
> *Yes, in these lands, the people surrendered their liberties and threw away their human dignity. They gave up their rights as individual human beings*
>
> Crowd: *Sieg Heil! Sieg Heil! Sieg Heil!*
>
> Voiceover: *And became a part of a mass, a human herd.*

Over the coming decades, these images returned to cinema screens — and then television — whenever repercussions from the Second World War made the news. Which was a lot. But the message became skewed. The footage of these mass gatherings reinforced two important ideas in the minds of the Baby Boomers:

1. Mass gatherings are politically powerful; and
2. Mass gatherings seemed frightening, intense, exciting, and maybe a little bit *fun.*

On the one hand, these films depict something vile. But on the other hand, in the Pan-American psyche, maybe everyone wants to be part of the unthinking mass. Besides, people could relate to this footage because this was the exact crowd behavior that they were seeing with Elvis. Then the Beatles. Then Hendrix. The tyrants of the Second World War were the original rock stars. Hitler was the archetype.

> Voiceover: *Stop thinking and follow me, cried Hitler.*
> *I will make you masters of the world.*
>
> *And the people answered, Heil!*
>
> *Stop thinking and believe in me, bellowed Mussolini.*
>
> *And I will restore the glory that was ruined.*
>
> *The people answered Il Duce! Il Duce!*
>
> *Stop thinking and follow your God-Emperor cried the*
>
> *Japanese War-Lords, and Japan will rule the world.*
>
> *And the people answered: Banzai! Banzai!*

After the Second World War, American designers took a page from the book of their defeated enemies. Post-Nüremburg, the manipulation of crowds became an art form of its own. And as we'll discover, the staging of both Woodstock and Altamont was indeed influenced by nefarious forces.

Woodstock features heavily in *A Venue for the End of the World* as a kind of antidote to these fascist rallies. The hippie movement, and Woodstock in particular, was permeated by the mantra *Think For Yourself, Question Authority*, one of Dr. Timothy Leary's catch phrases. This ethos underpins the Woodstock experience. So in order to properly honor the festival, to truly celebrate Woodstock for its fiftieth anniversary, we have to *question* it. We have to examine its mythology and think for ourselves in order to rediscover the *danger* that was inherent in the event itself. We're not here to debunk popular stories or to mute our appreciation, but it is important to balance our affection for Woodstock with critical thought. We owe it that much.

This book attempts to both appreciate Woodstock and to recover its archetypal element of danger. The fiftieth anniversary is a time to re-examine the reasons Woodstock captured our hearts, but it's also a time to enter the labyrinth. What we find is not always "peace and love." But what we find is most certainly human.

PART ONE
Woodstock

In the wake of the Second World War, society was hit with some sobering realities. Entire regions needed to be rebuilt. The world now lived under the specter of the mushroom cloud. Participants in the Woodstock Music and Art Fair were born during or in the immediate aftermath of the war. They were raised in the fifties — a difficult time for many, especially for people of color, for women, and for those with alternative political views. These kids came of age in the late sixties, where they began a movement to shrug off the cultural expectations of this previous generation.

So when the kids of New York were promised a festival in the country, where they could escape the realities of life and spend three days locked in ritualistic bliss with their fellow flower children, they *all* decided to go.

As people poured in, a labyrinthine system of passages emerged, formed by human bodies and their various detritus. The Dionysian elements are palpable — perhaps the ancient Greek god of wine and dance, of irrationality and chaos, was presiding over the festival in the guise of festival organizer, Michael Lang.

Thirty-two musical performances took place over three-and-a-half days in August 1969. Some of the world's hottest acts were billed — along with some new names that rode the Woodstock wave to the top of their game. Jimi Hendrix, Janis Joplin, Jefferson Airplane, Joan Baez, Santana, Joe Cocker, The Grateful Dead, The Who, The Band, Johnny Winter, Creedence Clearwater Revival, Canned Heat, Sly and the Family Stone, Crosby, Stills, Nash and Young, Country Joe and The Fish, Ravi Shankar, Richie Havens, and Arlo Guthrie were just some of the major draws.

Along with Michael Lang, the curly-haired face of the festival — the Theseus who would slay the untamed Minotaur and become King of Athens — three other men were key to the initial planning of Woodstock. The money came from John Roberts, heir to a toothpaste and denture fortune, and his partner, Joel Rosenman. The pair were putting together a sitcom pilot called *Young Men with Unlimited Capital*, a semi-autobiographical farce. They were knocked back by the major studios, so they decided to take out a newspaper advertisement to see what other ideas they could attach their money to. They used the title of their sitcom pilot as the header. Five-thousand people sent proposals. Among these, concert promoters Michael Lang and his promotion partner Artie Kornfeld brought them the idea of Woodstock.

After two failed attempts to obtain council permits, the festival finally settled its location as Bethel, New York, on the farm of a Mr. Max Yasgur. The people of Bethel were told to expect around fifty thousand people. The festival drew 456,000 people, defying even Michael Lang's most optimistic expectations of maybe a hundred thousand. Aerial photographs show roughly a million more who tried to get in before the New York State Thruway was totally clogged — traffic around Bethel was at a standstill for the duration of the festival as festival-goers simply abandoned their cars on the road and walked the last few kilometers. Fences at the festival site were not completed in time; what fencing did exist was promptly torn down and a great many thousands of people enjoyed the festival for free.

In her article for the twenty-fifth anniversary of Woodstock in *Life* magazine, Joni Mitchell writes that the people who were there "saw that they were part of a greater organism." We'll explore this concept in much greater detail throughout this book.

We're about to hear from the people who were there — major players in the heart of the most iconic music festival of all time. For each of them, we delve a little further into the societal context that surrounded their involvement. What brought them — and so many others — to Woodstock?

Chapter 1

Country Joe McDonald

Just across the Bay Bridge from San Francisco lies the university city of Berkeley, California. By all accounts, a socially liberal town with a strong tradition of protest. In the 1930's, students at the University of California, Berkeley campus led massive demonstrations against the end of the United States' disarmament policy and the approaching war. In the 1950's, protest centered around McCarthyism and prompted the largest student demonstrations in the U.S. up to that point. Larger protests followed.

Berkeley rose to notoriety in the mid-sixties as a hub for anti-war activity. Students at the U.C. Berkeley formed the Free Speech Movement, and in 1965, ten thousand protestors took to the streets in America's first major Vietnam war protest. The world was watching. Berkeley was news.

The Free Speech Movement had already gained political traction in October 1964 during an incident involving an impromptu sit-down strike surrounding a single police car on campus. Inside the car was one of the Free Speech Movement's founders, Jack Weinberg. Weinberg had been arrested for distributing literature in what had recently been designated a non-political zone. The crowd surrounding the police car quickly grew to an estimated three thousand. The car was unable to move for thirty-two hours, and demonstrators, including Mario Savio, climbed onto the roof of the car to deliver speeches and run continuous public discourse until the charges against Weinberg were dropped.

The Free Speech Movement staged one of the first occupation protests later that year. Joan Baez attended and performed in support of the demonstrators. Over two thousand students were involved. Then-Governor Edmund Brown Senior approved a mass arrest, and 773 students spent the night in county jail.

In 1966 Ronald Reagan won the Governorship of California on a platform that included "cleaning up the mess in Berkeley." He started an occupation of his own: the National Guard maintained a month-long presence on a patch of the university grounds that came to be known as People's Park. Rioting occurred intermittently throughout this period and resulted in the use of nightsticks, tear gas, and rubber bullets. Berkeley has remained a politicized locality ever since. A natural home, therefore, for the man who fronted of one of the first great protest bands — Country Joe and the Fish.

This part of Berkeley is a beautiful residential area, lined with trees, broad nature strips, and big houses. We knock on the front door. It opens quickly. Joe was expecting us, and we were right on time. Setup is quick; I don't want to waste any of Joe's time. He's a pro, and I get the sense he expects those he works with to be just as professional.

Joe is seated on a high-backed lounge chair with a sheepskin rug covering. Looking around the room, only a couple of small framed concert posters above the mantle give any clue to his rock 'n' roll stardom. And a star he is. At Woodstock he took total command of that crowd. Four-hundred-and-fifty-six-thousand people. All of them singing along in unison to words McDonald wrote.

His performance is immortalized in the *Woodstock* documentary. Upon release, theater audiences would sing along word-for-word with a little help from a bouncing ball above the words presented on screen. McDonald is wearing an old army jacket — a reminder to those in-the-know that his time in the military lends him a certain credibility when it comes to writing protest songs.

The protest anthem *I-Feel-Like-I'm-Fixin'-To-Die Rag* meant a lot to that audience. Every one of them would have known someone who got drafted, often a close friend or family member. Many would enter the next decade without a loved one.

And so a certain solemnity is blended with the irreverence of Joe's opening Fish Cheer: "Gimme an F!" "Gimme a U!" The audience roars. They really mean it. "What's that spell?" It was all directed at Washington.

Aidan Prewett: How did it come about, that you would perform the *Fish Cheer* at Woodstock?

Joe McDonald: I remember driving out really early. We were taken in cars through a back way on a little road and parked; walked up on the stage. You couldn't really see anything from the road. And then I walked up the steps onto that stage and looked out at the audience. It was a panorama of people. I had seen large audiences before, but this was really — I mean, it was so large that you had to turn your head to look at it. Really, when you looked one way, your peripheral vision didn't take in the whole audience. It was also upswept, so it went up and over a crest. I was really amazed and delighted that it was such a big crowd of people.

That Friday I had been on the stage most of the time, watching the acts and enjoying it — and I was going to play with the band on Saturday evening. On Saturday they had delays throughout the day. The Santana band had difficulty getting their equipment through, because of the crowd. The promoters knew me, and they came over and asked me if I would perform something — just to fill in the dead space in between the acts. And I said I hadn't counted on doing that, so I made a lot of excuses, and I said I didn't have a guitar.

They found a guitar for me, and then I said I didn't have a guitar strap — they cut a piece of rope and tied a piece of rope onto the guitar and just pushed me out there. I had no idea what to do because I had been working with the rock 'n' roll band for several years then, and my whole repertoire was geared toward the band. I had done folk music before that, just standing with my guitar, so I sang a few old songs — I sang a few Country Joe and the Fish songs, and nobody paid any attention to me at all.

It was a beautiful day, they were chatting amongst themselves, and picnicking — it was like a huge family picnic. The atmosphere was really grand. I sussed out that nobody was paying any attention to me after about half an hour. I walked off-stage and went to my associate, who was part of the production staff of Woodstock, Bill Belmont. Nobody even noticed I'd left the microphone. I asked if it would be okay if I did the cheer and the Vietnam song, because I'd been saving it for later on with the band. And he said, "Nobody's paying any attention to you at all, so what difference would it make *what* you do?" And so I was kind of emboldened and I went back and I thought, *okay*, I relaxed and I just yelled — "Gimme an F!" And they all responded, they stopped talking to each other, they looked *at* me, and then one thing led to another, I couldn't stop. They all started singing along and clapping and standing up. And it was filmed — that's just the way it happened.

AP: And of course, this is post-Monterey.

JM: Well, I think that people learn how to behave at concerts from what happens previously. So the Monterey festival had been filmed and people had seen it, so the attitude of audiences was changing in a way. So the audience that came to Woodstock was more used to being the new kind of sixties audience. As opposed to the old kind of audience. Because in the old kind of audience — I'm talking about how people would dress up and it would be a formal occasion, and you were often seeing people that you didn't feel you had much in common with.

If it was a classical event, they were wearing tuxedos and that sort of thing. Or if it was a band, they were wearing blazers with their name on it. And you usually saw one or two acts and that's about all. So this was a new way — '69… Monterey was '67, so people were pretty used to it. Also, the counterculture was happening, so the audience was — we were all part of the new, at this point, international counterculture. As opposed to the old establishment, which we felt pretty much estranged from.

AP: Did you feel that you were being subversive, in that estrangement? To highlight that?

JM: I think by '69 the division was being erased and we were becoming the status quo. And I think that was pretty much obvious as far as the audience is concerned. Because of this magnitude — the *size* of it — that *we* were the status quo. Because there were half a million of us. And there were so many acts. So it wasn't the beginning of a brand new thing, but it was a brand new thing that it was taking over. And we had that feeling of empowerment there. We hadn't been empowered in the box office yet, as far as film and recording and stuff. But as far as live performance, it was obvious that we had something. We had an audience, and we had a sound, a way of living, and a way of acting, a way of dressing. And it was taking over. We really felt it strongly.

AP: This kind of kinship that existed between the audience and performer, at both of those performances — is that something that is a common occurrence for a performer?

JM: Well, no. The sixties was a peculiar historical moment. Because the generation — the Korean war and afterwards' generation — felt estranged and divorced from the previous generation, the World War II generation. I think it was a thing that was happening *globally* actually. The tradition and the cultural expectations of that World War II generation were wearing thin, and they were boring. Pretty much boring, to us. We were bored with the music and everything. And we began doing our own thing.

But as an entertainer I have played to audiences that I didn't feel that kinship with. If you're showing up at your "job," then sometimes your job is just to play the music that the audience likes, and you don't feel that connection. You don't feel a kinship with them. But it began to change in the sixties. We began to have our own audience. We had a lot in common. And one thing in particular that we had in common was not feeling safe in the status quo. We felt they were out to get us. To draft us into war, or arrest us for smoking marijuana, or one thing or another. They didn't *understand* us.

Of course, it's different in America, because we didn't have a lot of thousand-year-old traditions. But in old European countries and such, you'd be playing the music that your great great grandfather enjoyed, and your grandfather enjoyed, and your grandmother. Everybody's doing the traditional dances that were done for hundreds of years. I don't know exactly what that feels like. But I did play in dance bands when I was in high school. And we would play Glenn Miller dance tunes, and the audience would do the foxtrot and that sort of thing. Starting in rock' n' roll, rhythm and blues eras, it began to change. It changed pretty quickly.

AP: Going back to Woodstock, for one second — was there a sense of power, standing in front of that many people?

JM: There was power in the event itself, and there was power in having them respond. I mean, I felt a part of – and the power came from the audience. Before doing the interview, I was thinking of different situations that you can have. Like, in a stadium, generally speaking, the people are observing something that's happening down below. And oftentimes, it's competitive. So, there'll be one team and another team, and ... it's a competitive spirit going on. Or in the traditional Roman stadium, the people in the stadium are oftentimes being killed — it was their *last* act. For us, at Woodstock, it was very different. We were all *one*. And we were one in a brand new way, and a real way. It made us — we were empowered, as a generation.

I've always loved outdoor events. When I was in high school, I was in the band and we played for football games and things. I like music outside. And I was enjoying that. And I was surprised that they responded the way they did to me. I was happy enough to just be a part of it, but when they responded so enormously.... In the film, it really pops out at you. But there, it wasn't quite so dramatic, I suppose. Because the sound dissipates, and the crowd was so big. But definitely there was something happening. And it was great. It was — I often equate it to a family picnic. It seems ridiculous, but it was like a huge family picnic. It was huge. And it was fun. It was great fun.

AP: We're attempting to investigate the sense of that power — as it was used at Woodstock in such a positive way — there's also the complete opposite, where it's used in a negative way. The most clear example of that that I can think of is the Nüremberg rallies where Hitler was getting out there in front of thousands and thousands of people and doing the complete opposite of what was happening at Woodstock. Do you have any thoughts on — as someone who has had command, in a certain way, of thousands of people — hundreds of thousands of people — do you have any thoughts on the relationship between the negative and positive?

JM: Well you're putting a label on it, negative and positive — but I don't think that the Nazis — and there have been many situations like that, where a particular group, an interest group, has a particular rally, and the focus of the rally is *us and them*. But I think that the dynamic is the same as at Woodstock. Somebody's doing something on-stage, and the people in the audience are digging it. They're *digging* it, you know? The theme is different — at Woodstock it was "Can't we all get along — peace and love," at Nüremberg it was "Kill those other people, and we'll take over and we'll kill those other people." But that's just the nature of human beings, I think.

I think it was unique — to have a gentle, kind, loving, cooperative.... But I wonder if there was a kind of cooperative spirit amongst the Nazis. Maybe somebody would get hurt, and they'd say "Can I help you out, brother? You seem to have hurt your leg...." Were they kind to each other? I don't know. Perhaps. There's always that dynamic.

But another thing that's interesting about Woodstock — using the Woodstock thing — is that they had planned staging, but it didn't work out. Like at the Nüremberg rallies, a lot of thought went into staging. And in most shows, a lot of thought goes into staging. How the staging will affect the audience, and the surprises and fireworks going off and that sort of thing. At Woodstock there really wasn't anything. There was just the music, and the vibe. And it worked, fantastically.

Just in the past couple of years, I did the Isle of Wight — like three years ago, where the Rolling Stones were the headliner. They brought with them some effects and staging, but generally speaking, it was pretty unelaborate. I think maybe this was a unique kind of thing. Where just the music and the vibe and the feeling is what people came for. And enjoyed. And that was enough. And it wasn't particularly leading to anything else. In your example of Nüremberg and the rallies, it was leading toward a political power. We didn't have a feeling that we were creating a Woodstock nation at the moment. And it was a leaderless movement, also. I think we were reacting to what had happened in the past, more than what would happen in the future. I don't think we were giving much thought to the future.

AP: Did you see a kind of collective consciousness?

JM: Yes, but I don't think that we knew we shared a collective consciousness before Woodstock. We were discovering that we shared it, when we came together. And I think in my moment when I sang the Vietnam war song, and people stood up, we were all acknowledging that *yes*, we all felt pretty much the same way about this particular war. It had that feeling to it, that we were meeting each other for the first time. Now, sometimes, when you go to an outdoor rock concert — it's not a first-time thing, or a second-time thing. It's a many *many* times thing. People say, "I've been to fifteen Rolling Stones concerts," or "I've been to fifteen Grateful Dead concerts" or something. It becomes a club. It wasn't a club then.

AP: Could you tell us about the army jacket you wore. The patch that read *Everett*?

JM: Well that's just a coincidence. We shared clothes, we didn't have *clothes* — it was just this army jacket that floated around in the band, and Barry Milton and I sometimes wore it, sometimes didn't wear it. And I just happened to be wearing it. It was one of those serendipitous moments, in which things came together. But it was a moment when the wearing of army surplus, military surplus clothes was — it's still trendy. Only now, they make military clothes that they sell in fashion boutiques. But we discovered that we were wearing cast-off clothing. With pride. Not because we were poor. We *were* poor, but we just wore it because — we would do anything but be like *them*. The status quo. The middle-class status quo.

It's also amazing to me that it was a feeling of shared empowerment among middle-class nations on the planet. So that the middle-class post-WWII generations were feeling the same disenchantment — an estrangement from the generation that came before. We're at a same kind of particular moment in history right now — with those same nations and other nations — the morality of the new generation is so in clash with the old generation. In this case, homosexuality or shared income or recreational drugs — a lot of issues. I don't know if this is a new thing or a cyclical thing, but it was certainly that kind of a moment. And it was a great joy in experiencing it collectively — without an agenda, a hidden agenda. Well, the hidden agenda I suppose, was from the promoters wanting to make money. But it wasn't hidden, because America is a capitalist country. You know, if you can make money, you make money. But they didn't make money. What was accomplished was something else.

AP: I was really fascinated to read about how Country Joe and the Fish got its name. I thought it was a very clever twisting of those words into something new and exciting. Could you tell us that story?

JM: Well, in 1965 I was putting out a little tiny magazine — by little tiny, I mean we sold maybe twenty-five issues or fifty issues of the magazine — listing shows around the Bay Area and music articles and some songs. We didn't have any copy; we didn't have enough material for the next bi-weekly issue and so we decided to record an album — a 7-inch extended play 33 1/3 album — and call it a talking issue of the magazine. And so, we did that, and there was a discussion of what to call the ensemble that was playing on the album.

This was a time in which a lot of middle-class college students were infatuated with communism. Discovering it for the first time. I grew up in a family that was in the American Communist Party, so I wasn't infatuated with it at all. But it was suggested that we call it Country Joe and the Fish because Mao Tse Tung, who was the communist leader of China at the time — communist China — had suggested in his military philosophies that "revolutionaries move through the people like the fish through the sea." And I said that was stupid. It just sounded stupid. Country Mao and the Fish.

Someone else said let's call it Country *Joe* and the Fish, after Joseph Stalin. Of course, if it was called Joseph Stalin and the Fish, that would have been stupid. But Country Joe and the Fish ... I thought it had a jug band ring to it, it had a nice sound to it. And it proved to be that too, because people remember the name. Country Joe and the Fish. Even if they haven't heard the music of Country Joe and the Fish, they remember it historically. So, it paid off pretty well, and that's what we did. I said, "Yeah that sounds fine, let's put it on the label." We sold a few copies of that record, and we began to use the name Country Joe and the Fish.

AP: And... could you explain to people of our generation that Country Joe was actually a pseudonym for Joseph Stalin?

JM: It was early Russian Revolution propaganda — to make him more relatable. He took on the nickname Country Joe, they used to call him that. He proved to be a lunatic on the level of Hitler, but at that time in history in the Great Depression, some Americans were experimenting with communism. My parents had come to be members of the American Communist Party, who were working for a lot of great laws and unions that we have nowadays, and we take for granted. And my father decided to name me Joe, after Joseph Stalin. And then, later on of course, the group was named Country Joe and the Fish. Which had nothing to do with me at all, it had to do with Joseph Stalin.

AP: You were in the Navy in the early sixties — were you involved in Vietnam?

JM: No. I wasn't involved in war. I was in the Navy from — when I was seventeen years old, to before I turned twenty-one, for three years and a few months. I was trained in air traffic control and I worked in flight operations. When I got out in '62 the Vietnam war was going on in secret, but it wasn't an active thing. And I never got recalled to go back in, so I had nothing to do with war, I'm happy to say.

AP: And yet you have taken on this veterans' advocacy role — how did you get involved with that?

JM: Well, I think being in the military — it makes you part of a fraternal order in a lot of ways. I think in every society, there's the military and the people in the military, and then there's civilians. And a lot of miscommunication and disinformation between the two groups. And I think just about everybody who was in the military identifies very strongly with that experience and other veterans. And so, when the war was going on, I was maybe the only popular entertainer who identified very strongly with the people fighting the war, the military personnel, and afterwards, and their problems. And I've always done that. But I don't do that with a separation. I do it as a military veteran, I feel very comfortable with other military veterans.

I realized that I had — one thing that enabled me to write *Fixin'-to-Die Rag*, and to perform it so comfortably from the stage for my generation, was that I had been in the military. It wasn't a mysterious thing to me. I was raised by people who were in the American Communist Party. They left the Communist Party because they didn't like it after a while and they realized that radical left-wing politics was wrong, radical right-wing politics was wrong, and I was also a hippie. You know, taking drugs and acting like a hippie. And so, I embodied those three things in the one thing that people think of as Country Joe McDonald. But not everybody understands the three groups that I come from. They … they're surprised to find out that I was in the military, or that my parents were in radical left-wing politics. But that makes me what I am today, and the attitude that I had toward those elements came together in the song, and my attitude towards performing it, too.

That's the difference, let's say, with the political rallies of Nüremberg. There's a fascistic, rigid attitude toward what they're saying. The right and the wrong of it. And I always shied away from that, because oftentimes when you're "right," you find out that you're wrong. And I liked the hippie thing because it was so loosey goosey. And what we were doing there was fun. I don't think Nüremberg was *fun*, in the way that Woodstock was fun.

I was thinking about professional sportspeople in a stadium. Is it fun the same way that going to an outdoor rock festival is fun? I don't think so, because there's always a loser, isn't there? So there's always that edge, that competitive edge, taken to a level of where people sometimes kill each other at these events. A level of winners and losers. But at a musical event, particularly the kind of event that came from the sixties and Woodstock — there really aren't any winners and losers. Most of the people didn't even pay, so it's very different. It's very different, and I love it. I'm so lucky to be a part of it, to make a living out of doing that. It's an incredible gift. I've always felt comfortable doing that. Being on stage in front of a large audience and seeing the way things will evolve and go. Sometimes you can feel a tension building up in the audience, and musically you can let it out — it's magical. Really, it's magic. You never really know where it's going to go. But for the most part, it always ends well. Very seldom does it end in bad way.

* * *

Joe insisted that he drive us a few blocks to the nearest BART station — San Francisco's Bay Area Rapid Transit. "Getting a taxi across the bay is stupidly expensive." We weren't about to argue.

I explained to Joe that his interview had really connected some dots — we were now sure that we had a film. Joe's answers delved into the history of performance in ways that I had never considered. In the space of a few years, the music scene went from fairly traditional dance music straight into electrified rock and roll. The cultural effect of this went far beyond just musical sensibilities. The cultural shift, the new ideas being presented socially and lyrically, was a key inspiration for the protest movements. The movements themselves had a power to them — and the musicians that came during and afterwards — Dylan, Baez, Seeger, McDonald — latched onto the zeitgeist and provided anthems for the people. Joe McDonald tells us that he was in fact *not* in control of the crowd at Woodstock, but he provided an outlet, a tangible expression of a feeling that was already there. Joe McDonald was a celebrity of the counterculture movement. He became a conduit for all things anti-war. His art gave voice to the crowd, leading them in a cathartic way to vent their frustration. In this way, Joe became a kind of benevolent demagogue.

In our next chapter, we'll discover some incredible parallels between the world of demagoguery and the world of rock. And one of the most important voices from Woodstock will take us into the heart of the Third Reich.

Chapter 2

Chip Monck

The voice hits you first. Deep, instantly familiar Matter-of-fact, but there is a warmth here and a discernible calmness that held sway over half a million people for three days in August 1969. As principal announcer, Chip Monck's voice curated so much of the Woodstock experience.

And suddenly I'm on the phone with this voice. Unmistakably.

It's a Friday night and I'm just getting back to my car. The phone rings, and the butterflies which have been threatening my guts all day suddenly kick into high gear. Chip had sent me an enthusiastic email earlier in the day and now he was calling to arrange the finer details.

"Hello, this is Chip Monck calling for Aidan Prewett."

He knows my name. The voice of the Woodstock Generation. The man who designed every Rolling Stones tour between 1968 to 1973. Tony Award nominated for set design of the original *Rocky Horror Picture Show.* Speaking to me now. But two sentences in, I'm completely at ease. Chip's intonation and turn-of-phrase is hypnotic. Ten minutes later and it's confirmed — two days of interviews over the coming weekend, plus access to a cache of original photographs from Stones tours and everything in between.

It turns out Chip lives in Fitzroy, just half an hour away. He's as charming in person as on the phone, or the record. We sit around his kitchen table, chatting about the project and ideas we both have for the project. It's only at this point that Chip fills me in on his encounter with a man named Albert Speer. I'm gobsmacked. Not only at the incredible paradox — the Rolling Stones head of production meeting with the designer of the Nüremburg rallies — but also at the notion that my degrees of separation from Hitler have just been dramatically reduced.

A quick tour of the house. Spanish Mission style. The front room features a large table covered in staging plans and diagrams. Next to it is an architect's drawing board. This is the house of a craftsman. A craftsman in the middle of a complete renovation. It's a constant work-in-progress, and Chip does all the work himself. More than fifty years in the business of designing and building sets for concerts and theatrical productions comes with some serious carpentry training. The backyard is messy — who has time for gardening with so much else going on? We stroll through to the biggest tool shed I've ever seen. It's old. Brick, with a flimsy wooden door. Once inside, a space that was probably built to hold two T-Model Fords is currently home to every variety of imaginable hardware, meticulously organized and clearly labeled in shelving. The wooden shelves are as old as the shed itself and seem mildly unstable. But if you needed any specific power tool, gauge of wire, plank of wood, nuts, bolts, screws, or rope you'd find it here.

I got to know Chip's place quite well. We spent two days recording as many of his stories as we could. This was followed by a third day a couple of months later to fill some gaps. Over the course of these interviews, I was taken through the breadth of Chip's life experience, from running away to join the circus to his time at John F. Kennedy's private home in Hyannis Port. And then there was his meeting with Albert Speer, Hitler's Chief Architect and Minister for Armaments and War Production....

Chip boils the kettle while I set up the camera gear. Checking the mic level, there's a touch of road noise — he lives on a tram line — but it adds to the atmosphere. We settle in. Let's go to Woodstock. I ask about the now-famous Brown Acid speech.

Chip Monck: "There's been a warning that you stay away from this, but it's your trip, so be my guest, but please be advised that there's a warning on this." And then I went right into another announcement, because there wasn't anything else to do. How many people had taken the brown acid? It was one of the most difficult announcements I'd ever made. Because *how many people were in danger, or how many people are now in danger?*

Aidan Prewett: So the audience could have gone either way with that — they could have panicked, or...

CM: Sure. Luckily enough there wasn't enough around. Or, who knows whether it was good or bad. I always make a joke about it, that I was selling the blue acid — I had to make the announcement. But it may have been just as silly as that. There's no way that any of us know. Because the doctor who's treating this person who is on a trip that is not working well, has told him he has taken acid and "what color is it?' "I think it's... *brrw.*" "That might have sounded like brown. So, all of a sudden, I get tapped on the shoulder, and brown acid is not a good idea. *Oh, great. Here comes another stone through the glass wall.*

There was a shortage of paper — so by the time you got an announcement again, you'd have to look on the reverse side and remember whether or not you'd already given that one. "Doris please meet Harry at tower number four to get your diet pills

— or your diabetes formula — because it's time for you to take your next pill." Which meant, "Bring me a joint."

I became sort of — the audience's information font. And whenever they got a little out of hand, the parenta l… a little more than guidance. There was a bit of: "Sit the fuck down, and if you punch him, I will come out there and punch you." And John Morris was great for his *love your brother* and all that crap, but I mean, for all intents and purposes that was not my existence. That's not what I was there for. I just performed a duty that I was tapped on the shoulder at seven o'clock in the morning the day we opened, and Michael Lang said, "By the way, I've forgotten to hire an MC and you're it."

AP: So did you feel like a shepherd in that sense?

CM: In a certain sense, yeah. But no — I'm not a shepherd. I might have had that position for a few moments and had to sustain it when it became a little touch-and-go at times. The best thing that happened to the audience and to the acts and the technical department, with the exception of the damage that it also caused, was the rain. The rain at Woodstock was magnificent, in as much as everybody looked exactly the same. They were all covered in cow shit and they all looked like drowned rats, nobody could tell one from the other. And basically, without that, we would have been in a very unpleasant place.

The other thing that was interesting was that everybody came up on-stage — all the other acts — and stood on the giant turntables that we were using to revolve the stage between acts. So, the turntables broke, and all of a sudden, we were *un-Fillmore-like* again. Where we had no immediate ability to change over one act to another, whether or not they were pre-set, sound-checked or anything else, we didn't have two front-of-house consoles, we didn't have two-monitor desks, so we couldn't pre-check anybody. If we had been that efficient, the point is — what would that audience have done for the twelve hours that they had off if we presented all of that day's acts in a twelve-hour period, then they had twelve hours off … *uh-oh.* Trouble. When you combine the rain, as well as the technical inability that we were left with, everything worked out just fine.

AP: Would you say that the crowd at Woodstock had a particular character?

CM: The Hog Farm made every effort to make it a particular character. It wasn't necessarily Monterey Music Love and Flowers. It was just — their orientation was one of a commune. And they expected everybody else to treat each other in that fashion — with great care and courtesy. Watch out for them, make sure they don't get hurt. If they are, get them to a hospital tent. Yeah, there was a solidarity there that was quite rewarding.

With 456,000 people, which was our pin-count — because we didn't have any scanners or computers — and the people under the trees couldn't be counted. We got past 456,000 and we figured, "ah well, we've counted enough. There are enough pins in that map." Everybody acted quite well. I think because, also — they were just so tired, and so beaten by the weather, and perhaps the lack of food and this, that, and the other thing. If they came there in a hostile mood for any reason, I think it ended by the time they broke down the fences. If there were any left by the time they got there. I mean, getting to Woodstock was a monumental task. One of John Morris's famous announcements: "The New York State Freeway is now a parking lot — it's closed!" Right? He was very pleased about that. He also found a copy of the paper — "This is a free festival! Everything's fine, isn't it wonderful?" He always brought the best aspects to the fore.

AP: Was there a particular moment at Woodstock that summed up the atmosphere for you?

CM: Well, there were twelve follow spots, which are carbon-arc, hard to operate unless you knew how to do it. So, when operators are getting a little tired of a three-day experience that happens to be disagreeable and uncomfortable, they would just leave. So, while there were people underneath the deck of the stage, loading film magazines, we ran follow-spot courses down there during the day. So, I'd go down and work with the people that had been literally dragged out of the audience when I'd made a couple of announcements — "Anybody ever run a follow spot? Raise your hand?" "Anybody ever run a carbon-arc follow spot?" And unfortunately, there weren't many hands. But I said, "Okay, you've got a job, and we'll pay you. Go to that point, tell them Chip says to let you in." So, they became follow-spot operators.

So, most of my time was consumed by trying to get done what I felt was necessary to get done — what I was hired to do. And dealing with John Roberts running up and down and screaming and yelling about the fact that the wires that took power to the follow spot positions on those four towers were unsafe because the mud was getting so thick that you would sink down and your foot was going to touch those wires. But they were heavily insulated.

Roberts was taken somewhere and sedated so he wouldn't keep running around worrying about people getting electrocuted. So there was some interaction with the audience, but it was — "I need you, you, and you because you raised your hand, come this way and I'll take care of you and get you fed and you'll work your ass off, but … there'll be somebody on the tower who if you don't know what you're doing, will help you."

AP: How did you feel that they reacted to *you* when you were…

CM: Well, I was scared to death. Michael Lang's second sentence after "You're it," was "and I think you'd better move that barrier back because with the crowd pressure they're going to be pushed against the camera platforms and they won't be able to see anything." So I explained to the audience that I needed their help. I said, "Alright, I know you've all got nice indentations in the mud, and you're probably feeling fairly comfortable and fairly well-oriented and you're ready for some entertainment. Well before we do that, I'm going to have to ask you a favor. Grab all your stuff, and I want all of you to stand up." And everybody stood up. I thought *well, maybe this is going to be okay.*

AP: How big was the crowd at that point?

CM: A hundred or so, more.

AP: A hundred people or a hundred thousand?

CM: A hundred *thousand.* They just kept coming. And I said, "Now we need each of you to take ten giant steps backwards. And I'll count them off for you. Here we go. We'll start with ten, nine...." *Holy shit it's working!* "Eight, seven.... Now, you'll probably find somebody else's imprint there in which to sit. I'm terribly sorry to have inconvenienced you."

"Now two guys are coming out with hammers, and we're taking our barrier, which happens to be two fence posts and a clothes line, and we're moving it back to where you are *because*, when the pressure comes from behind, you'll all end up with your nose against the plywood and you won't see anything for three days. So I think this is probably a worthwhile thing for you to have done, and I'm particularly grateful for you following my directions."

AP: So to see all of them moving, at your direction, what did that feel like?

CM: Lucky. Because otherwise there would have been inordinate difficulty and problems and very unhappy people, whether they paid or not. You knew something was going to break out because

I can't see anything. I can hear something, and I want to see it. So there was no way, without a proper barrier having been built, that our wooden barrier would have held itself together if people started pushing. Nowadays you push against it and you're standing on an L-shape – it's not going to allow that vertical to fall over. That's the way all barriers are made now, where the audience themselves are the counterweight that holds the barrier up, not the security that's behind them. Kinda simple physics, isn't it?

AP: And then when Hendrix played, was it a kind of culmination of everything you'd all been through?

CM: Absolutely. It was over, it was finished, it was done with. It was just something — you stood there with your mouth open. In his white leather — better-than-Daltrey fringe, with the beadwork. It's a stunning shot that will always remain in my mind.

AP: What was the feeling?

CM: Well, unfortunately there were only about forty-five or fifty thousand people left. But it was — they were absolutely awestruck. What a wonderful way to begin a week. Here's Monday morning. Some people saluted.

AP: Beautiful. So now the absolute flip side of Woodstock: How did Albert Speer come about?

CM: A trip to Switzerland, to Geneva. It was something that I thought I should do – lots of people thought I shouldn't do — but I got on a plane and I went to Geneva, and I made all the enquiries necessary, and I finally ended up having coffee with Albert Speer. Who, for those of you who might not be familiar with the name, wrote a book called *Behind the Third Reich*, and basically was responsible for the Volkswagen, for the armament of the German forces, and was a stellar designer. Everything that Hitler would appear at or be anywhere around was done by Herr Speer.

I brought a roll of plans and he brought a roll of plans, his wife translated. After I showed him the mirror and things I was doing for the Rolling Stones and what *I* did — and he had a good laugh at it — he then brought out the plans of Nüremberg. I was totally amazed that they were all hand-drawn — they were more like color washes that you would do with a little paint box.

And I only got him once, just before we were leaving, which was very amusing. There were vertical banners that were hung all along the stadiums at Nüremberg where there was the cathedral of lights. Where all the searchlights — carbon arcs at that time — were focused to create the illusion of being inside a gigantic glowing cathedral.

All the banners were hanging very close to the audience. That's where they should have been as far as design required them. But it came to light there were quite a few bloody noses and a lot of scars and sore heads — because he had put a piece of inch-and-a-half pipe in the bottom of each of the banners to keep it hanging correctly. So I sketched out on a yellow pad — which is my usual fashion when I'm not speaking the right language — that a water pocket or a sand pocket would have probably been more comfortable for the audience. And I got a "*hmpff*." And that was about the end of the interview.

AP: What was it about him that drew you in to that situation?

CM: The massiveness and the care and the meticulous design, I think. The ability to handle something that large, so well. It must be quite easy when you have the entire army and the force of the nation behind you, because they're told to. So you have every stagehand that ever was, taught or told to do whatever you told them to.

AP: Could you describe his character for us?

CM: I didn't feel any character at all. I just felt responses. There was no interaction, there was no interplay. I was a foreigner who was a young pup doing music, and here he is, basically designing armament and vehicles and huge staging. Too far apart. There was no mesh whatsoever. I was just curious. I just wanted to see — I wanted to take away with me more than I possibly could have. I just was interested to see — *how did that happen?* And not for my use to rush off to the Forum or Madison Square Garden and duplicate it. But, strangely enough, Van Halen picked it up. Lots of acts have picked it up. The vertical banner and all that stuff is very popular. And summons you back to a certain point in history, I suppose.

AP: Did you ever wonder about the possible, sort of — brain-washing aspect of that — the way it was designed as a collective consciousness-type thing.

CM: Never really thought a lot about it except for the fact that that's what design does. When you walk into a theater and the curtain opens or whatever it does, you are taken away. And that is a brain-wash for all intents and purposes — you are sucked into whatever the element is that you are going to see. Plus that fact that you've already paid for the ticket — you've already committed to it, because you wanted to see it. It wasn't because you were told you had to see it — to be in the group. You wanted to see it.

AP: So is that a key difference between the Nüremberg audiences and a musical audience — would be that the Nüremberg audiences—

CM: *Had* to be there. Yes, they were told to be there. Nowadays, peculiarly enough, with the way the media and electronic media is working, it's possibly getting nearer to the fact that you have to be there, because you were told by a certain amount of people or a person, that this is something you can't afford to miss. So it could be parallel to a certain point, I suppose. It's turning — it turns, it always changes — what's popular and why is it popular. And unfortunately, it seems as though in music — even in Coachella, the actual quality of the music isn't as important as the gathering. Where there are people who would much rather — in Gen Y shall we say — who go for the spirit of the gathering and being together, rather than for what the actual draw was supposed to be, as set up by the promoter. Which is supposedly the music and the excellence of — and what they paid for, to get you there. But now the younger people use it for a different purpose. It's the fact of being a unit.

AP: Do you think that Albert Speer would have had similar moments with Hitler, that you had with Jagger?

CM: [Laughs] If he was allowed to. It's an entirely different — you know. All I ended up doing was being a thorn in his side and kept pushing him, and was a rebel — and he wished I'd get the fuck out of the theatre. *Why do I have to now do this when I was doing that so successfully for the last four months?* "Because it's time for a little improvement. How long do you want to be a garage band — or would you like to become a brand?" "Don't you think it's time we made a little effort?" I could get one of those sentences out maybe once a month. And I'm sure that maybe Herr Speer would not have spoken to the Führer in that fashion. Although, he may very well have done exactly what he wanted to do. I very seriously doubt that he would have expressed it in that fashion.

* * *

In his 1959 novel *Sirens of Titan*, Kurt Vonnegut suggests that the primary difference between good and evil is in the goals, rather than the methods or organization by which they are obtained. The means may be similar, but the intended result of these actions — in our case, manipulating and controlling a crowd — define the nature of the people and groups using these methods. Ergo, the techniques developed by the Nazis can be used for benevolent reasons, too. These methods can be taken to other levels and employed for a higher purpose. Woodstock certainly achieved that.

Later on, we'll come to something of a Freudian analysis of these situations. For the time being, suffice it to say that human beings both love and hate. People themselves are not inherently evil, but history shows we often become part of something bigger than ourselves, that is. This psychological duality brings us to the 1969 Altamont Speedway Free Festival, the West Coast's answer to Woodstock, where the character of the crowd became the antithesis of *peace and love.*

Chapter 3

Michael Shrieve

The club is called The White Rabbit. It's night in Seattle, the day after Christmas. Snow falls outside. Inside, the club is smoky, hot, full. A giant hypnotic spiral hangs behind the stage. The crowd is excited. They're already down the rabbit hole, and they're about to share a drink with a man who changed rock 'n' roll forever.

The door swings open and a short burst of wind brings a fresh dusting of powder. A man with a bleached-blond Cobain haircut and a flannel shirt walks in. He holds the leash of a full-grown husky. He takes his dog to the bar and orders a drink. Nobody bats an eyelid. This is Seattle, after all.

The crowd tonight is chasing a different rabbit, from a different time. They're chasing a man who provided a leg-up to the Cobains and the Vedders. In 1968, Michael Shrieve introduced Latin drum grooves to a band that rode a *wave* of Latin drum grooves all the way to the top of the charts. Shrieve played drumkit in that band, Santana, from its conception until 1975; the group's rhythmic backbone for six studio albums. In recent years, Shrieve rejoined Carlos and his bandmates for a new album and a reunion performance at Madison Square Garden.

But tonight isn't an arena show. This is more personal. Mike lives around the corner, and his new band Spellbinder plays here every Monday night. Even so, there is gravity in the room tonight. This crowd has ownership. This is *their* Mike. The man whose drum solo at Woodstock has — for fifty years — provided inspiration for generations of kids to pick up the sticks. Bonham, Moon, Mitchell, Shrieve. As a kid, these are the four drummers who knocked me over. They continue to push me to be a better drummer every time I hear them.

Earlier that day, I spent a couple of hours with Michael at his home. Our conversation took some interesting turns. Along with Joe McDonald, Shrieve remains a highlight of the *Woodstock* documentary film. His drum solo is mesmerizing, the crowd pulsating in time with him as he cues the band to return to the groove of *Soul Sacrifice*. Shrieve was the youngest performer at Woodstock; he turned twenty just a few weeks before. But the crowd isn't with him because they identify with a youngster. They're with him because he's *so damn good.*

Shrieve was also present at the Altamont Speedway Free Festival. This is the festival where the hippie dream is said to have died. The Rolling Stones headlined, along with Santana, Jefferson Airplane, Crosby, Stills, Nash and Young and others. Three hundred thousand people attended. Crowd violence punctuated the event — several performers were assaulted — songs were interrupted by scuffles on and off stage, vehicles stolen, two hit-and-run deaths and one fatal stabbing, captured by the Maysles brothers' cameras in the documentary *Gimme Shelter.*

Shrieve is seen in the film detailing the violence for members of the Grateful Dead: Marty Balin of Jefferson Airplane had jumped into the crowd to try to stop a fight and had been knocked unconscious. The Grateful Dead never went on stage. More about Altamont later.

Shrieve left Santana in 1975 to work on more personal projects. He played in a host of supergroups, high-profile session gigs, film scoring, and solo work. The soundtrack to *Apollo 13* is his, as is *Tempest*, directed by Paul Mazursky.

In 1998, Shrieve was inducted into the Rock and Roll Hall of Fame. In 2011, he was listed tenth in *Rolling Stone* Magazine's Best Drummers of All Time. And I'm now a guest at this gig. His partner Pamela has saved me a seat. Also at the table is Lee Oskar, harmonica player for War. Eric Burdon and War were the last people to jam with Jimi Hendrix, at Ronnie Scott's club in London on September 17, 1970. I wish I'd known that as we sat together at this table, waiting to hear from another icon of rock.

Shrieve and his band take their positions on stage. The air tightens. This is a home crowd, and one that returns on a weekly basis to brush shoulders with rock royalty. They begin. It's instantaneous — sounds are coming at me from all angles. It's monstrous and delicate at the same time. There's a kind of spirituality happening on stage, and it's all from the music. These are serious players. No gimmickry, just absolute respect for the collective focus that is resulting in this new ethereal sound.

The audience is with them.

Shrieve's Woodstock drum solo is one of the most famous in history. Tonight, Shrieve proves that he has spent the last half-century pushing further. The music is tighter. The drum solo is even more impressive.

Michael Shrieve: At Woodstock — because I used to surf, and I used to spend a lot of time at the ocean, my first reaction standing on stage was *This is like standing at the ocean, and the water is the people.* Then there's the sky. As far as you could see, there's the water and then the horizon. That's exactly what I felt, standing at the ocean. Then I guess I had to think *oh my God, we have to play for these people.*

But it was very difficult to feel connected on an individual level. Understanding that we were a brand new band to everybody, we didn't have a record out or anything like that, and that we connected with them in the way that we did. Although that didn't happen from the first note. Soul Sacrifice — which was the one in the movie — that was the last piece that we did. So in listening to it some years later, I realized we were struggling a little bit. People didn't know us. We won them over, but it wasn't just a given.

But here it was documented and it's an amazing feeling to connect with that. And we knew it was, you know, the intensity. The drums, the percussion that connected to this tribal experience that everybody was feeling. Because everybody was feeling connected there, for even *being* there. Just being there alone and making it through the night or whatever they were going through.

Sometimes you do shows and you don't really connect. It's just too much. You can't really see anybody, you can't really connect with anybody unless you put yourself in the *whole soul mode*. And I think that for a lot of groups, playing huge places all the time, you end up kind of playing to yourselves, and inspiring yourself to do a good job. Because you're not really connecting with this huge crowd of people. Maybe you'll find one person, somebody to connect with. Otherwise it's just a sea of people.

Aidan Prewett: Could you take us to Woodstock, from the moment that you flew in?

MS: We kept hearing about the concert on the news, about the interstate being closed down. We were staying in a house in Woodstock for about a week prior, after being on the road and doing a lot of festivals. And so we knew something was going on. Then we found out we had to go by helicopter. As soon as we took off, we saw the crowd. It's nothing like you could relate to. It seemed like it was pretty phenomenal. It wasn't all a shock because you'd been hearing about it. But *seeing* it really was a shock. And then we landed. I think we flew over Jerry Garcia and some other people and, you know how it was, everybody was feeling good. Backstage anyway, everybody was feeling good. It was really the height of *everything's groovy*. So we were informed that we would perform at a certain time later in the day, and then it seemed like not too much longer, they said, *You've got to go on now. If you don't go on now, you're not going to play*. So that's what we did. But I remember hanging out with John Sebastian's brother, Mark. We were kinda the same age.

Everybody was blown away by the feeling of the thing as well. I remember I had, as a kid, hitchhiked from my parents' house to Monterey, California for the Monterey Pop Festival. And I was by myself and I was one of those kids that slept overnight on the lawn and stuff, because I just wanted to be there. That's kinda my only experience of that, aside from going to the Fillmore. But, feeling that this is something really special happening, and I want to be there. You know, I took off. I was sixteen or something. So I was familiar with that feeling of why people want to go to those concerts. And there was nothing quite like Woodstock. I never had that feeling again of *Oh I really want to go hang out with thousands of other people*.

AP: You were the youngest performer at Woodstock.

MS: It didn't really feel like, "oh, come on kid," or anything like that. The crowd was like this ocean, but they were open. It didn't feel like it was a tough crowd, it was just so frightening that it was so huge and as far as you could see. I didn't feel like because I was the youngest, they made me feel more comfortable or anything like that.

Backstage I was just another musician. A lot of the people that played there, we knew already. The Dead and Sly and his guys, we were good friends with. And Jefferson Airplane and Janis Joplin and her band, and a lot of those people we'd seen on the road so it wasn't like… I mean yeah, people were kinda like I was the kid, but *everybody* was pretty young. I looked younger than I was as well. But no, it was just camaraderie. I was just another musician with them. I mean, even before playing with Santana I was seriously about to play with Jefferson Airplane. And so I had known those people even before I met Santana, and I had made a trip to L.A. with them and with Yorma and Jack so I knew all those people. So it was more like family, youknow? Yeah maybe I was the young kid in the family. But I wasn't treated specially — *Don't do it around Mikey* — you know, that kind of thing.

AP: The documentary is overflowing with a sense of achievement — a huge cultural achievement.

MS: I think Arlo Guthrie sums it up, watching him in the movie, or John Sebastian, where they're really feeling it, "We did it, man, we did it! Can you believe this? We did it!" You know, there's something happened there. It reminds me of the scene in *Close Encounters* where everybody just comes together, and they don't know why. Woodstock…. When I say that movie, it felt like Woodstock to me. That gathering of the people and they didn't even know each other, but they were all compelled to go to this place. And I think that's what happened at Woodstock where this whole hippie thing and so much was going on culturally in terms of the war and politics and things were changing. People were experiencing things they hadn't felt, and drugs had something to do with it. People were feeling liberated that they can break away and make a new way in society. So I think that Woodstock was the culmination … it said, "Look, there are this many of us. We are standing to be counted."

AP: *Stick it to the man* comes to mind.

MS: In terms of Woodstock, I think most definitely. That was the vibe, then. Sticking it to the man. We can do this, and we can do it peacefully and have this many people. I mean obviously there they even won over the cops, you know. So that was the thing. Stick it to the man.

AP: Who was the man?

MS: It was the authorities, it was your parents, it was the police. It was your teachers, it was your politicians, it was — you know — a, those people who tried to tell you to live a life that you didn't want to live or didn't believe in. The biggest thing was that people were being sent to a war that they really didn't believe in. What they really thought was an evil war that was manufactured by Nixon and people like that. They knew it was wrong. And they saw, when they started to speak out about it, the way that police and government reacted in such a violent way. And that drew some lines. When they got violent it made people more aware. And then other people like the Black Panthers and others saw that this is not going to happen by peace and love. So motherfucker, we're going to do it our own way. So there was a lot going on.

I mean, frankly, I moved through that whole period looking at myself as a craftsman, as a musician, growing up in these times. It wasn't like the reverse, like "I'm a hippie, and this is my movement, and I play drums in a band." It was "I'm a drummer first." So I moved through that whole thing as a working man. That's how I felt, not so much part of that culture, I just was like, this is my time. And there's a difference. Some of these things I can speak to now, looking back and getting a sense of what the feeling was among other people, even though I may not have been, I mean, I never even considered myself a hippie. I was a musician, and this was the music that was happening.

AP: You were at Altamont too — what was the feeling at that concert?

MS: Altamont had the strongest negativity of any group environment that I've ever experienced. From the moment we got there, it was palpable. And this was after Woodstock. It was the extreme opposite of the feeling that was at Woodstock. I mean, literally it felt like evil in the air. It felt like this weight that was … there wasn't the lightness of all the hippie movement prior to that, living in San Francisco and the Bay Area. Never really considering myself a hippie, but being around that and knowing what that feeling could be — this was the exact opposite. And that became … I'm not saying the crowd was dark, but something was permeating the air there, that certainly caused that emotion to be there. And certainly that negativity did come to light. I just wanted to get out of there. We chose even, to not be in the film, because it was so weighty and negative. Even though we performed there and were filmed there like the other groups.

AP: Do you feel that some of that negativity was due to the presence of the Hell's Angels?

MS: I mean obviously it was miscommunication and it was the wrong idea to use Hells Angels for security. Even though what they did, in their mind, they saw someone with a gun. And so they did what they thought they had to do.… They thought a performer was going to be assassinated or something like that. But it was just very dark, it was an unbelievable feeling. I think there's so much, and I could talk at length about why that thing went wrong, and I think it probably starts with the intentions of why it was even put together. And then the way it was put together. It was different to Woodstock, the reasons for being put together were more pure with Woodstock, with Michael Lang and John Morris. It was a mess, but it was a different energy. Here it was put together by the Stones, rushed together. It was a disaster.

So that's one place, I mean, there's other things. I've done a concert in Italy years ago with Santana where people were throwing bricks and stones — and this is apparently when they love you. Or places in South America when we were playing before bands went down there. And they didn't necessarily pay the right guys for security or something. And bodies were being lifted over the crowd onto the stage and into ambulances in the back. Just because there was no crowd control. It can get frightening really quickly. All those pieces need to be in place for the crowd to be secure and for it to be a safe environment. That way the audience can either go to a beautiful place or it can turn ugly really quickly.

And there've been others, throughout concert history. I remember when Pearl Jam went through that thing, the Roskilde Festival in Denmark I believe. And people died and they just couldn't believe it. But sometimes stuff like that happens. Same with The Who in Cincinnati years ago. The band is always shocked that where people should feel so joyous, people could lose their lives.

* * *

Altamont brought to light the Jungian duality of music festival culture, which has been repeated in various guises in the ensuing decades. In such a short span of time — four months post-Woodstock, in the same culture, the same factors became a malevolent force. This was an unexpected, undesirable outcome, and we'll soon learn more about why events unfolded in this way.

Stick it to the man was a catch-cry for the times. But pushing back against the system doesn't work all the time. At Altamont, the people seemed to be pushing back against a system of their own design. *The man* was suddenly one of them — namely Mick Jagger. The organizers of this festival were largely flying blind and hoping for the best, and it didn't work.

At Woodstock, despite similar chaotic elements, the organizers managed to curate a festival experience that was something truly special. Our next guest was the head of production at Woodstock. He was in charge.

Chapter 4

John Morris

Nestled in the hills above Malibu Beach are a series of winding, interlocking roads which are home to some of the most successful people in the world. It's not at all like I pictured. Many of these roads are unmade, single-lane, and badly signposted. The people who live here like it that way. Vegetation creeps right up to the roadside. As our taxi winds its way toward our destination I wonder if our driver has any real idea of where he's going. He does. We pull into a driveway and suddenly the vegetation clears away and we see the frontage of a two-story flat top beach house. It's modern in a classic 1970's James Bond kind of way. I ask the taxi driver to wait for us to confirm we're in the right spot before he leaves. The door opens. The beaming face of John Morris greets us. I wave to the taxi driver and we enter John's house. It's another world.

John's life as a music industry luminary has changed a lot. He now runs a business as a curator and distributor of original Native American art. This was his first love, even before music. Morris's career in music really began when Bill Graham employed him to manage the legendary Fillmore East — Graham's venture to take the magic of his San Francisco Fillmore Auditorium to New York City. John Morris knows *everyone.* After Michael Lang employed John as Head of Production for Woodstock, he was approached by the post-Altamont Rolling Stones to manage their return to the U.S. in 1972. In the mid-seventies John owned the London club Rainbow Lounge, which drew many of the decade's best acts and many old friends and Woodstock alumni.

Now that we've seen some of the horrors of Altamont (we'll return there shortly), we've come to John to find out just what it was about Woodstock that went *right.* What was done at Woodstock to quell the many tensions and to frame the festival — for the audience, performers, and crew — to promote a gentler, more loving spirit?

We're here to meet John and three of his dear friends who were instrumental in the creation of the *Woodstock* documentary. We'll hear more from each of them in the following chapters. As we set up the cameras, lights, and sound, John is already proving his chops as a raconteur. I'm taking mental notes to make sure I get these stories while the cameras are rolling.

One story I wish I had captured was about the time that John got sick of Jim Morrison's increasingly outrageous antics during rehearsal at the Fillmore East. He had a stagehand connect the fly harness to Morrison's belt. In the middle of a diatribe, Morrison suddenly went sailing into the air. The diatribe continued. Morrison stayed up there alone for a full hour while the entire crew — and the rest of The Doors — went to lunch. When John Morris returned, he had stern words with Morrison before letting him down. Jim Morrison was good as gold from that moment on. The Doors played a great show that night — possibly one of Jim's most sober performances. But of course, they never played the Fillmore again.

Aidan Prewett: So can we talk about Max Yasgur's farm and how that was in the days preceding Woodstock, and how that changed as people started to arrive and the stage was being built....

John Morris: Nobody had any idea that there were going to be as many people there as there were. The largest two performance events that you had before that were the Beatles at Shea Stadium, about fifty thousand people, and Monterey Pop, which was about thirty-five thousand people. And that was as far as it went. Nobody knew about the size of gigs that happen now, and we had planned for fifty to seventy-five thousand, which was really pretty unthinkable, outside of New York. Chris Langhart, who was our technical director for the whole thing, built everything to stand four times that. Just for safety. Which is the only reason we got through what we got through. 'Cos there were forty miles of underground pipes carrying water. Everything worked except the fences. The fence guy never finished.

I'd actually taken my crew out to dinner in town the night before, figuring that it was going to be a little hectic and we probably wouldn't have a lot of time — having no clue. And we came back, and Bill Handley had been testing the sound system and put it up so that they could hear. And I walked up to it by accident, walked up to a live mic, and looked out and saw the field was totally full. And went: "*Holy shit!*" And about three or four hundred thousand people laughed at me. And that's how we actually started. We just at that moment figured, *okay* — you know — *we're in it deep, so let's go to work*. And that's how it was established, that way. That was where we were going to go. We had the equivalent of a small city.

JM: It was probably five or six o'clock in the morning, and I said, "Get the yellow pages, and hire every single God damn helicopter that you can lay your hands on." And we had sixteen of them in the end, including the army ones. Because the first thing we had to do on the first day was to fight with the chief of staff of Nelson Rockefeller, who was the governor and wanted to shut the whole thing down. Send in the national guard, shut everything down. Do what he in fact did at Attica. The prison, where forty-three people died. I spent my first waking hours arguing with them about how stupid it would be to try to move them out.

I can't remember the guy who was the chief of staff, but he was in fact a reasonable human being, and we got away with it. And in the end he said, "what can we do for you?" I said we could use medical facilities, because there's close to half a million people out there, and we have some, but...." So they sent us National Guard medical units. We had three of them who set up tents and took care of a whole bunch of things. So what could have been a disaster turned out to be much better.

When those helicopters flew over the crowd, they came over from behind. It's in the film — where you can hear the whooping, and so can the audience. I was the one who could see them, as I had been pressed into services as an announcer. And I went: "Ladies and Gentlemen, the U.S. Army." *Boo Hiss*. "Medical Corps." And the crowd's sentiment changed just like that, in a second. It was — you know — un-accidental good timing.

AP: The symbolism of the helicopters coming in the midst of the Vietnam era...

JM: Oh, it froze everybody. It was amazing, looking at those faces, *that way*. And that's when I realized I could get off a good line. And if I couldn't, then we were going to be in trouble. Because a lot of the kids there thought the army, or *they*, would come and kill the festival. Do them in, whatever.

AP: So, at what point did it become apparent that this was going to be a really historic event?

JM: I don't know that anybody thought in terms of historic right away. I think everybody's first thought was *how the hell do we cope with it?* I don't know who the hell came up with the idea to get NYC Disc Jockeys to be the announcers. And we had ourselves a bunch of "Hi, groovy guys and gals, welcome to N.Y.", that kind of stuff. But I heard that with one of the first announcements, somebody introduced Richie Havens in that manner. "Hey hey,

Richie Havens!", you know. Totally antithetical. And so I just said to Michael Lang, "Uh-uh, this ain't going to work. Let's get rid of them." So we gave the hook to them. And then it was *who's going to do it?* And then Chip Monck and I ended up doing most of it. And Wavy Gravy.

You're standing there looking at half a million people, and you've got in the back of your head: You can't get the artists in — you can't get the film in — without the helicopters. Had it not been for the helicopters, we'd have been in deep shit. Actually, there were about fifty things that had it not been for the helicopters, wouldn't have happened. And it really was a confluence of lucky things. To a degree that's amazing. And that first day we were scrambling. We knew what we were doing, but we really just had no idea in this situation.

Richie Havens got slapped on stage because he was there. And Joe McDonald did a solo because he had told me someplace in Europe that he wanted to try doing solo. And I looked around and there's Joe standing around with us. Hanging out. He came early, so he could see the whole festival. And I said, "You're on next." And then John Sebastian, who was not on the festival billing. He was, believe it or not, walking down the dirt laneway, dressed from head to toe in tie-die, stoned out of his skull, carrying a guitar. And somebody said, "There's Sebastian!", and somebody else goes, "Well, go get him!" So they went and got him and they slapped him on stage. And that's how he ended up on stage.

Richie's freedom song is because — you can see it in the film — he starts to get up, and I walk up behind him and push him back down in the chair and say, "You've gotta play for longer, I haven't got anybody to follow you." And that's where he started improvising *Freedom*. Finally, the way he got offstage was getting up out of the chair playing *Freedom Freedom Freedom*. He kept playing and walked all the way around the corner, and walked back to the corner of the stage as if to say, "I'm getting outta here."

AP: During the festival, was there a sense that the audience was its own, kind of collective character?

JM: The audience, I would say, definitely had its own — built itself its own character. And then went in different directions. There was not a recorded incident of violence from one human being to another. There were some pretty damn close calls, but the audience wasn't in that place … they were there to have fun. In spite of all the rain, all the mud, all the bathrooms that were a mile-and-a-half away. I mean, the lack of food — they shared with each other tremendously. People were there to listen, get high, have a good time.

As announcers we were not encouraging people to get high or whatever. We were just — "We're doing a show — for you." There was lots of talking — Wavy Gravy does a great thing in the film of — "Good morning, here's Breakfast in bed for four-hundred thousand." And they threw oranges and food. One of my ushers from the Fillmore who was working for us read the funnies on Sunday morning. There were all sorts of little great moments like that. And nobody had a tendency to do a negative thing.

It was interesting too, to be an announcer up there — there's stuff going through your head about what you can and cannot say. I mean at one point we talked about creating a special sign — a three-finger salute that forms a "W" for Woodstock. And it would probably still survive today. And I thought, "That's corny." We forgot about it.

I've done a lot of announcing at a lot of places in my life, but I've never seen anybody successfully lead something in a negative direction. I mean, they've put down riots in some places in the country where the kids were all excited. And you come to the mic and you talk to them and ask them to be sensible. You ask them to share with each other. What are you here for, are you here to have a hassle, or are you here to listen to the music? Do you want to listen to Jim Morrison, or do you want to make trouble? And they're very logical, in most cases.

I mean, the audience really was there for the greatest music in the world. We had almost every major artist, with the exception of the Stones and the Beatles. Everybody thought Bob Dylan was coming — he lived up the road — even though he had no intention of coming. But aside from them, we just about had everybody across the spectrum. From the San Fran acts — Santana, who had never had the exposure before that — we paid them $2,500 to come. And he just blew it out and became world-famous. Joe Cocker — Michael Lang and I had seen him in England, and I'd had him at the Fillmore East in New York, again, twenty-five hundred bucks — world-wide reputation.

AP: What were the audiences like at the Fillmore?

JM: Our ushers were great. We trained them up. If there was a problem, they knew how to swoop in and just pet it down and get it to go away. So we rarely ever had any problem with the audience. And I watched — we did a Black Panther benefit, and the funny thing about it was that we had more cops than Black Panther members, because every department of the New York Police Department would call up and say, "We'd like to send some undercover guys." Oh, God help me. I mean, that was the danger. The only real problem we had with Pete Townshend was when some cop from the TPS — Tactical Police Force — decided to stop Peter in the middle of a performance. And it was all a gentle audience, it was all nice — but the guy's lucky he didn't get killed, because he was interrupting the music.

The only problem I've ever had in thirty-four years was in London where I had a theater called the Rainbow Theatre. Frank Zappa was playing, and he had finished about his third or fourth encore. Some guy charged up out of the audience while the security was just changing from looking from one direction to the other. He got past them — and as the English say — barged Frank, knocked him into the air, down into the orchestra pit, which was built up with scaffolding over the orchestra pit. Frank caught his leg, and it twisted, and broke it. The guy was immediately pounced on by the ushers. He did three years for grievous bodily harm. But that's the only time I remember that happening. The guy was whacked out of his head on meth, and he just got it into his head that his girlfriend loved Frank and not him. I mean, there are isolated incidents like that, but nowhere near the rule. And at Woodstock, not at all.

AP: Did you feel a sense of responsibility toward the crowd?

JM: Oh Christ, yes. I mean, you stand up there looking at a sea of faces — you've got a microphone, you realize you're the only one talking to all of these people. And things go through your head about whether things can be turned and twisted. They can be turned and twisted in very positive ways.

One of the things at Woodstock on the Friday night — Joan Baez had played, which was a very peaceful thing. It was like: "Okay, goodnight. Say good night to each other and we'll see you in the morning." It wasn't being patronizing, it was just, "That's it for the night, we'll be back tomorrow. Get a good night's sleep, be kind to your neighbor." That is easily done. The whole feeling that I got throughout the thing was a feeling of cooperation. I mean, you could literally say, "We're running out of food. So if you've got some extra food, give it to the person who's next to you." A lot of that went on. And of course we were reading announcements sent up from audience members. Of, "Sally — go meet your sister Katie at the information booth."

We suddenly had a bunch of these messages in French — we had a lot of French Canadians. A friend of mine, Roland Griot, who I knew in the Virgin Islands, had come up with his wife to work on the festival. And … and so I said to Roland, "Go out there and read them." And he went out and read all these things in French. And I said, "You know what I just realized? You've spoken to more people in the French language than De Gaulle or Napoleon," anybody else you want to think of. And he had come back from throwing bricks in Paris in '68. He said, "Oh good. The Left gets the last word."

AP: In your position, there must have been moments of extreme stress.

JM: One thing to remember is that we all were not a bunch of hippies. We were adults. Most of my staff just kept going until they dropped. They weren't doing drugs — they weren't doing anything else. You couldn't. Nobody told you that you couldn't, but you couldn't *and get it done.* It got done. Including that maniac Wadleigh, who was the main camera.

But what I will never forget — the moment I came closest to a nervous breakdown in my entire seventy-two years — was when the roof, which was badly designed, started flapping all over the place. We had fifty-mile-an-hour winds. Cocker was singing. My wife had broken her ankle in the mud; my dog had disappeared. All the rest of this. And I'm up on stage saying, "Get off the towers," 'cos they're forty feet in the air and there are super troupers on the top that could fall on people, and I'm trying to get everybody to calm down. And the mic is shocking me. And by the way, down at the bottom of my feet, is this whacko with the beard who is still bare chested — Michael Wadleigh got to show more of his body on that thing than anybody needs — with his camera right up in my face. And he knew what was going on with me, and I knew that he knew. And it was just like — *couldn't panic.* Had to keep it calm. Although you'd like to go somewhere and climb in a big bed and go to sleep. But that I think was the attitude that everybody had throughout.

AP: And it ended beautifully.

JM: Oh yeah. Toward the end of the Sunday night we decided we wanted to keep the acts going through the night, so people wouldn't leave and drive home in the dark. We thought that would be dangerous. People paid no attention, and went home — a lot of them — 'cos they had to go to work the next day.

But I got Jimi on stage after literally three days of him riding around in circles, with Mike Jefferies — his manager — and saying, "Can we come in now?" *No.* And they were great about it. But I finally got them on stage, then I went straight up to my trailer and lay down, straight out like a light. And I was out until I heard the first chords of the Star-Spangled Banner. And I sat bolt upright on one elbow, listened to it and went: *It's over. It's done. That's good. This is the perfect way to end it* — and lay right back down and went to sleep. And probably woke up about four or five hours later and looked out the window.

The whole area where the show had been, ninety percent of the people had all gone. They'd left sleeping bags and cooking pots and pans and all sorts of other stuff. It was a muddy mess. And it looked exactly like the civil war photographs of Matthew Brady's, of different battle fields after the battles had happened. With no artillery or anything, but it was just totally desolate, totally done. So I dragged myself up and I went for a walk, all over the site. And it sticks in my mind as one of the most amazing parts of Woodstock. I thought somebody might be dead somewhere, somebody might be hurt somewhere. I didn't find anybody, which was wonderful. It really was, for me — *okay, it's over. Nobody's been harmed.*

A while after the festival I went to 81st and Broadway, to the editing rooms of the documentary. I saw the six projectors linked together, projecting on a wall at the same time, six different angles — and to me it was like the start of a whole other festival. Because the view of it, the look of it — what it created… it proved that we did something — we were *involved* in something that was very very major. What Margaret Mead called "*one of the most important examples of social action in the world.*" And we're here and grey and talking about it. That's a pretty nice experience. You don't get that in wars and that kind of stuff. It was a great experience.

* * *

John's more peaceful mechanisms of guiding and regulating a crowd seem to have had a direct impact on calming the tensions that existed due to food, water, and space shortages, sewerage issues, and heavy rain. John's ethos set the tone for all crew at the festival — and by extension, the crowd as well. His announcements, along with Chip Monck's, are exemplary in their direct, optimistic nature. In much the same way as a performer, authenticity is key in catching an audience's attention. They have to *believe* you. In the *Woodstock* documentary, John and Chip can be seen giving the most earnest performances of their lives. The subtext: *If this doesn't work out, all of us will be in a world of trouble. So please listen.*

The sincerity of the announcements is endearing. The editors of *Woodstock*, Thelma Schoonmaker and Martin Scorsese, used the announcements as a kind of narrative backbone for the documentary. It's reassuring, providing a punctuation to the film's three-hour runtime. There's something parental about it all. The documentary audience is guided by the same voices that guided the concert audience.

But we're about to find out that the *Woodstock* documentary very nearly didn't happen at all.

Chapter 5

Dale Bell

Woodstock saved Warner Bros. Pictures. The sixties was a rough time for cinema, with television and the new suburban culture blamed for a decline in attendance at the city theatres. Multiplexes at suburban shopping malls were yet to take off, with only a handful of successful titles released in the sixties, including *My Fair Lady* (1964) and *Who's Afraid of Virginia Woolf* (1966). In 1967, co-founder Jack Warner sold his controlling interest and the company soon ended up part of a car park conglomerate which happened to include a minor R and B label called Atlantic Records.

In 1969, Ahmet Ertegun, head of Atlantic, signed a deal to release the Woodstock album. Only as a last-minute afterthought was the deal updated to include film rights for Warner Bros. But who was shooting the footage?

Dale Bell put together the team that did. This team went on to create a film that took out the Academy Award for Best Documentary and went on to huge box office success. Warner Bros. suddenly had the financial means to start again in the new decade.

Sitting opposite four people who were instrumental in the production of this film is daunting. It's hard to believe that these people who helped shape the way the counterculture was received around the world would be happy enough to get together to chat with me. Yet here we are.

Dale Bell was associate producer. In practical terms, for this film, this meant on-site management of an entire film crew in a disaster area. This was followed by several months overseeing Thelma Schoonmaker and Martin Scorsese in the editing process.

Dale is co-founder of the Media and Policy Center, where he has devoted his career to the creation and promotion of social justice programming, and the support of public television.

Aidan Prewett: Can we begin with Max Yasgur's farm in the days leading up to the festival?

Dale Bell: I went up with half a dozen other film people on the Saturday, before the music began on the Friday. So it was just six days in advance. We looked out from the hill and the stage and saw these little two-lane roads. Some of them were even one-lane farm roads. So if you were going down the farm with a tractor, you'd have to get off one side or the other. I remember looking out and somebody like John Morris or Mike Lang had said they were expecting fifty thousand people. And I turned around and said, "Guys, we're going to have to get our team up here by Thursday. Because if we're aiming to do Friday, it's going to be impossible." Thursday morning. That was really the goal. It was absolutely essential. Because the crowds — even with fifty thousand — they would not yet add the extra zero — with fifty thousand it was going to be incredibly crowded. Incredibly claustrophobic.

AP: And you had to get a film organized.

DB: On the first day, we determined that it was possible for us to really put a film together if we could find enough synchronous cameras and enough magazines. We rented from every film house in New York. So what we had was essentially about fifteen cameras and about fifty to sixty film magazines and a batch of 5.9-mm lenses, and a couple of 25-250-mm. But the thing that we didn't have was the raw film stock to put into the cameras. And we called Kodak. Michael Wadleigh and I had determined that we would need certain batches: 72-42, 72-41, and 72-55. But he had no estimate yet as to how much we would be shooting that would be nighttime, how much would be daytime, and what kinds of stock, what grades of stock, we would need. So we just called Kodak on Monday — I did — and said, "How much do you have?" and they said, "Oh, we've got it all here. It's right here." I said we'd probably need about fifty to sixty boxes. "Don't worry, we've got it, we've got it, we've got it." When we came to split the order, and order a specific amount of 42, 55, 41, we called in and they did *not* have it. They had misinterpreted or whatever, they had made a major mistake. And we found out that there were only ten boxes of raw stock in their New York vault.

We had the team going up there. There were ten boxes, maybe fifteen boxes in Paradigm films' ice box, and a lot of those were short ends. Michael Wadleigh and the rapidly expanding team of camera people were arriving each day of the week at Max Yasgur's farm. They had very little raw stock. So my production manager Sonya Polonsky and I had to find raw stock in places like Rochester (where Kodak made its film), in Chicago, in Denver, in Los Angeles, in Atlanta, and have it flown in — as many boxes as were possible — into La Guardia. And then by airplane up to Monticello, and then distribute it from Monticello to White Lake. And that's where John Morris and the helicopters came in. These helicopters that were bringing in the people and performers and medical facilities were also bringing in the raw film stock from all over the country, so that we had an opportunity to do the filming that we had to do. And they were coming at least until

Saturday afternoon, when we got our last shipment. So without the helicopters, we never would have had a film.

AP: The logistics of dealing with so much film, and such a big documentary crew — I can't get my head around it.

DB: The crew were all working on 4x8 plywood, which the festival people had put on the ground for us because the mud was ankle-deep. And then on sawhorses we had another batch of 4x8 plywood, so that people could be in film change bags up to their elbows, changing one kind of emulsion, and other people were making notes on clipboards. *This was a Dick Pearce camera roll, something or other, or this was a Mike Wadleigh camera roll, something or other.* This was absolutely the most critical part of finding out what we had shot for the editing. This was all taking place underneath that stage — a batch of people who finally got credit in the film, but we can't possibly give them enough credit for what they were doing. Because it was all unseen stuff. They would come to the edge of the stage where we had the lip, and they would hand up a magazine and it would be labeled *Dick Pearce — Camera Roll something or other*, and it would go up on stage and it would go to Dick Pearce.

But the day before the festival started, we still didn't have an official deal to actually make the film. We just showed up. The *New York Times* had a little article on the front page, far left, on Wednesday. On Thursday morning, another article, more into the center of the page. Come Friday morning, it had started on the right side of the column, which was the highest urgency, and went across with a massive picture of the N.Y. state throughway threatened with being closed. Miles and miles, you could just see, eons of people crawling — ants — towards White Lake. As soon as I saw that article, I called Wadleigh and said, "You know, we're on the front page of the paper, we've got to have a deal. We've got to make something of this deal." There was still no deal.

We didn't know it at the time, but Paul Marshall, a lawyer who had been hired by the festival people, had offered and sold the sound recording rights to Ahmet Ertegun, the head of Atlantic Records. Seventy-five-thousand dollars. No one had at this point even *conceived* of the movie rights. Because nobody thought that the film rights would be worth anything at all. Paul Marshall went back to Ahmet about two or three weeks later and offered him the movie rights for an additional $25,000.

And Ahmet says, "Oh, $25,000, of course, I'll take it." For $100,000 he's got the soundtrack rights and he's got the movie rights. The irony is that Paul Marshall never told Porter Bibb, who was producing for Al and David Maysles, that he had sold the rights to Ahmet Ertegun. And Porter Bibb went around trying to get rights to the individual performers — but he never knew that the rights had been sold.

Atlantic belonged to Warner Bros. And at this time, also remember that Warner Bros. was moribund. It was up for sale. It had just been purchased by Kinney, which was a parking garage conglomerate with funeral homes attached.

Our approach — we were saying to ourselves, "You know, if we put somebody up on the site before the music begins, and they shoot negative, and we own it — we will be the magnet to which whatever this conglomeration becomes. They've gotta come to us." So while Porter was out here doing his thing, trying to protect and support and get an "in case it rains" insurance policy, we had no concern like that. We had guts. We had daring. But we also had skill, and we had technique, and we had a design.

We showed that design to the Maysles on the Friday, a week before the festival. The Maysles brothers and Porter came to 81st Street and Broadway where the three projectors could illustrate what they had just edited with Aretha Franklin doing *Respect. Respect* was song number one and song number two was *We*

Shall Overcome. The images were on this big white wall, shown by three projectors and one common Magnatec sound machine and everything ran in sync. And you looked at these images, first images, second image, third image. They bounce back and forth. The Maysles brothers were in the room that Friday evening, And they looked at it, and they were blown away. They were coming to us, asking us to "shoot the performance." They thought *they* would do the documentary portion, and I remember coming out of that room and saying to everybody, "We know how to do this ourselves. We don't need them, we can do it ourselves." Larry Johnson, our sound designer, ran David Maysles down the stairs. They actually came to fisticuffs.

We knew that Friday night that we could do it. And it was that decision — a week before the festival — that really propelled us forward. The next day we all convened and drove up there to White Lake. That was the decision point, no turning back. And that was lucky. It was not lucky so much as it was design. I got it back to the notion of design. With Michael's skillset, my skillset, Larry Johnson's skill set on sound, and Thelma of course. And we had Marty Scorsese. And Marty knew all about the music. He knew about *music*. And then there was a record guy — Eric Blackstead knew about the music.

I do remember when he came to 81st street and Broadway, and we had the rough cut in late November–early December. And Fred was there, and we … and Ted Ashley was there. And Fred did not want us speaking directly to Ted Ashley at all. We were supposed to be directing all of our questions, or comments, if you will, to Fred. And we refused to do that. Fred had been on our backs from the beginning, theoretically on the behalf of the entire Warner's conglomerate, to have a single-image film made by December, so that when kids came home from college in December 1969, they would throng to the theaters. And thank God for people like Bob Maurice, and people like Sid Kiewit, and other people, because we kept all of that push on Warner's side at bay, until we were able to complete the film in March and Ted Ashley was able to say, "Thank God you held out for the legacy part of this film. That its integrity is sacrosanct." A lot of arguments along the way, but the integrity remained.

And at this time, also remember that Warner Bros. was moribund. It was up for sale. It had just been purchased by Kinney, which was a parking garage conglomerate with funeral homes attached.

I noticed that on our invoices from Technicolor, that they would be processing our negative, but making two prints of it. One print would go to us and I called Technicolor and asked "where's the second print going to?" They said, "Oh, it's going to N.Y. The people in N.Y. are looking at it. That's our contractual arrangement with Warner Bros." And I said, "oh, that's curious." And Bob and I talked, and Michael talked, and said, this is totally against our relationship with the lab. We are the vendors of record with the laboratory, it's illegal for them to be sending a print to their client.

AP: So was Fred Weintraub added to the thing? In New York? Was that what he was doing?

DB: We were fearful of whatever they might be doing. So we took the negative out of the negative cutters hand. Remember this is 375,000 feet of 16-mm in hundreds and hundreds of cans, all well-labeled and everything. We brought it into our office, hired a twenty-four-hour security person with a gun, and went right on editing. But told Warner's that we were stopping unless they no longer requested a copy from Technicolor. That was issue number one.

Issue number two occurred in the first week or so of March, by which time we had mixed most of the film, and we had made an optical of the images at six different optical houses and married it all together. And we had at that point a four-hour cut mixed of the entire film. Warner's — we had a screening with Warner Bros. on March 10, and the movie was to open on March 21st. On March 10, with five hundred people in the screening room, and a lot of grass, we looked at the film, and we thought at that point, that Warner Bros would be cutting their own version of it. Because they wanted a two-hour film to give to exhibitors, not a four-hour film that we'd created. And that's the point at which we went in at night, to the Warner studio, and purloined the soundtrack and a lot of the work print. So it would be impossible for anybody to cut it. We thought perhaps John Cowley was cutting it. And it turned out that that was not the case. But it proved a negotiating point that still controlled the material until it got exhibited. We negotiated down from four hours to three hours four minutes, dropped some acts to which Warner's did not have rights, and then put out a three-hour, fourminute film in eight cities, on I think it was March 21st, 22nd … something like that.

AP: Could you tell us about Hendrix?

DB: It was funny, because he was working with a new band, and they had not practiced or rehearsed very much. And he was saying at some point in there, something like, "I'm just noodling, I'm just trying to find a tune, and we're just going to play slowly, and maybe it's going to be a little bit off-tune as we're trying to search to really synchronize our harmony," if you will. And then he explodes into this most disharmonious — if you will — musical explosion of sound. And you really wonder what it was that Jimi was looking at, or what did he see when he was playing that? What was going through his mind as he cascaded these chords, these riffs, and exploded?

He visualized it musically, or it almost wasn't music, it was a sound effect, or a series of sound effects, I think, that culminated what was going on in the sixties and I think maybe even was looking forward. To what he saw — the disharmony of the sixties, had actually represented to him, and to the people he represented.

"'Scuse me while I kiss the sky." That to me was like, "I'm not singing only to those who are left, the stragglers on the Matthew Brady landscape — I'm really going for the world. "'Scuse me while I kiss the sky." That was his sort of homily to all that *was*, all that had been before, and all that was to come afterwards. It was an incredible moment. He defied Michael Wadleigh to continue filming. You know, when he put his foot down on the foot pedal and he stared straight in to the lens. It was like, "you're never going to watch this — you're never going to believe what I'm gonna do next." It was that sort of arrogance, pride, humility — marvelous. Marvelous.

Country Joe has taken on the advocacy for veterans since Vietnam. And he is called upon all over the country and I'm sure in parts of the world, to talk about the role of veterans in society. He's a tremendously commendable force in that, and particularly now, we're welcoming home and sometimes not welcoming home so many people who have fought in Iraq, Afghanistan, and other places. Joe is going to be there and going to be more necessary to our society to raise the questions about how we are transitioning our warriors into citizens now that we're bringing them home finally, after the horrendous ten years. A really horrendous ten years. And Joe is still there and doing what he ought to be doing. Joe was an activist before Woodstock, during Woodstock, and after Woodstock.

DB: Now, Shrieve was the youngest performer on that stage. Before I did my book I did a little bit of research on this subject. And it also turned out that Michael had come to live in the same town that I was living — Grand View on Hudson. And he became a mentor to my son Jonathan, in drums and in music. Michael is just a — really an incredible *hero* for so many people who don't think it's possible for people to make the big time.

Except if they follow the example of his kind of persistence. Practice, practice, practice. You might not just get to Carnegie Hall, you might get to Max Yasgur's stage. You might be able to perform with Carlos Santana. Michael is just a phenomenal person to watch.

AP: Can we talk about the legacy of Woodstock, and the film? In your new introduction to the book, I found it very interesting to hear your observations of....

DB: ... by and large, we knew what we were doing, and we wanted the optical house and the mixing house to come to learn what we wanted to teach them. And that was very very important to us. So in the one incident that I cite, and there were many, but this is really a symbolic incident — was in the Warner Bros. mixing studio. Which had not been upgraded technologically for probably twenty years. And where we were assigned by Warner Bros. to mix our multiple tracks, the studio was in no way competent to be able to handle it. And it took hours and hours of time and repositioning and re-patching different plugs and cables and everything else in order to try to upgrade the technology. And while we waited we had a ping pong table brought in. And we would play ping pong while the technicians were trying to get it together.

The head of the sound department at Warner Bros. was George Groves, who mixed *The Jazz Singer*, the first talkie film in history. And he stood proud that the studio had not changed since then. I mean, if he was raising his right hand, that's what he was really kind of doing. And we just looked at it and just said, "We cannot mx here unless we do some upgrading." And so in the process of mixing, we had to do a lot of this upgrading.

* * *

That the film was completed at all was a minor miracle. But that the team was able to hold their own against the studio executives, who would have homogenized it, is remarkable. The film stands today as a living record of the festival, in the true spirit of *peace and love*, but also a shining example of Timothy Leary's *Think For Yourself, Question Authority.*

The people who made this film were already making their mark on the world, as we're about to see. These filmmakers drew on their previous experiences as part of the anti-war movement. They knew all about sticking it to the man.

Chapter 6

Jeanne Field

As New Yorkers prepared to usher in the new year 1967, a crowd of one thousand people gathered in Central Park and set fire to a Christmas tree in an impromptu protest against the Vietnam war. This gathering of early hippies brought with them rudimentary musical instruments and a flock of geese. Later that year, further protests in the park numbered in excess of one-hundred thousand. Police cars were politely turned away, covered in flowers. "We love cops, turn on cops." Turned on by the happening; the scene; the smoke; the crowd chanted. Draft cards were burned. Celebrities made appearances. The organization of these events promoted a community spirit that created a kind of social contract among the participants. An informal agreement was reached: the people could exist together, promote peace together, and just *be*. These demonstrations came to be known as be-ins. They set the scene for Woodstock. Jeanne Field was there.

Jeanne is the reason we were able to focus the film on Woodstock. My original correspondence with Jeanne led to her recruitment of Dale Bell, John Morris, and her husband John Binder to the project. From this vantage point we were able to interest Chip Monck, Michael Shrieve, and Joe McDonald.

Jeanne's career began with assistant camera work with the Maysles brothers on *Gimme Shelter* and Michael Wadleigh's documentary *Woodstock*. She was production coordinator for Martin Scorsese's *The Last Waltz* and David Lynch's *Eraserhead*. Jeanne spent much of the seventies collaborating on film projects with Neil Young, co-writing and producing the feature film *Human Highway*, among others. At one point during filming, Young seemed distracted and Jeanne asked what was troubling him. Young replied: "Oh, it's just America, man." Jeanne offered her commiserations about the war in Vietnam, but Young interjected. "No not the country — it's that band America! Everybody thinks I wrote the song *A Horse With No Name*."

Jeanne now runs an agency, Windfall Management, to represent writers, directors, and novelists in Los Angeles. I reached out to Jeanne through IMDb Pro agent listings and received a prompt reply. "Sure, let's talk about Woodstock. Can I bring some friends?"

Jeanne Field: I lived around the corner from the Fillmore East. And there was this attitude in St Marks place in the West Village — *peace and love*. I mean, it really did exist. We had preparation for it though. There had been be-ins in central Park that Allen Ginsberg and other people had formed, and a hundred thousand people would come together, and it was just lovely. You'd be on Sheep's Meadow and people would just be grooving, and music playing, I'd been part of a lot of peace marches or anti-war marches or civil rights movement marches — I mean, there was a lot of emotion attached to these gatherings. They weren't frivolous, they weren't just for fun — they really had a purpose. And I really felt like at Woodstock, that purpose really coalesced. I remember thinking, *my God I had no idea that there were so many people in agreement*. And that was the big word — *agreement* — and that's really what civilization is.

It's agreeing that we're all going to drive on the right side of the road, or whatever. We agree just what our social rules are.

Aidan Prewett: How did you get to Woodstock?

JF: I actually had tickets. I was living in the East Village, and Jim Rose's Eastside Bookstore was across the street, and it had one of the early posters. So I thought that sounded like fun, and Michael Wadleigh had a camper. So I talked to him; he was up for going up with his wife Renee, so I bought early tickets to Woodstock. Which I can't find. They'd be worth a lot, wouldn't they?

Once the filming had been somewhat organized, I came up on the Thursday night, the day before. Van Schley and I drove up Eddie Kramer, Jimi Hendrix's producer, who was the music recordist for the concert, and the car was on the shoulder of the road to dodge the traffic jams. Van said, "If we want to get there, this is what we have to do." It was terrifying.

AP: And you also worked on *Gimme Shelter* with the Maysles brothers?

JF: Well, I knew the Stones' road manager; he would just give you a backstage pass. So I went down to Madison Square Garden, standing by the stage door. And here comes Al Maysles in his van. He pulls up, all by himself, and he starts to unload equipment, so I go over — "Can I help you, Al?" And he says, "Yeah, take my tripod and put it right in front of Mick Jagger's microphone." So I say, *hey!*

So I do that, there's a security guard there and say, "I have to stay here. I have to protect this little tripod here." And so Al comes in with his camera; puts it down. And I just stay there with Al, while he's shooting Mick, and pretty soon, the crowd surges, and we get crushed. We are literally crushed together against the stage. We have to be pulled — the Stones had to be pulled aside, and a couple of guys come and pull Al and the camera and me up and over the stage to rescue us.

AP: Can we hear about Hendrix?

JF: I thought that he was supposed to end the show. I mean, I thought that was all planned. And I thought, *how perfect.* Sha-Na-Na had been on — such a crazy little act, and then here comes Jimi Hendrix, who was like a God in our world, really. And he started out rough. I figured he was either exhausted from staying up all night, or disconcerted that there were so few people he was playing to. So he was kind of noodling. His act had no real center to it, it wasn't like he was really putting it out there. I mean, everybody was so wasted, by that morning. Not necessarily on drugs but just by the experience, and filthy, and there are some shots of the audience in the film and it shows how people were not at their best. But that's as it should be.

And then all of a sudden — you know. He *got it.* The first chords of the *Star Spangled Banner.* And literally, he was electric. It was electrifying to us. I was at his feet, which was pretty amazing. Michael Wadleigh literally was under his microphone. Dick Pearce, who I was working with was off to the right a little bit, but we were right there. It was such a great ending to that. And then he shifted down into *Purple Haze*, and it was just perfect.

AP: Do you feel that Woodstock had an effect on society, moving forward?

JF: For me, Woodstock was the beginning of that realization that you can say you want to change the world, but before you can do that you have to change yourself. And that fed into what the seventies became for us. How do we change ourselves, if we don't want to be part of the conglomerate that's feasting on the icons. For a lot of people, it was a spiritual thing. People reaching out, whether it was yoga or Buddhism or Hinduism — George

Harrison goes to India and brings all of that back. And people kind of opened up their minds as much as their hearts have been opened up at Woodstock. People did change. I know people make fun of the seventies, but I thought it was a great decade.

* * *

Woodstock took advantage of the pre-existing protest movements and the crowd's knowledge of their expected behavior patterns. The people of New York knew how it was done — they had been staging successful be-ins for two years prior.

The spirit of organization that Jeanne witnessed early in 1967 was growing into an international phenomenon. The year 1968 saw the rise of student movements across the world, in the vein of Mario Savio and Berkeley's Free Speech Movement. The most successful of these student movements was in France, where for a brief moment in time, the entire nation was brought to a standstill.

Chapter 7

John Binder

As location supervisor for the *Woodstock* documentary, John Binder was the first member of the film crew to set foot on the festival site. He held the fort for a full week before the festival, secured liaison with the organizers, and directed new crew arrivals in the ethos of the film: *Film What Turns You On.*

Dale Bell gave John Binder and Michael Wadleigh (*Woodstock* director) their first professional film gig at WNET public television in New York. Together, Binder and Wadleigh started a production company, Paradigm Films, which produced a number of documentaries for WNET along with editors Thelma Schoonmaker and Martin Scorsese. This formidable team also worked together for free on anti-war films, including *No Vietnamese Ever Called Me Nigger*, which is now in the Smithsonian's African-American Museum.

Binder and Wadleigh were responsible for the split-screen effect used throughout *Woodstock*; they had travelled to Germany to bring back a state-of-the-art editing system (KEM), which they first experimented with on their film of Aretha Franklin live in Detroit.

On their way back from Germany, Binder and Wadleigh found themselves in Paris in May 1968.

What had begun the previous year as an innocuous request by University of Paris students to loosen restrictions on male-female dormitory visits, soon turned into demonstrations, arrests, and shutdown of the university's Nanterre campus. This led to a three-hundred-student occupation of the Sorbonne campus, which was met with tear gas and clubbings from riot police. Forty thousand students took to the streets, constructing makeshift barricades and throwing cobblestones. Five hundred students were arrested; hospitalizations numbered at roughly 250 police and many more demonstrators. Over the next week, more than eleven million French workers walked off the job, joining students in the street or occupying their workplaces. The country was locked in stalemate. Shaken, President Charles de Gaulle announced the dissolution of the National Assembly and called a general election for the following month.

In June, de Gaulle won the election, rioting ceased, and life and France returned — for the most part — to normal.

Aidan Prewett: How did you wind up in Paris?

John Binder: We were going to buy a Steenbeck editing system — D.A. Pennebaker and those guys had Steenbecks. And this guy said there's a better one, but you'll have to go talk to him in Germany. Michael and I wanted to go to France anyway. We went to Germany, and bought the biggest KEM unit that they had there, and some other stuff that was a little bit more experimental. We went back to Paris and the riots broke out — the '68 Revolution broke out. So we were there for that; we spent a couple of days running with those kids. I got slugged on the chin by a teargas grenade. There were irate old ladies dropping flower pots from their window boxes on the would-be revolutionaries in the streets below. I saw the famous Vogue model Verushka chased by a *flick* wanting to crown her with his long baton. I listened, half-comprehending to the students in the Sorbonne, with their streaming red freedom scarves, proclaiming their dreams of revolution as their ancestors had two hundred years before. It was great — really a great moment, to have been a part of that — and then to be a part of Woodstock too.

AP: And also to have been a part of Bobby Kennedy's campaign.

JB: My partner and I were filming Senator Bobby Kennedy at a political convention in Albany N.Y. We arrived in a limousine at the Convention Hall, where a crunch of screaming fans greeted him. We made it into the building and down a long hall into a "green room," here he was to wait before making his speech. The bodyguards couldn't keep part of the crowd from pressing into that room behind us. They just had to be near him. We were right behind Bobby, filming until the floor lamps were knocked over and the room went dark. The crush was so great that Bobby and I were smashed together and pushed across the room. There was a sofa, which caught Bobby's legs. He tumbled backwards over it and was turned upside down. I stayed on my feet, but we were sandwiched in the corner like sardines or two pieces of bread. I was screaming for the bodyguards to rescue him, but they couldn't reach us. Bobby's head was between my feet and his shoes were in my face. For some minutes we remained in that absurd posture, long enough for me to reflect that this was going to be another of life's moments to remember.

AP: Hendrix at Woodstock must have been another one of those moments.

JB: Jimi finding those chilling first notes of the *Star Spangled Banner* after twenty minutes of stoned noodling, searching for a tune, was about the most powerful dramatic moment of my life. We'd been half a decade trying to stop a genocidal war in Asia and to discover a decent America again. Jimi found it in that sacred anthem by the dawn's early grey light in a muddy cow pasture full of grimy hippie children. I cried.

AP: When you first arrived at Woodstock, I'm guessing the Yasgur farm must have still been a farm?

JB: It was — just a pastoral farm with a little road that they'd built. The organizers somehow had to leave Woodstock — didn't get the permit in time — so they had to quickly assemble that stage. They were working long hours day and night. But it was otherwise this pastoral farm with all the fencing and all of that. And then people started pouring in.... Michael Lang seemed to be the most aware of this youth movement phenomenon that was going on. Wadleigh and I had been to Haight-Ashbury, and we'd been around some of it. But the day the kids started coming in was a little terrifying. I remember being really anxious. A guy came up to me — this guy had been a very successful photographer. He gave it up and was living a counter-cultural life and he said a couple of wise things. He looked at me and said: "What's wrong with you?" and I said, "Jesus Christ, they're not ready for this!" He said, "Can you do anything about it?" I said, "No," so he said, "Well then, quit worrying about it." And it was that moment when somebody tells you the right thing. It was like stop motion when you see those shots of an empty stadium — somebody should have had a fixed camera to see it fill up, because that phenomenon was as powerful as anything that happened up there.

You know, just in terms of the ambience, being there initially — when I showed up I asked around for Mike Lang. There were guys doing a certain amount of organizational work in this green farmhouse. And there's all these long-hair kids running around doing various things and there were a couple of moments that I noticed. One of them was — I'm standing there, waiting for Mike, who's on two phones, and in walks this hippie-style guy, and another guy behind him with trays full of marijuana. They were cookie sheets. It was green grass, and they took it in and — "Excuse me," and they go into the kitchen and put it in the oven and dried it so that it could be smoked. That was the first vision.

The second vision: While I'm waiting, finally about to get to talk to Mike, and a Crosby, Stills, Nash and Young album was playing. I'd never heard of them, 'cos we were just hardworking filmmakers, and not as culturally hip as some people. Everyone was just listening; grooving. And then the whole place was buzzing, and a Joe Cocker record came on. We *all* stood at attention. It was like, who the hell is that guy? And it was — for me it was a great transitional moment.

So Mike and I talked about the film. Warner Bros. had actually sent up a traditional filmmaker, whose name was Arthur Barron. He was a good fellow, and he was a good filmmaker, but he was used to scripted documentaries. So Mike said, "Can you get rid of this guy — just tell him whatever you want to tell him 'cos we're busy up here." So I took Arthur over and he was very nervous about what was happening. He said, "What are you going to do, how are you going to do it? What's your organization, what's your thing?" I told him we weren't organized. He goes, "What?!" I said, "Well, that's the point. If you look at this, there's no way to centrally direct this." I wasn't being a smartass; it was just an intuitive answer. I said, "These guys don't need direction. We all understand the stage is covered, and we're just coordinating who shot what, let's get some more around the site." That way we couldn't be stopped. If we had an organization, that would have broken down a couple of days prior. Anyway, he got on the phone and called Warner's and said, "This place is a disaster and these guys don't know what they're doing. So cancel this thing!" I mean, he got pretty vehement, especially with me. So that was kind of a funny button at the end. We could laugh at that when the deal was finalized.

AP: As you were moving all around the Woodstock site, what kind of energy did you sense from the crowd?

JB: As I circulated around before the music started, I sort of listened and talked to the people, and you got a sense that there was something quasi-sacred about the whole thing. There was this one moment where a bunch of us were sitting up at the Hog Farm's camp in teepees one night. I'd never been in a teepee I assure you. And we're sitting around a little fire in the teepee, passing a joint, and a lot of silence went on. And there was a hubbub outside. I said, "What's up?" and they all seemed to communicate in some kind of spiritual way — honest to God — the hippies who had been in collectives. They all just moved out of the teepee. It was the Hog Farmers greeting the Merry Pranksters.

Ken Kesey wasn't there, but Ken Babbs was — he was a kind of leader, an elder statesman. They came together, and Wavy Gravy, the Hog Farm guy, came out of the teepee. These other guys came in with their bus, *Further*. What was great dramatically — I didn't film it 'cos I didn't have anybody with me and there were no lights — but in the headlights of the bus, Wavy Gravy and Babbs threw the I Ching to see how this was all going to work out. It was very exotic to me. I asked how it was going to turn out and they said, "It's gonna be great."

Through the whole thing, there certainly was no centralized thought from any individuals. But there was a preparation. The Fillmore East was a preparation for the music side, in really a lot of ways. What had gone on for a couple of years in San Francisco was coming east, and they came with intention. There were a lot of groups that saw this instantly. And before — maybe even before all those people arrived, this was going to be an opportunity for those philosophies.

For the film, our people — most of them — had been at and filmed peace and anti-war demonstrations. Which were not, in physical terms, not that much different for a cameraman. Because you never knew where the next eventful moment was.

AP: The rain was quite eventful, I'd imagine.

JB: Well, in the dark, after the big rainstorm, some time had passed since John Morris talked about getting away from the electrical towers — and God knew where that electricity might be running. These guys had a caucus, all the guys in charge. I just joined the group and listened. And there was a whole discussion, it went on and on. *Dare we turn the electricity back on?*

It was a terrifying moment. I wasn't part of the decision, I was just a witness, but they were seriously considering canceling everything at that point. It was, *My God, what if we electrocuted someone?* The people weren't all crowded right up against the towers, but there were a lot of people in the mud. I think it was Steve Cohen as I visually recall, broke away from the group while these grown-ups were talking — he was a tough roadie, you know — and ran the stage, I believe. He just went up to the big box, and he grabbed that handle and pulled the switch. The electricity came on, and nobody fried.

AP: Did you identify with any of the film movements that were big at the time — *Cinema Verité*, or *Direct Cinema?*

JB: When Michael Wadleigh and I came out of NYU film school, we were hired by Dale who was producing three hours of social documentaries a week for public television. So that was a progression that started more or less with the *Cinema Verité* people in N.Y. like Ricky Leacock and Bob Drew and D.A. Pennebaker who were really great filmmakers. And they were better initiators of films than we were. But they had a philosophy where you just film what's going on, no interviews, no interaction. Michael Wadleigh and I and some others were a little bit at odds with them. We never quite adhered to the rules. There was a little tension about that.

But I think what Wadleigh achieved — aside from having the ego to hold this whole group together on a film side — he thought we could do a technically better job than what was the norm. Most of the people who worked on this film thought that we could get better sound and get more consistent pictures if they could fit on a television, which was very conservative. Technically they didn't even like a camera to shake. That was the major change, the transformation that Wadleigh brought to the project.

But what Wadleigh and Marty Scorsese — who was a key editor up until the finishing of the film where they let Thelma's taste rule over Marty's, and perhaps wisely — and Thelma Schoonmaker achieved: those three people and everybody around them took *Cinema Verité* to a point where they could make it closer to rock 'n' roll, and closer to that kind of art, where you can shape it. Just to put those multiple images on the screen, would have driven the Maysles and those other guys crazy, because that wasn't the way life is — *in black and white and through my lens.* And you don't even get close with that microphone.

That's why we got a lot of those early jobs. And that's how we formed our group, because Marty would do some editing, Dale would hire us, or get us hired, Jeanne would get things set. But we were all employed by that — our ethos. So Michael took these ideas further and said, "This is the reality we shot, but we can shape it like music." In film terms, I think that was a legacy that's taken for granted now. Indie films, everybody's films. You can use the real thing, real acting, real stuff, and then orchestrate it. *Woodstock* was an orchestration of a very complicated event.

AP: *Woodstock* was a big part of why I went into documentary filmmaking. I think the spirit of *disruption* that carries throughout that film was really inspiring to me and to a lot of other people. Do you see *Woodstock* reflected in filmmaking today?

JB: We came in and it was a lot simpler technology, sixteen-millimeter film. But it was disruptive to a small circle of people, as your technology and your attitude is to a very large number of people. It's pretty much one-to-one. And that's the way change seems to come. I mean, rock 'n' roll was disruptive. I thought rock and roll disrupted our entire culture. I mean, it pushed jazz out of the way. And then film at least settled down for a while, and suddenly digital technology really exploded. So it was an experimental age.

AP: Did *Woodstock* inspire a generation to stand up for what they believed in?

JB: I think the whole era did. Woodstock was an artifact of that attitude. But today you have the Burning Man festival, and that goes on — which is another big sort of moving Woodstock, and it's annual, and it goes on — I haven't gone to them, but it sounds like it's in the spirit of Woodstock. On the other hand, you have the Occupy movement, where they arrest fifty people for speaking out. So we're still fighting this tension. So when you assemble politically, you might get shot in America now. That's literal. But if you assemble and keep it within the annals of commerce — I don't want to get too heavy on capitalism, but you know. It's still a tension. You know, what's a gathering. How dangerous or how fruitful is a gathering to the people who think they're in charge of something?

What was good about Woodstock, in a sense — culturally, politically, to me — was that the gist of what everybody's saying here was: *Not only did that thing occur, but the people behaved like grown-ups enough to see it through.* And some of the establishment was very happy when Altamont became a disaster. Because it said, *well, now we're back to normal. You need Daddy and Mommy.*

* * *

Woodstock was the product of a number of top professionals — talent, staging, organizers, filmmakers — who came together and did what needed to be done. Once the festival began, it worked without much central direction because it was clear to everyone that if they didn't make it work, this was a disaster area waiting to happen. Re-starting the power after the rainstorm was a risky move; a mass electrocution would have made Altamont look like a picnic. But as Jimi Hendrix played his final notes on Max Yasgur's stage, the remaining stragglers in their muddy encampments witnessed the conclusion of a festival that succeeded in ways that nobody anticipated. The muddy mess had turned into a victory dance for the counterculture, for the anti-war message, for civil rights, for free-thinking.

For the two men who bankrolled the festival, John Roberts and Joel Rosenman, the debts incurred by the festival and lawsuits from farms surrounding the festival site, followed them into the 1980s.

Michael Lang's career burgeoned as a producer and investor in recorded music, festivals, and films. He is the curly-haired organizational face of the festival and has resurrected the brand for several anniversaries, including Woodstock 50.

The Atlantic album arranged by Ahmet Ertegun and recorded by Hendrix producer Eddie Kramer went on to release a triple album soundtrack in 1970. It hit number one on the Billboard albums chart. A further double album followed the next year. A photograph by Magnum photographer Burk Uzzle was featured on the album cover: a couple wrapped in a blanket amid the mud and chaos. The couple are now known to be Bobbi Kelly and Nick Ercoline, who were married in 1971 and are still together today.

The *Woodstock* documentary turned one of the biggest profits-on-return of any film in history. All told, Warner Bros. and Wadleigh/Binder's Paradigm films outlaid roughly $600,000 for the shoot, editing, and distribution. The film returned over $50,000,000 in domestic returns on its initial cinema run alone.

The bands that played at Woodstock were furnished with a post-festival calling card for life. Bands that were relative newcomers, like Santana and Joe Cocker, suddenly gained international followings. Established acts were cemented at the very top of their game: Hendrix, Janis Joplin, The Who, Joan Baez, Jefferson Airplane. Crosby, Stills, Nash and Young were a new supergroup who quickly attained legend status. The Grateful Dead and Creedence Clearwater Revival elected not to have their material released in the film as they felt that their performances were underwhelming due to a variety of technical issues.

After all, these musical heroes are real people, going about their lives and encountering obstacles along the way. A year after Woodstock, Jimi Hendrix and Janis Joplin succumbed to overdoses within weeks of each other. The conflict in Vietnam continued until 1973; the last Americans left in 1975. The people continued to struggle for peace, civil rights, and women's rights. Woodstock was an image, an icon. What it represented — and continues to represent — is more important than what it actually achieved.

When it comes down to it, maybe these heroes aren't the Gods we wish they could be. By conferring deity status upon them, we're doing them a disservice. They deserve to be recognized as true achievers, not just geniuses who were born with amazing talents. By calling them Gods, we're doing ourselves a disservice, too. As humans, we have more in common.

Leni Riefenstahl was aware of this. By painting Hitler as a God, she cast him as an omnipotent force, someone completely apart from and above the people. Someone born with supernatural abilities who could change the world. Surely only a sociopath would truly desire this kind of fervent mass adoration.

Woodstock worked, and was *witnessed* working, thanks to the documentary work of John Binder, Dale Bell, and Jeanne Field.

Their team's film output stood on the toes of the previous generation. The old studio system was dying and making way for new ways of filmmaking — more accessible equipment, more "real" filmmaking. The film world was changing in the same ways as the wider society. Protest movements were stepping on a lot of toes. Disruption was their *modus operandi.* They scared the hell out of the older generation: *This is simply not the way things are done.*

As John Binder mentions, Altamont must have been something of a relief to certain parts of the establishment. Just four months after Woodstock, this new festival put a damper on the dream of the hippie utopia. The organizers' approach to Altamont was perhaps an early expression of the next decade. Misplaced self-assuredness — the *me* decade. If Woodstock could succeed, despite all the chaos, surely other large-scale festivals would be easy. The success of the approaching Altamont Speedway Free Festival could be taken for granted.

PART TWO
Altamont and the Aftermath

In a short span of time, within the same country and culture, the same factors that made Woodstock a success melded to construct something that became its very antithesis. On December 6, 1969, another mass gathering numbering around three-hundred thousand took place at a motorsport venue outside San Francisco. The venue had changed, literally the day before, as the Rolling Stones and their organizers faced contractual issues at the previous site. Similar location issues faced Woodstock, and the Stones brought in Michael Lang to assist with the logistics of the last-minute relocation.

Rolling Stones tour manager Sam Cutler was in charge of organizational details, including the hiring of the Hells Angels as a security team. The Stones had previously used the British Hells Angels in London without incident. But it turned out the British Hells Angels were not the real deal. At Altamont, the Angels did what they were told to do: guard the stage and performers. They were paid in amphetamines and alcohol. Four deaths occurred; one was a stabbing incident at the foot of the stage. The day after the festival, Cutler released a statement in which he took responsibility for the disaster. But there were other factors. It was a perfect storm of chaos.

In the way Woodstock haphazardly become an icon for peace, Altamont's lack of clear organization unearthed the darker underbelly of the counterculture. The Maysles brothers captured this twist of fate in their documentary *Gimme Shelter*. While *Woodstock* portrays hippies dancing and sliding through the mud, *Gimme Shelter* depicts brawl after brawl in the dusty barren landscape of the speedway. The film leads to a brutal climax; the Maysles camera team captures the infamous stabbing in front of Mick Jagger's microphone stand.

Chip Monck was also on the team, as the head of production for the Stones. There were other bands on the bill, but as the Stones were headlining, Chip was in charge of all staging and lighting. We're about to hear more from Chip and our previous interview subjects. They weren't all in the same room, but as this and several future discussions centered around a common theme, the conversations have been curated here into a cohesive piece.

Chapter 8

Altamont

The man who was stabbed and died in the crowd at Altamont was Meredith Hunter. He was an eighteen-year-old black kid who was there to see the Stones. He was right at the lip of the stage, right in front of Jagger, when he was hoisted up by his hair and punched by a member of the security team. As Hunter scrambled back into the crowd, he was pounced on by four other security personnel and was kicked and beaten. A minute or so later, Hunter returned with a long-barreled pistol.

For a moment, the crowd split apart around him, then a member of the Hells Angels burst forward, stabbing Hunter four times. Hunter fell to the ground where he was further kicked and beaten. He died in a first aid area behind the stage.

Three others died at the festival site. The edge of the speedway was available for parking, but the space quickly became a drag-race area. Two were killed in a hit-and-run incident; one person drowned in an irrigation canal. Hospitals around the Bay Area were inundated with festivalgoers. A lot of bad acid and pills were circulating, but the most common hospitalizations were injuries incurred from drag-racing cars and brawls. The Angels' weapon of choice for this festival was pool cues — sawn off to a little longer than a billy club.

There was a lack of genuine authority at both festivals, but the same disordered approach that calmed Woodstock helped to create the violent scenes at Altamont. The crowd at Altamont fashioned its character around the environment that was laid out for it, as we'll discover shortly.

Santana was the first band on the bill. Even their mid-afternoon set was punctuated by violence.

Michael Shrieve: Altamont had the strongest negativity of any group environment that I've ever experienced. From the moment we got there, it was palpable. And this was after Woodstock. It was the extreme opposite of the feeling that was at Woodstock. I mean, literally it felt like evil in the air. It felt like this weight that was … there wasn't the lightness of all the hippie movement prior to that, living in San Francisco and the Bay Area. Never really considering myself a hippie but being around that and knowing what that feeling could be — this was the exact opposite. And that became … the crowd … I'm not saying the crowd was dark, but something was permeating the air there, that certainly caused that emotion to be there. And certainly that negativity did come to light. I just wanted to get out of there. We chose even to not be in the film because it was so weighty and negative. Even though we performed there and were filmed there like the other groups.

Chip Monck: Well, we started out with the Fillmore in sight, which was on top of a hill. And the audience was at a slight incline all the way down. Which was a great idea, because all that crowd pressure was delineated. Therefore, here's a stage that was available that was one meter high. So we put it at the top of the hill, and everybody could see nicely, and all the pressure was neutralized by the fact that it was an incline. They weren't going down a bowl into a hole.

Then all of a sudden, the Fillmore, who owned that site, decided if they can't have a piece of the "feature film" that's being made, and nobody thought of it as a feature at that time — the venue was not available. The Fillmore said fine, get off the land.

Well I think we had four days, if not two. So finding other staging elements, or getting a scaffold company in to help you out, and then deck it, and put plywood on top of that. But unfortunately at Altamont, the performance area was at the bottom of a slight incline. So all of a sudden, stage is without a sufficient barrier.

We'd gone through most of '69 and a lot of '70 European, without ever using a barrier. It was great. In 1972, when we had the audience right up against the deck, the deck was at five-foot-two. Just perfect. 'Cos they weren't going to hop up. They'd have to stand on somebody to do so. And they had some sort of respect, to not do that. So, barriers never really came in until this assault on the acts started to happen. I mean, when you get up on stage what do you do? The easiest thing to do is dance with Bruce Springsteen, or be kissed by Bono. That's about the only time there's any necessity for you to be there. So, here we are at the bottom of a hill, and here comes all this pressure. And the Angels weren't helping much at all. And it got pretty ugly.

MS: It was the wrong idea to hire Hells Angels as security. Even though what they did, in their mind, they saw someone with a gun. And so they did what they thought they had to do. They thought a performer was going to be assassinated or something like that, but it was just very dark, it was an unbelievable feeling. I could talk at length about why that thing went wrong, and I think it probably starts with the intentions of why it was even put together. And then the way it was put together.

It was different to Woodstock, the reasons for being put together were more pure with Woodstock, with Michael Lang and John Morris. It was a mess, but it was a different energy. Here it was put together by the Stones; rushed together. It was a disaster.

John Binder: I think those naive Brits didn't know what the biker gangs were.

John Morris: That's it exactly. Sam was an Englishman, who was used to Hells Angels who were London lambretta riders. And he just didn't — he just had no clue. He thought they were mild and peaceful and it'd be fine. He worked with the Grateful Dead, and he worked as an English roadie, and he was that hard-ass English attitude of *do it my way or not do it.*

JB: The Oakland Angels were something else.

JM: I think that's really what happened, is — and I've talked to Mick about it — they had no intention that it would be as negative as it was. I mean, Mick got smacked in the mouth the minute he stepped out of his trailer to go on. One of the Angels hit him. They also beat up Marty Valen from the Airplane. The Airplane were not an aggressive or antagonistic band. And I don't think you can blame it on the Maysles — but I don't think they were antithetical to that situation. I think the Woodstock situation created itself. And the film crew were of a like mind — "Yeah, hey, this is really interesting. It's an historic thing, and it's positive — let's go with it."

Dale Bell: There was such real difference between what went on in Altamont and what we were a part of.

JM: It was day and night.

DB: It was like animalistic at Altamont. That the Maysles would go on and make a film called *Gimme Shelter* about this — and that we would make the film about Woodstock. I mean, the positiveness of Woodstock and the negativity that was infused in every part of *Gimme Shelter*. I mean, I think as an audience one has to think, what really might have happened, had the Maysles made a film about Woodstock? Would it have been the same kind of film that we had? And Al would tell me *no*. Not at all. They never would have conveyed the ebullience, the camaraderie, the commitment to each other in the way that we did.

CM: Most of the Angels' superiors were at a meeting somewhere else, so the juniors, as it were, were in charge. And since the payment for their security was a bushel basket of assorted pills, and a U-Haul truck full of beer, they didn't really have any balance to help anybody out. So they reverted, I guess, to punching the shit out of people. So they started doing that. Then they brought the Harley Davidson choppers in, set them in front of the stage, to "help" the security. Yeah, sure. They just wanted some other reason to be able to punch somebody out, because they pushed over the chopper or something. And it just got out of control. Because there was basically no way to talk an angel down. There's a stare-down technique that I understand that the angels use. And if you break away from that confrontation, you'll usually get punched up, because you weren't up to it.

I spent fifteen minutes trying to get the stage rug off the truck. I'd pulled the rug off the truck when they were leaving at about six in the morning, and a chopper came off with it. And I actually had a conversation that lasted fifteen minutes before I got it with a pool cue. But — I think that's the longest I've ever had their attention. It's usually much shorter than that.

AP: I'd like just a little more detail about the pool cue…

CM: They knocked all my front teeth out. So then I bought a case of brandy and I found out where they'd gone, and I traded it for the rug. Then I went to see the dentist.

AP: You went to speak to the family of the person who was killed.

CM: Well, I went to try and find whatever family he had. I finally found the address, I knocked on the door and introduced myself, and she had a cup of tea in her hand, and she threw it in my face and slammed the door. I decided, well, I'll wait a week and come back.

We sat on the porch — I wasn't allowed in the house. And I wasn't offered a cup of tea or anything — it didn't make any difference. I wasn't looking for hospitality, I thought something should be said. And I said it. That it is — an absolute disaster has happened to your life, and we caused it. I'm not a Hells Angel. I'm a technician. A designer. I work for some of the acts. And I'm terribly sorry.

AP: Why did you feel that was your responsibility?

CM: It wasn't my responsibility; it should have been done by fuckin' Jagger. Or anybody else that had any clout. It should have been done by Sam Cutler, or Emmett Drogan, or Rock Scully. They're the ones who made the decision to use the Angels. And possibly, there should have been a foundation set up or something.

I don't think Meredith was a meth dealer. I don't know why everybody — all of a sudden these stories came out, about what a bad person he was. I'm not quite sure. I don't have that ability. I'm not able to find out that sort of information. I don't have that sort of underground — I don't want to have that sort of underground in San Francisco. I already got shot once in San Francisco, while sitting at a table, talking with — I'll just give you her first name — Kathleen. And we were talking, and suddenly it's "Fuck you, whitey," she pulled out a .38 and shot me in the shoulder. And I said, excuse me — if you don't mind I'll go pick up the check now. And I said to reception, would you mind calling me an ambulance. Paid the check, walked out again, and she'd gone. So I don't go to San Francisco anymore.

JM: I have had a conversation with Jagger about it, and it embarrassed the living daylights out of him, because they did sing *Street Fighting Man*, they did have a lot of songs in that direction and that level. It destroyed it for them. I mean, it ruined their whole American tour, and they didn't want to come back for a while. And there were reasons why they didn't come back for a while. I mean, there were threats from the Angels to Jagger. And I worked with him on the '72 tour and helped plan a lot of it. And he was very paranoid about going on stage. We had conversations like, "Look Mick, if somebody's gonna get you, they're gonna get you. I can hire the best security, you know, we can sweep the halls, this, that, and the other, but if somebody wants you, they're going to get you. You've got fifty to sixty thousand people out there, and you just can't control all of them." I remember saying to him, "We can get you a Eichmann style booth" — and he started laughing, but that was the first break of the fear. But that was the choice.

JB: The Popemobile.

JM: Right. Either be Mick Jagger, or put yourself in a bulletproof box. And he eventually didn't do that, but he was terrified. With good reason.

JB: I think it has to do with the music too. Nobody was singing *Fighting Man.* That ambience is carried, and I wonder about Hollywood pouring out everything of violence it does today. But at Woodstock nobody came up and sang an inflammatory song of that type. Everybody loved the Stones, but when you bring out the content of their stuff, and then the mistake of hiring the Hells Angels, it's what happens.

JB: David Myers — who did the Port-o-San section at Woodstock — He was asked to go film the Angels reactions to the *Gimme Shelter* film. The Hells Angels had a three-storey Victorian that was their headquarters in Oakland. And David Myers and a sound guy go over there, and Al Maysles has a projector that he'd brought over there, and he's going to run some of the footage. Something happened, and I don't know what it was — and not unusual for those guys, they got very upset. Some of the Angels felt insulted by something, And Myers says — he goes into the men's room, they had a large bathroom, and he goes in there, and one of these Angels has Albert Maysles against a wall and wants to beat him up.

He was the kind of guy — he was a non-violent person, but he was sort of fearless, ‘cos some of those camera guys are. And he went through this whole thing of trying to diffuse the situation, but he's dealing with a loaded gun in this Hells Angels guy. He said Maysles looked totally shocked that he was in this position. And later David said he was naive. He had no idea of the dynamite he had here, And I think the guy finally punched him. But if you look at the film and you look at Mick Jagger's face, he's terrified when he's trying to calm the audience. So I think there are people who can't grasp that here in America there are a large number of people who are very violent. And Altamont — I think the people responsible at Altamont didn't understand that.

* * *

In January 1970, *Rolling Stone* magazine published a comprehensive feature detailing the extent of the Altamont disaster. Causes listed included the last-minute venue change, the vehicle access, the low stage and a poor-quality sound system. In some ways, the failure of Altamont and the success of Woodstock came down to luck; the chaotic elements of both were very similar. With just a little push, both festivals could have become even greater disasters.

The *Rolling Stone* article details how observers were quick to shift the blame from Sam Cutler to the Rolling Stones themselves. The hasty organization, post-Woodstock, to demonstrate that the Stones could also draw that kind of throng, was seen as self-aggrandizement; a public display of the Stones' power as the biggest touring band in the world. How badly did they need to prove this? Were they troubled by their apparent inability to outsell the Beatles? At the festival, the Stones sequestered themselves in their trailers behind the stage and seemed intent on cultivating their untouchable superstar image by surrounding themselves with their burly security guards of choice.

Five months pre-Altamont, at the Hyde Park free concert that was policed by the London Hells Angels, Jagger is on record as detailing to his financial manager how easily he could move a crowd to violent action with his voice in the same way that Hitler did. It's not exactly maniacal for a performer to believe this, but it is an ego trip. And Jagger took things one step further in 1972, hiring Leni Riefenstahl to take couples' shots with his then-wife Bianca.

In a Freudian kind of way, it is easy to be absorbed by something morally repugnant. The Rolling Stones won't be the last rock stars to be inspired by the propaganda techniques of the Nazis. Well-documented examples also involve David Bowie, Lemmy Kilmister, John Lennon, Bryan Ferry, the Sex Pistols, and Siouxsie and the Banshees, among others. *Triumph of the Will* is almost a necessary study piece for anyone playing to stadium audiences. So when our questions about the feeling of power drew frequent responses referencing Hitler, we knew we were onto something.

Chapter 9

Ian Anderson

It's dark backstage. We're ushered through a decrepit corridor behind the cyclorama and given our position for the interview. We're on prompt side — the wing of Stage Left. While the corridors of Melbourne's Palais Theatre may lack some of the usual updates, the stage and wings boast an impressive array of technical equipment. The publicist who brought us through knows this venue well — this is a great backdrop for an interview.

"You guys will need to keep this to about ten minutes. The sound check isn't going well."

We're right next to the band. Sound check is happening in front of us, but we don't have time to appreciate it. The usual rigmarole of setting up lights and camera takes time — mainly due to the need to make alterations for the specific venue.

We hear feedback through the speakers. Somebody swears. The song dies.

"No, no — take it from the top."

The song starts again. *Aqualung*. This has bought us a few precious minutes. A moment of relief, followed by the realization that our subject may not be in the best of moods. Any second now Ian Anderson — front man for Jethro Tull — will exit the stage. We'd better be ready.

Anderson has been the undisputed leader of Jethro Tull since 1968. To date, the band has sold an estimated sixty million albums worldwide. Their career was evidently not adversely affected by Anderson's decision to skip Woodstock. He didn't want to spend his weekend in a field of unwashed hippies. He's a no-nonsense kind of guy.

In 1988, Tull took out the Grammy for Best Hard Rock/Metal Performance in a surprise triumph over Metallica. When Metallica picked up a Grammy in 1992, drummer Lars Ulrich thanked Jethro Tull for not releasing an album that year.

Our cameras are finally ready. *Aqualung* draws to a close. A few seconds later Ian Anderson is shaking my hand. The sound check is forgotten; he's a pro. We know that Anderson has a storied history. What we're not prepared for, however, is just how profound his insight would be. What we were told would be a ten-minute interview quickly turned into a stellar discussion. We left the Palais with twenty-eight minutes of excellent footage that would become the backbone of our film. It all came back to the Nazis.

Aidan Prewett: Do you ever feel that there's a sense of power when you walk out and there are thousands of people cheering for you?

Ian Anderson: Not in the sense of the National Socialist Party doing a Hitler rally or something like that. It's not a sense of going out andworking people up into a frenzy. I know there are bands that do that ... the raised fists, heavy metal hard rock kind of thing. We're not like that, it's a bit more invitational — come and find us. Meet people halfway. If you get out there and try to get all over them with this rabble-rousing behavior, I think it's rather vulgar. I think you have to let people make their little journey to you. So you try to create the environment where there's that meeting of minds and souls half-way, rather than you just being all over them. Like a ton of emotional bricks.

AP: You've sung before about the misuse of that kind of power, by religious organizations — particularly in *My God*.... Do you understand the temptation that people might feel to use that power?

IA: Well, I think everybody does. Parents will do it with their children. Teachers will do it with their pupils — and vice-versa, pupils, once they realize they can get the upper hand with their teachers too. I mean, we're all guilty of, or at least guilty of wanting to misuse power when we think it's in our hands. It's a very easy thing to start using it. And seeking some gratification or some tangible end result by using that power. It gets dangerous when it's politicians and dictators. And I guess dangerous when it's the kind of mumbo-jumbo of organized religion.

I'm a — loosely speaking — a religious person. I'm quite involved, as it happens, with the Church of England with charity work, and supporting our great cathedrals and churches — I do a lot of things with the church. But I'm very critical of the church — I'm very critical of the role that it plays — and the role that it *doesn't* play — that it fails to adapt to in modern society. But particularly Catholicism, which is bound *horribly* in the chains of its own history. To kind of re-write the rulebook just seems not to be possible. Even in the Church of England, the Anglican churches, certain things, it just seems impossible to change. It just goes fundamentally against the basic tenets of the religion. So you've got some real, real problems with adapting to live two thousand years on from Christ. It's just — it's a real uphill battle to get things to change.

So of course I want to be really critical of it, but at the same time, I value the church and the role that it plays, even churches that I don't personally get involved in. But you know, it doesn't stop me getting angry or getting mad about it. Overall, I still think religion is a good thing. And if people derive some real solace, something positive from going with the cant and occasional hypocrisy which is contained therein, then I don't have a problem with it, so long as they realize they are kind of going along with a lot of myths and legends rather than real stuff. But it beats going to a shrink.

AP: Have you ever experienced a situation where an audience has given you that kind of reverence, as a kind of a pseudo-deity?

IA: I don't think audiences are usually that stupid. They're just there for a good time, and to be entertained primarily. Of course there are some who are a little more obsessive about it, but I think for the most part, it's good to realize that your audience is not really *your* audience. It's the same audience that will be there for a dozen or two-dozen other acts that they'd like to go and see. You're nothing particularly special. There'd be some people in the audience who are just besotted with what you do, and don't actually like anybody else, but they're a tiny fraction. For a majority of people, you're just one of a hundred bands that they'd rather like to go and see if they were in town and the money was right. I think you've got to keep it in perspective — your audience is not really yours. You share it with a whole bunch of other performing artists, who just don't happen to be in town that night competing for the same ticket.

AP: Do you believe in the idea of the collective unconscious, in the way that it might relate to an audience?

IA: I think that there is always going to be some of that sort of thing, that strange crowd empathy that occurs. Whether it's at a football match or a rock concert, or in the hallowed halls of some great cathedral at a Christmas carol service. Those things happen.

I like to think that in a positive way you can just dance around the fringes of that phenomenon, if indeed it exists, but you've got to be a little careful about getting too deeply into those more spiritual aspects of what entertainment, what worship, what being at a political rally is all about.

There is a danger — regard it as an infection. Not necessarily a bad one, it isn't going to ruin your life or bring an untimely end, but you've got to be a little careful about getting caught up in that stuff. I mean, collective consciousness, it's only just a little step away from falling under the spell of a Reverend Jones or an Adolf Hitler. Obviously Adolf Hitler had a charisma and a real power as a speaker. He could tap into that collective consciousness and turn it into something where a whole nation set its face against the rest of the world and decided to go to war. That's scary stuff.

But I think you have to be a little wary when you think collective consciousness is at work. Is there something behind it that you really could be better off without? Regard it all as a potential infection rather than something to enjoy. Collective consciousness — you can define it in different ways — but I'm a little wary of that. I suppose it's in my nature anyway, if I think there's a bit of that going on, I want to be somewhere else. I step outside of it.

I think you can look at the politicians in any civilized western country and see that some of them know how to do this stuff. I mean, Tony Blair was pretty good at doing it for a while. Especially when it came to controlling his own cabinet and his own supporters. I mean, he knew that he had this knack to be able to do it up to a point. He's not a bad guy; I think he made a couple of really really big mistakes. I think he was also a very good politician who did some very good things. But the danger is that you start to believe, if you're in that position, that this power that you have is actually something that raises you above everybody else. I'm not saying Blair is one of those, but he's an example of someone who could be.

George Bush — I didn't mind George Bush because he didn't have that. He struggled with the idea of presenting himself to people. He was always making terrible gaffes and fumbling and falling over and mangling his words, but he knew his own weaknesses. And in essence, whether as a politician or as a world leader you think he was a good or bad guy — as a human being, I think he was probably a pretty good guy. He probably still is. So I didn't mind him at all. But he didn't have that. He just really sorely lacked that kind of — that huge sort of personality. Powerful personality. People like Churchill had it in spades. Some of the guys we think of as the good guys had it. And some of the bad guys had it too. And there'll be more to come.

But I don't feel that at all when I'm on stage. That's not what's going on in my mind. I'm not thinking about controlling, or dominating, or being powerful. It's my job to be a performer, and to some extent between songs, a master of ceremonies — trying to push things along. I try to remind myself that when I shamble out of the stage door in some sordid, rather scruffy theatre somewhere, I'm just another little old man walking down the street back to my hotel, which sometimes is not a very nice hotel. It happens to be a very nice hotel I'm staying in here. But you get enough sore reminders that you're just another guy once you step off the stage, indistinguishable from the average stagehand. Or the average film documentary maker.

* * *

We'll hear more from Ian Anderson as we return to these central themes and our other interview subjects. I needed to know more about the political implications of performance, and the psychology of it all. The bond between audience and performer was also something I wanted to explore further. And not just from the stage. The post-war era was dominated by a new medium — television — which offered the rich and powerful their own soap box in every living room in the country.

Chapter 10

Dick Cavett

I make it down to the hotel lobby just in time. It's the end of the working day, people are moving in and out with purpose. I see a man in a white fedora walks in. He heads toward the front desk. His head is down — he's avoiding attention — it must be him. I hold my hand out.

"Mr. Cavett?"

"Yes?"

He wasn't expecting me to pounce like that. I introduce myself — at least we're both prompt — and we head for the elevator. When the hotel heard that Dick Cavett was coming, they insisted on giving us the luxury suite they used when Oprah Winfrey was interviewed here. It's called the Author Suite. It overlooks Madison Avenue.

The hotel staff are aware of Mr. Cavett's *gravitas*. He was the face of intelligent late-night television from the late sixties through to the eighties, and is currently a New York Times columnist. His career began in stand-up comedy and as a writer for Johnny Carson. When he picked up his own talk show at ABC, Cavett became a bastion of smart conversation on-air. He has an intimate knowledge of the power of broadcast television. Guests who chose to sit opposite him include Vice President Spiro Agnew, Vice President Gerald Ford, congressional candidate and later presidential candidate John Kerry, Salvador Dali, Alfred Hitchcock, Fred Astaire, Katharine Hepburn, John Lennon, George Harrison, Janis Joplin, and Jimi Hendrix.

The Dick Cavett Show was chosen to celebrate Woodstock in a special live broadcast the day after the festival ended. Hendrix was booked to appear but had to cancel due to exhaustion. In attendance were Crosby, Stills, Nash and Young, Jefferson Airplane, and a young Joni Mitchell, who pulled out of Woodstock in case the traffic congestion prevented her from getting back to the Cavett Show. Her management felt that the national TV exposure would be vital at this early stage of her career. In any other circumstance they would have been correct. She wrote the song *Woodstock* in her hotel room while watching TV reports about the festival, lamenting her inability to attend the counterculture event of the century.

The last hour has been stressful — trying to get the camera and sound gear set effectively in a hotel environment. We expected the setup to be easy. But nerves kicked in and with the luxury of setup time comes self-doubt. But now I'm in the elevator with Dick Cavett. And some other people.

"Excuse me, are you Dick Cavett?"

"Uh, yes — on my better days."

The gentleman who asked the question explains that he was once on Mr. Cavett's show for one reason or another. He explains how fortuitous it is that they should meet again. He proceeds to tell Dick about his life now.

The elevator stops at a floor. Nobody's getting out. Nobody's getting in either. I'm certain Dick and I have the same thought: Are these people staying in the elevator just to spend a little more time with Dick Cavett? The man continues to give Dick his life story. Dick remains cordial throughout. Finally, we reach the top floor. Dick offers the gentleman:

"Well, it was lovely to see you again."

The man showers praise. The elevator doors close and Dick and I are alone in the hotel corridor. We hear the elevator descending. Dick turns to me.

"I have absolutely no idea who that guy was."

"That was just weird. I expect you must get that a lot?"

"Oh sure, in different ways though, I suppose."

From this moment, Dick has me completely at ease; the skill of an experienced interviewer. This is something I hope to learn from him. We head through into the corner suite.

Aidan Prewett: We spoke to Country Joe McDonald, in Berkeley, where we spoke a little about the Chicago Seven. And you had them on your show after the trial.

Dick Cavett: I remember sitting there thinking that Abbie Hoffman is a much more brilliant manipulator and practitioner of media manipulation than any of the people who are supposedly the geniuses at it. He was just wonderfully smart and effective in how he managed to annoy the right people and influence the right people — get himself seen. And the interesting part of that was that the network was not going to run the show, which I somehow managed to make known. So that there was an outpouring of these chickenshit people — *why won't you let us* *see it.* And they did run it. It was a very effective show, and it's just that whole *time* seemed so nightmarishly strange now. We haven't lost our wonderful ability to get into unnecessary wars. Because what would we do for entertainment? It's funny, isn't it, all the draft dodgers who are running for office and were in office, and...

AP: And then there's you, who boiled your draft card.

DC: What a memory you have for an old joke from my nightclub act — yes, I didn't have quite the nerve to burn my draft card — so I boiled it.

DC: It's amazing that you remembered that. You should use your head for better things.

AP: Did you feel you were being subversive at all?

DC: Subversive, *moi?*

AP: In support of the Chicago Seven and John Lennon and that kind of...

DC: Well not exactly, but I just thought, well, I don't want to do a show that's just *namby-pamby* — dreadful phrase. I've never used it before. And colorless and stays — avoids controversy. I like controversy, it gets your blood circulating and can be very entertaining. No, I didn't go out of my way to do it. Shows that sell controversy are usually short lived.

AP: Is there a sense of power for you, walking out in front of the cameras each night, knowing that millions of people would be seeing you, and hearing your voice?

DC: Well, you can't think about that very much when you're doing it. Sure, there's a sense — because you get feedback. Like,

"I saw this", or "that guest changed my life," or "that thing you said was so funny," or — all of that has to puff you up a bit, or you'd be … odd. But somebody said, "Don't be nervous about going on television. Whatever you do, don't think of it as, say, forty million people looking at you. You can't comprehend that. Think of it as eighty million eyes." I forget what comic did that. But you couldn't really go — you'd come apart if you sat there thinking….

Actually, I did once, the sort of thing you were saying. A guest was going on boringly, and I felt my eyes glazing over. And I chanced upon the thought of, *at this moment, I must be being seen in a bar in Cody, Wyoming, by a murderer in a cell in Florida, some old maid school teachers* (as they used to be called), *some … maybe Greta Garbo has her set on* — (she was alive at the time — she'd have to have her set on to be watching me, I guess), and *some people falling in love, and some people having sex, and some people in the act of strangling someone, maybe.* And a thousand other things — *things* — and people, are watching this. *Phew!* Better get off that thought.

I remember once I saw Johnny Carson on — actually I was in a bar in I think Wyoming or Colorado, late at night, and Johnny was on, and I thought — I'm sure of all the things he's thinking, one of them isn't *Dick is watching me in a bar in Wyoming* … but it is kind of a strange thought. A man I have sat next to and worked with and written for, and so on. And now we're connected by an electronic *band* of some sort, that's totally artificial, I can't touch him, I can't speak to him. But I will a couple of weeks from now, when I go back to work.

AP: So there is a connection there? There's a real … kind of a bond between an audience that you've never met — will never see…

DC: Yeah. If you could once see a picture, taken by a million cameras of all the different kinds of people and places you're being seen in — now in the back of a cab — in tourist busses with TV kings on them — in a mob family's room where they're sitting around planning a murder. And you're on their screen. *Maybe my favorite movie star is watching me now.* Best though, and this would be solid advice to you, young man — don't let anything remotely resembling that cross your mind while you're doing a show.

AP: I'm very interested to hear your thoughts on the differences between performing for a television audience and performing for a live audience, such as Broadway, or a concert.

DC: I've thought about that, and I'm not sure there is much difference. First of all, my television work was always in front of a live audience. If you mean the difference between standing on stage and in a studio, I think it's essentially the same thing — you want to get laughs where you're supposed to get laughs. It's better if the audience doesn't dislike you intensely — you can usually figure that out. Often they do suddenly, or off and on. But I think if you're — you'd better be a born performer if you're in the business. I don't know of an adjustment like that, nothing that would compare with the difference between acting for movies and acting for stage. That's a vast difference. But as long as the audience is facing the stage — and alive — I think you'll be fine, most of the time!

AP: Do you liken your style of performance to acting, then? When you're delivering your opening monologue and that kind of thing?

DC: No — *everything's* acting that you do in front of the public; you're never the exact same person you are *off.* One of the weirdest illustrations of that is — I came home once — somebody said, "How'd your taping go?" I said fine. It had been a one-person show. And somebody else said, "Who was it?" and I said, "It was … oh my God … they sat right there…." And it took some minutes to come up with the obscure name Lucille Ball. Whom I had just faced for ninety minutes. I mentioned this to Johnny Carson, who was worried, because his doorman one night had said, "Who'd you have on the show tonight, Mr. Carson?" and he said, "We have four guests usually — we had..." He said he couldn't come up with any of them. And he was worried — he was drinking a bit, then. And some horrible personal problems at that time. I felt sorry for him, because he came in looking a wreck, and would pull himself together brilliantly to do the show and seem like a man without a care in the world. But the thing was, why should *he* or *I* not be able to think of people we just sat with. Because it's not *you* out there. It's the *you* who does the show. The slightly false version of your real self. And that person stays there. You have to get out of that in order to go on with the rest of your life. I'm not saying I could never think of a guest — but there is something to the idea that the performing self can be totally separated mentally — *mentally* — from their own self.

AP: Did you ever come across or interview a person who was very close to their own self, in their performing self?

DC: Well I think some people — people are to a more or less degree. And there are people who are not — usually not performers — people who you might say are sophisticated enough to have devised a personality that they use in public. Some are genius at devising one. And you wouldn't recognize them, talking in the back seat of a car with them, as the same person — the love on the screen or whoever. It's easier. Everybody in the business works behind a mask to one degree or another. And a good thing, because they themselves sometimes are terribly uninteresting.

AP: One of Jimi Hendrix's personality traits was this sort of flamboyant style that he had, not only in his appearance, but in the way that he moved on-stage and then — from what I've heard, he came off-stage, and then was a very demure kind of a person.

DC: Oh, yeah. True. I rather enjoyed that. I like when somebody has created a persona, and plays it well, you don't know whether to believe it or not. If they're good, they convince you that that's how they are. And I also enjoy seeing people meet them backstage, or at a party or somewhere, and say "Gee, he wasn't like he was on your show. Seems like an ordinary guy." Or "He seems likeable, and he didn't on your show." Not about Hendrix — I loved Hendrix. I loved the moment when — I didn't quite know what to say next to him, and I think I said, "Do you try to get up every morning and get some work done?" and he said, "Well, I try to get up every morning...." Or possibly "in the morning." Wording is important in comedy.

AP: I liked where you mentioned people writing nasty letters, and he was confused as to why anyone would want to write a nasty letter after his beautiful rendition of the *Star Spangled Banner.*

DC: Oh, that *Star Spangled Banner.* Yes, there's hardly anything you could do to the *Star Spangled Banner* that isn't going to upset some idiot.

AP: Could you tell us about a particular person that you've worked with, or interviewed, who has really had some kind of strong command over their audience.

DC: Command over the audience — well certainly Katharine Hepburn did, although the show I did with her, we didn't have an audience to begin with. 'Cos she surprised me. We were supposed to do it two days late — she came in merely to check the set — and then said, "Why don't we just do it now?" And we did, to my amazement — for hours. It became two ninety-minute shows, and some more. Actually there's twenty-five minutes that never even got on the air, and I've never seen. But that was a stunning and unique experience, to have such a fabulous personality to display — sitting there with a woman who's utterly un-gettable for television to that point. And seeing her a little nervous at the beginning. I mean, a woman known for her guts throughout the years in the profession. To see a little bit of nervousness in one cheek — it was the up-camera cheek so it didn't show — that completely liberated me. It relaxed me, because I thought *this poor kid needs my help*....

We got on great, and that had an influence on me, I don't know what ... permanent influence in terms of — it didn't change my style in any way. I suppose it's conceivable to be vastly influenced by ... a great educator, or a great ... someone who could convert you to or from a religion *on the spot*....

AP: In terms of religion, did you ever have anyone on the show who was a very strong religious figure, who...

DC: I had Bishop Fulton J. Sheen, who long before you were born actually ended the career of the comedian Milton Berle, who was the king of television for years, by going on opposite him and commanding a vast audience. Sheen was a character with very dark, penetrating eyes and spoke straight to *you* through the camera, and never had a note or a prompter or anything. Really a genius of the medium.

And I've been moved by people — Richard Burton was quite moving, to me personally. When I asked him if he would talk about booze, since he was a drunk — and he said he would, and he did. And when he turned to the camera and expressed his sympathy for, "I know how hard it is for you — I've been through this hell myself." I just got goose pimples now under here — I could show you — thinking about the effect of that. And those moments are wonderful.

* * *

It turns out that Dick Cavett is mentioned twenty-six times throughout the Nixon tapes. In the heat of the Watergate, The Dick Cavett Show featured interviews with guests relating to the scandal throughout 1972–1974. The most notorious of these appearances was G. Gordon Liddy, who masterminded the raiding of the Democratic National Committee headquarters at the Watergate hotel. Liddy detailed the break-in for Cavett and explained why it had to be done — he was hired to set up espionage equipment for the Committee to Re-Elect the President (derisively known as C.R.E.E.P.). The espionage equipment was seen as vital to Nixon's campaign. Liddy seems almost proud of his achievement. Also featured as Cavett's guests were *Washington Post* reporters Bob Woodward and Carl Bernstein, who broke the Watergate story.

Dick Cavett's lighthearted coverage of the complicated Watergate proceedings gave the public an accessible way to understand what was really going on. Cavett went to Washington and broadcast after trial days from the actual hearing room. His reputation provided access.

Access is also vital to documentary filmmaking: access to a key person, a location, or an event. Our next guest made his career combining all three. We're about to be given backstage access to the Monterey Pop Festival, to Bob Dylan going electric, and to the JFK White House.

Chapter 11

D.A. Pennebaker

As a documentary filmmaker, there are few artists who have influenced me more than D.A. Pennebaker. So I'm terrified. We've spoken on the phone once before, to arrange this moment. Today, I step inside the headquarters of Pennebaker/ Hegedus films.

Pennebaker has run his filmmaking operations out of this building since the 1970's. This is the Upper West Side of New York, a short stroll from the Park — why move? The taxi drops me off at one of 91st Street's ubiquitous brownstones. I grab my gear, and find the number I'm looking for. It's a converted basement apartment. I'm greeted at the door by a very enthusiastic personal assistant. I theorize that once a person reaches a point in their lives where they are satisfied with their achievements, they're happier to share this knowledge with others. They're secure in themselves. And they hire assistants who display similar qualities.

It's cold outside — mid-January — and it's nice to be greeted at the door with sincerity and warmth. As we're led down the stairs, we enter a veritable museum of pop culture history. The walls are covered, every inch, with original posters from JFK's political rallies, concerts flyers from the Fillmore East, and every other performance venue important enough to have Pennebaker make a film there. Shelves are lined with artefacts from this storied history. The original portable film cameras, built by Pennebaker to gain ease of access in cramped backstage environments. The real revolution that Pennebaker started was to incorporate synchronous sound. Camera manufacturers quickly followed suit.

We're following Penny's PA; she has to slow down a little while we take in our surroundings. We continue through one room which is stacked floor-to-ceiling with sixteen-millimetre film canisters and logging equipment. The labels on the cans are yellowing and handwritten. Clearly legible are *Ziggy Stardust and the Spiders from Mars*, *Don't Look Back*, *Monterey Pop*, *Sweet Toronto.*

Walking through a room containing original footage of these performances is a big deal for me. They're some of my favorite films. But the knowledge that just through the next door sits the man who captured this material … Hendrix setting fire to his guitar. Bob Dylan going electric. John Lennon on stage with Chuck Berry. Pennebaker is a witness for us all. Together with his wife, Chris Hegedus, Penny took his revolutionary filmmaking in the 1970's through to more politicized works in the subsequent decades. The pair were nominated for an Oscar for *The War Room*, their documentary film of Bill Clinton's 1992 political campaign. Their most recent film *Unlocking the Cage* deals with a groundbreaking court case involving animal rights. Pennebaker was awarded a Lifetime Achievement Oscar in 2012.

After spending a few moments trying to absorb the energy of the celluloid storeroom, we break through into daylight, and there's Penny. Unassuming, sitting at his computer in a large office space. A Jimi Hendrix action figure sits near him on a shelf, setting fire to a plastic guitar in full Monterey regalia. Pennebaker was always a little older than his rock star friends and subjects. But here he is — a survivor.

Aidan Prewett: How did you find your way into filmmaking?

D.A. Pennebaker: Well, I worked with a filmmaker named Francis Thompson, whose film — it was a very abstract film, a beautiful film — I worked with him in that I drove a car while he went around and made the film. So I thought of myself as a car driver, not a filmmaker. So one day, I saw — we had a screening in my apartment, because he was going to show it to somebody who was going to write about it. And I saw the film itself, in somewhat of its entirety, and I realized that he'd done it all by himself. And that was it. I saw instantly that it was something I could do. Up 'til then, I hadn't thought particularly to do it.

AP: And these are the cameras you used for all the early films, up here on the shelf?

DAP: The one with the green on the handle was Chris's — I made one for her specially. And the one with the red on the handle is mine. But there were four other ones. When we did Monterey we had — a great source of anxiety for me throughout that whole festival, was the thought that we had six homemade cameras shooting, and I couldn't believe all of them would work. It was a horrible time. I was happy to get an ATON when they finally came out, although it was kind of copied from this camera.

AP: The first formal question that I've got is — have you guys ever seen a performer really take command of an audience — possibly in some kind of controlling way, or in some kind of way that everybody seems connected?

DAP: Well, I met Leonard Cohen at Albert Grossman's office — 'cos Albert was his agent at the time — and I had to take him down to the Fillmore East, where he had promised he would make an appearance and sing. And this was, I think, the first time he'd done it — at least in this country. I took him down there, and I remember he had a big wooly sweater on. We were off-stage together. Whoever was on there beforehand abandoned the stage and Bill Graham said, "Okay, get him on" — and he said, "I can't do it." I said, "Well, you've gotta do it, they're all waiting!" And he said, "No, I can't do it." And I had to actually push him out on to the stage. He went out there, looking back hopefully — that he could run back again. Everybody started cheering for him, because of course they knew Suzanne, and he was already a celebrity before he even set foot on the stage, really. But we weren't thinking about that. And he started to sing, and it was amazing. He kind of like — he'd come to a place where he was completely happy. And I kinda watched him change from this frightened rabbit that I had been pushing out there, to this guy who had total command of that theater, in five minutes.

AP: Was Bob Dylan like that?

DAP: The audience for Dylan was interesting, because here, rock stars and musicians would appear, and there would be thousands of children squealing at them. That was kind of the expected reaction to when they appeared. But in England, the audiences were much older. Much more serious people — it was like they'd come to hear the poetry, and not the music. And Dylan could appreciate that. He really dug that. So when he started to sing, it was just dead silence. And only a couple of times did people break out — they were … he had a few where he himself broke out and started yelling at people. But in general, his command began before he even got there. We would go to a town and there would be no posters saying he would be there. But out the front of the hall, there'd be a hundred people sitting, waiting — a day before. I found that really interesting at the time, because that was not the case with most people here.

AP: And I'm sure Monterey would have been a different experience altogether.

DAP: Well, Monterey was like a big party. They were all — they were kind of mixed between San Francisco types and Los Angeles types. And between them, there was not a lot of love lost. Between them, they each had their own kind of singers. And the singers were now going to sing for everybody — the audiences were totally for them. I mean, Janis — a lot of people had not heard Janis before. Or Hendrix. Or even Otis — this was not an audience that Otis Redding sang for, because he was thought to be a black singer who sang for black audiences. But the fact is, he was looking for bigger audiences. And he knew that this was the next step, even though the record company he played for didn't really go along with that. We just watched. The chemistry that took place … was in place before we even got there. So we just watched what happened, and filmed it. Filmed everything we could film.

AP: We talked a little bit on the phone about Ravi Shankar, and the Monterey audience reaction to him was quite unique — could you tell us a bit about that?

DAP: Well, I'd never heard of Ravi Shankar when I went to film with him, so I didn't know what it was going to be. But I thought that it would be an obscure and probably not too popular moment at the festival for people who were there earlier — Janis, or Jefferson Airplane, various well-known groups. And the audience was sort of interesting to us, it involved some well-known people. People from Los Angeles, San Francisco, it was kind of an interesting audience — at least we thought it was. So we got the cameras filming the audience. There were these two guys who had been working with me, they came to work and said, "We just want to work." I think they were working for nothing — or at least, they were kind of apprentices. So I thought, we'll let them film this Shankar act, whatever he's doing down there, and see what happens….

About half-way through the Raga, I began to listen to it — and the whole audience was just rapt by it, and I thought this is not going the way I thought it would go. So I went down to see what was happening with the filming of it — there's two guys, there's Ravi Shankar and then there's Alla Rakha on the tablas. And then there was a woman who was playing this long string instrument, who was smiling this wonderful, strange and mysterious smile.

And these two guys were really into it. I could see they were filming everything that moved on those two guys. So I thought, they're getting it. There's nothing more for me to do. So I just turned around and filmed the audience from in front. And the thing ended, and the audience just went wild. And I thought, boy, did I call that wrong. But we got it.

And it became kind of a high point for the film — the film kind of built to that. The whole film is about music, and this was really about music, in a way that we hadn't anticipated. So I knew from the beginning that that's how the film would end. I hadn't even seen the footage, but on the way back to New York I made little notes, and I could see that that was going to be it.

When I finally saw the footage that they shot — we had a double-headed Steenbeck, or maybe a Moviola — I could see both images at the same time. And I realized that these two guys knew how to use the camera. I still find it so exciting because in that scene, which goes on quite a ways, the beginning part of it is played over the audience and happenings going on. So you see it partly the way I saw it, which was interesting and different, to where it's just absolutely fundamental.

When you watch them build up and do that, it's like watching some kind of conversion, it's like watching a minister convert somebody who believed in the devil. And it takes place right before your eyes. But also, it takes place with the audience too — the audience was so into it; they were responding to every note.

Everything would happen. And there would be some sort of a musical joke, which Ravi Shankar would do sometimes. He had these little things he would do. And he and Alla Rakha would laugh, and the audience would roar. It was so interesting to watch how that music taught everybody something they hadn't expected to find. That's an amazing piece of film, for me, to watch.

AP: What about with Hendrix? Most of the audience at Monterey had not seen him....

DAP: Well I'd never heard Hendrix either — John Lennon had told me about him. He said there's this guy, a blues player, and he sets himself on fire. And I thought, well that's blues like I had never thought about it. I don't know what to make of that. And when I heard him in the beginning, he was chewing on his — he had a pick, a flat pick that he was sometimes using, but he was chewing on it — I thought he was chewing gum, and I thought, this is really laid back. He's chewing gum and he's going to set himself on fire? What kind of blues is this...

And then, as you listened.... At the beginning I just thought it was a racket. I didn't know what I was listening to, I had never heard him before. I couldn't make sense out of it. And about ten minutes into it, he just — it just stopped. As everybody in that audience did. It was just such an amazing kind of sound that he could conjure up out of that — I don't – it was like he was going beyond music, in a way that nobody understood.

AP: Was there a kind of shared consciousness going on in the audience?

DAP: Well I think the thing that was interesting about that audience — the audience was watching a once-in-a-lifetime scene, through the whole thing. And that audience had such a feeling of depth. That was such an amazing kind of aspect for those three days.

I've since met people who were there. For instance, I got a traffic ticket out in East Hampton, for parking my car near a street that I shouldn't have. And I had to go into court in South Hampton, and I went in there dreading it, because I thought it was going to be like a hundred dollar fine or something. And this woman, who was the judge, said, "Is there a D.A. Pennebaker out there?" And I thought here's where the shit hits the fan. And I said, "Yeah," and I raised my hand. She said, "You made *Monterey Pop*?" And I said yeah, and she said, "I was there, and you're free."

I met her again recently, and she still remembers it — she's such a terrific person. She said, "You changed my life." She was a young, whatever, sleeping out on this football field — it was such a collection of people, that you would never expect to spend time with. There were the motorcycle gangs — it was kind of an amazing moment in music, for everybody.

Woodstock was an amazing moment in crowd study. It was like the next step, which was to overrun the world, which is kind of what it did. But Monterey was an extraordinary musical event. And these were raucous, populist singers, who had big record contracts, but who were all suddenly doing it in your backyard. That was what was amazing.

AP: How did *Ziggy Startdust and the Spiders from Mars* come about?

DAP: I was on this barge in the Mississippi, making a film with a friend of mine about a theatrical group that was going from town to town, putting on this goofy little play they had written. And RCA called and asked me if I wanted to go to England with Bowie. I thought they were talking about Bolan — Marc Bolan. I knew about Marc Bolan. I'd never seen him, but I loved that music, and all the stuff that went with it. I said, "Well, I can't because I'm doing this thing on the river." RCA came back about three or four days later and said, "No, you've got to go because we need you to make this film which is going to be an experimental video device."

They had invented this device which was like a video thing. And they wanted me to make a half-hour film of Bowie. The reason was that they already had a contract with Bowie, so it wouldn't cost them anything. So they thought they were getting off free, and I was just supposed to make a half-hour, and then I could come back on the river if I wanted.

It was a little bit difficult to get to England. We got there on a Saturday because all the planes were on strike. We had to go to Italy, and fly up from there. I saw him perform on the first night. Right away I said, "I don't give a fuck about the half-hour film that RCA needs, this is a movie."

Bowie would go from being this plain-talking person in his dressing room, who was sort of like an accountant or something, talking about what he was doing — to this mercurial creature on stage. It was just extraordinary to watch. Two guys came with me, Nick Doob and Jim Desmond — Jim had been at Monterey with me, and Nick Doob I knew about — because I was up at Yale in the film department there, and he'd made a very short film which I'd seen and liked. But this was his first trip with me. So it was a very small group to be making a film, but … we just figured out how to do it. The next night we put up signs around saying *Bring your cameras and shoot all the flash bulbs you can afford*, so that the place would be lit up like a circus. We filmed the whole thing, then we came back.

And then David came to the U.S. with a big sack full of drugs, I think. It was hard to communicate with him for about a year. And then later, when he saw the film, and he really liked it, he came back and spent a month here, helping me re-mix it. And we did it — RCA had nothing to do with it — we did it all ourselves. In the end, we released the film, and it was such an interesting thing to watch a person on-stage, where we didn't make a neat film. It was very rough, very unplanned. But it had a kind of edge to it that I thought was what worked. Because of just the way he performs. And he liked it, so we released the film that way. It was a surprise to me that it ever was successful, because it was so strangely shot.

AP: A couple of weeks ago, we were in Berkeley, and spoke to Country Joe McDonald — is there a chance you could speak a little bit about his performance at Monterey?

DAP: Yeah — I didn't know Country Joe — later, Janis [Joplin] told me a lot about him, because she'd spent a lot of time with him. But he — everybody had a very anti-government view. Because we were in Vietnam, and that was bothersome, especially to younger people and younger musicians. So you didn't — you weren't going to get any God Save America music out of any of them. What he played was kind of interesting, and complicated, and in a way, I kind of liked it. It was not what I expected to hear. And I used it as a sort of a bridge between two sections. I don't remember exactly how, but I liked that it was not what you expected from Joe McDonald. And his agent came to see me about it. He said, "Why didn't you use his big record?" and I said, "Well you don't need me. Your record's doing fine. I wanted to hear something that you don't often hear." So it was all okay.

I mean, I had trouble with Simon too. Paul didn't like the song we used, which was the 59th Street Bridge song. And he had this other long song he sang that put everybody to sleep — he wanted to use that. It was a good song, but I mean — it was not what people wanted to hear at this kind of a music thing. But 59th Street Bridge was perfect. And he came and said, "If you use it I'm going to sue you." And I said, "Okay." And he said, "Oh, I can't sue you." He came later and apologized; later he used something else from the film. But we got along pretty well.

Everybody in that film — it changed their lives in some way that they hadn't expected.

* * *

Monterey Pop kicked off the Summer of Love in 1967 and laid the immediate groundwork for Woodstock. Pennebaker's film provided a blueprint for audiences, who now had a motion picture demonstration of what *peace and love* looked like.

Monterey became a three-day festival at the site of the Monterey Jazz festival. The festival was the brainchild of entrepreneur Alan Pariser, the Mamas and the Papas, and their record producer, Lou Adler. They saw it as an opportunity to promote rock music as an art form in the vein of Jazz and Folk festivals. They recruited Derek Taylor, publicist for the Beatles, in the hope of a live performance from the band. The Beatles had just released *Sgt. Pepper's Loneley Hearts Club Band*, another key element of the summer of love, but they had no wish to face the seething throngs of Beatlemaniacs again.

Monterey was the first festival to include big acts from each major city music hub: San Francisco, Los Angeles, New York, Memphis, Chicago. This was the first time many of these performers were to meet each other in person; in many cases they enjoyed each other's company. There were major names on the bill, many of whom went on to play at Woodstock: Jimi Hendrix, The Who, Jefferson Airplane, Janis Joplin, Country Joe and the Fish, Ravi Shankar, the Grateful Dead, the Mamas and the Papas, Simon and Garfunkel, and Laura Nyro, among others.

Paul McCartney attended and was involved in the planning, as a kind of talent scout. He had seen Jimi Hendrix perform in London and insisted that Monterey was the place to debut The Jimi Hendrix Experience in the States. He also suggested that The Who could use a re-introduction to the American public.

Hendrix and The Who knew each other well, and were fully aware of each other's stage antics. They had to flip a coin to see who would follow the other. Hendrix lost. Both acts pulled out all the stops. The Who obliterated their equipment and employed the use of rudimentary smoke bomb effects; Hendrix set fire to his guitar and smashed it to literal pieces as the climax to his version of *Wild Thing*.

Also making a big career move at Monterey was Otis Redding, backed up for this performance by Booker T. and the M.G.'s. Redding's act was high on audience participation, drawing the crowd in with classic soul begging and pleading, such as *I've Been Loving You Too Long (To Stop Now)*.

Up to this point in Redding's career, he had been performing in America for mainly black audiences. Meanwhile, his European tours were selling out. His manager, Phil Walden, had been pushing for the unofficially still-segregated airwaves to play more of Redding's music. "Race records" were still in recent memory. Rolling Stones manager Andrew Loog Oldham was aware of this and suggested that Redding appear at Monterey Pop to boost his profile with white American audiences.

In 1965, Redding had penned the song *Respect*, which became an impromptu anthem for the civil rights movement. *Respect* was a personal relationship ballad, but it spoke to the need to stand up for one's self – or for one's people — in the face of adversity. *Respect* defied a social order that continued to uphold historic injustices. The song was released just days after the signing of the Voting Rights Act (1965). The act outlawed redistricting, literacy tests, and other measures designed to prevent black men and women from voting. Reverend Dr. Martin Luther King, Jr. had been arrested in Selma, Alabama in February 1965, demonstrating in support of this very issue. On March 7, at the Edmund Pettus Bridge outside Selma, state and county police shot tear gas into what had been a peaceful march. Many were beaten or trampled by police horses. Televised footage of the brutality enraged viewers around the country. When the Act was introduced to Congress a month later, civil rights leaders — now under federal protection — led a five-day march of twenty-five thousand people from Selma to Montgomery, the Alabama capital. The Voting Rights Act went on to become a highly effective piece of civil rights legislation.

Otis Redding died in a plane crash on December 10, 1967, just five months after his success at Monterey Pop. His swan song *(Sittin' On) The Dock Of The Bay* was released posthumously and went to number one on the Billboard charts.

Respect was taken on by Aretha Franklin, and became an anthem not only for the civil rights movement, but — as we'll soon see — for the women's movement as well.

Chapter 12

Chris Hegedus

Chris Hegedus has produced, directed, shot, and edited social commentary and music documentaries since the mid-1970's. Hegedus was Oscar-nominated for *The War Room*, a film that followed Bill Clinton's 1992 presidential race, was awarded the Directors Guild Award for *Startup.com*, and won an Emmy in 2004 for *Elaine Stritch At Liberty*. Over the years she has worked with Samuel Beckett, Jerry Lee Lewis, Isaac Hayes, Wilson Pickett, Carol Burnett, Germaine Greer, Sam Moore, Susanne Vega, Branford Marsalis, John DeLorean, Depeche Mode, Bruce Springsteen, and President Jimmy Carter, among many others. The gravitas she brings to a project has earned Chris a serious reputation. Doors are opened and filming access is granted for people and locations that are usually off-limits.

Chris is married to D.A. Pennebaker and the pair have collaborated on many projects through their company, Pennebaker Hegedus Films. With their back-catalogue of more than fifty performance or political films in as many years, they have become the interface between politics and music. Their first collaboration was *Town Bloody Hall* (1979), which centered around a 1971 public debate between Norman Mailer — whose published works were cultural commentaries, frequently on sexuality — and the head of the National Organization of Women (N.O.W.), as well as outspoken feminist writers.

Earlier, in 1960, more than fifty thousand women took to the streets in cities around the United States to protest nuclear testing. This became known as the Women's Strike for Peace. In 1963, Betty Friedman published *The Feminine Mystique* which advocates for deviation from traditional gender roles. Also published in 1963 was Gloria Steinem's explosive exposé of the misogynistic inner workings of New York's Playboy Club.

In 1966, Friedman co-established N.O.W. in response to the federal government's impotence in the enforcement of anti-discrimination laws. Their goal was "to take action to bring women into full participation in the mainstream of American society now, exercising all privileges and responsibilities thereof in truly equal partnership with men." Key issues were abortion and reproductive health services access, violence against women, constitutional equality, promoting diversity, lesbian rights, and economic justice.

In 1968, a group called New York Radical Women joined with N.O.W. to protest the 42nd Miss America Pageant. A group of four hundred demonstrators gathered outside Atlantic City's Boardwalk Hall with placards and banners. Telecast around the country, the pageant was interrupted by the unfurling of a giant banner inside the contest hall. The banner read *Women's Liberation.*

Outside the hall, protestors used a large metal trash can to symbolically dispose of items that reflected the oppression of women: high heels, makeup, girdles, and bras. The media ran with an analogy equating this N.O.W. action to the anti-war movement's burning of draft cards. The headlines of the day coined the phrase *Bra Burners.* The trashcan was never set alight, nor was any other part of the pageant. Many years prior to this, however, suffragettes had symbolically called for the burning of whale-bone corsets.

In 1970, more than one hundred demonstrators from N.O.W. and New York Radical Women stormed the head office of the largely male-authored *Women's Home Journal.* Their sit-in occupation lasted eleven hours. Banners displaying the words *Women's Liberated Journal* hung from the office windows. The occupation led to the resignation of the magazine's editor-in-chief, who was supplanted by senior editor Lenore Hershey — one of the publication's few female employees.

By 1971, Norman Mailer had just published *The Prisoner of Sex*, a kind of treatise rallying against N.O.W. leaders and a response to *Sexual Politics* by feminist author Kate Millett. An on-stage panel was formed with Germaine Greer, Jill Johnston, Diana Trilling, and Jacqueline Ceballos. Betty Friedan and Susan Sontag were seated in the front row. Captured on film, Mailer received the rebuke of his life.

Chris Hegedus: It was advertised as a battle of the sexes. One of the interesting things on that night, was that one of the speakers, Jill Johnston, who wrote for the *Village Voice*, and was a highly regarded lesbian writer, decided to do a stunt and have her girlfriend come onstage. So they drop to the floor and start rolling around and kissing each other. And the audience at that point is like "Ohhh, what's happening?" And Norman of course is really like, "Oh my God, I can't believe this is happening." So he makes them get up off the floor and he decides to put the vote to the audience whether Jill will finish her speech or not. Norman announces, "Okay, we're going to put the vote to the audience, whether you should stay or leave, but I'm gonna do the counting. Any of you that think that I can't do the count fair enough can come and take this mic away from me." And so the audience does a kind of *yay* or *nay* to each of them. And in the end the nays were louder, so Jill gets booed off the stage. In a sense the audience *is* part of the event, in that film.

Aidan Prewett: What was the kind of progression, that led to these beginnings of your filmmaking career?

CH: Well I started out in the art world. I went to art school for college during a particular time in the art world when art was deconstructing itself and there was no more art *object*. It was the beginning of conceptual art and performance art and a very exciting time because it was the beginning of a movement, but in the end these trends didn't interest me enough to go in that direction.

I was working in photography and doing experimental films a little bit. But it was really such a political time. It was the Vietnam war, the Women's movement and the Civil Rights movement. Doing very formalist experimental films didn't seem interesting to me anymore. It was also at this time that sync-sound cameras started to become available. and so everybody's goal was to get their hands on equipment like that and make films.

AP: And now everyone can, and it's kind of become … it's just part of the process now. But that must have felt *freeing*, in some way. That you could suddenly go out and do all this.

CH: Well, it was freeing. But it was very hard to get the equipment. And in some ways, that's how I met Pennebaker. I knew I needed to find filmmakers who had the equipment, so I first went to Bob Drew. I had read that he produced some of the early verité films. I went to Bob Drew and asked, "Do you have a job?" and he said, "No, ask Pennebaker, he's just up the street."So that's how I landed on Penny's door — to get cameras. And eventually, we had these two matching cameras that Penny built.

I did buy my own camera though, because every single time we filmed, Penny would be on the floor with the camera taking it apart, right before we had to start shooting — and it was a source of so much anxiety for me.

AP: In your film career, is there a performer who stands out as really taking control of their audience?

CH: I always thought that the thing about the Bowie film is that it's so difficult for a performer to have the kind of charisma and power to hold the stage for the whole performance, by themselves, pretty much. And David Bowie is totally that. I mean, he's just unbelievably sexual — to men, to women — animals — whoever. He just exudes it. The audience is so wild in the film — they're so emotionally attached to Bowie. I mean, they're weeping, at times. It's an amazingly powerful Frank Sinatra type of performance reaction.

There have been few performers, I think, that can do that. And Bowie was definitely one of them. In terms of other concerts that we've filmed, the one for me was filming *Depeche Mode*. What I thought was interesting about the audience for *Depeche Mode* – as opposed to the audience for *Monterey Pop* or some other audiences, is that the audience had such a close relationship with the band. They had a unique style that they were all wearing, and they had hand signals that they were developing. I think it was the beginning of when audiences started doing the *wave* in stadiums. Whereas people in the sixties were dressing in ways that really expressed their individual creativity, everybody was *out there doing their own thing*. This audience invented a whole new style identity that I thought was really interesting.

David Gahan is a very strong performer, and the audience really connected with him. One of the interesting things about filming David was that he and the band decided to take an incredible risk as a band and rent the Rose Bowl in California. Everybody said, "No-one's filled the Rose Bowl for ten years," since some metal band — I don't know who it was. Everybody doubted they could do it. And they did fill it. It was an incredible concert. And to film in a concert space like that is amazing, because it's a beautiful venue. And I remember at one point right at the beginning, it was getting dark and the sky was this deep blue color — then it started to rain a bit which is always a very precarious time for a performer on stage. It was so beautiful. Then it stopped raining and the crowd was totally excited and supportive *for* the band. That's an amazing time to film, when that happens.

AP: My next question is about politics — because you guys covered Clinton's presidential campaign. Is there a difference between a political audience and a musical audience?

CH: In many political crowds, people are searching for answers, and in politics especially, they're looking for somebody who's a leader. Clinton had a huge amount of charisma. That was one of his strongest points. People hear him speak and they come away with a lot of admiration for him. Not all politicians can create that effect. One of the most interesting politicians we started to follow was Reverend Al Sharpton when he ran for president in 2004. He was an interesting person to film, because he was a preacher, basically. And so he really knew how to move an audience and control an audience and speak to them in a very Southern Baptist kind of way. You don't usually see that type of thing on the campaign trail.

One of the people who we did do a film about, who ended up being a politician, although he wasn't a politician when we began filming him, was Al Franken — Who has subsequently become a senator. But he was at a point in his career where he was transitioning from his comedy SNL persona into writing political satire and really wanting to change things and talk about the way that politics was going. And we decided to follow him when he had just put out his latest book, *Lies and the Lying Liars Who Tell Them*, which was bashing Bush and Fox News and the right-wing establishment. The audiences for Al were really interesting because they were looking for somebody to give them answers. It was a point in this country when a lot of different comedic and television figures like Jon Stewart — and Al's one of them — were starting to be looked to for political news. And one of the great things about Al is that he's a really powerful speaker, and he can also make people laugh. The power of being able to tell jokes while you're delivering a serious message is an amazing skill, and not very many politicians can do that. So he was unique in that way, and it was interesting to watch audiences for that reason. They loved coming to hear him, because they knew they were going to get something besides political knowledge, they knew they were going to be entertained.

* * *

The debate in the 1971 film *Town Bloody Hall*, produced by Hegedus and Pennebaker, exemplified politics as entertainment. The audience was taking part in the proceedings and seemed to enjoy exercising their power as a mass. But at the crux of this debate, serious messages were being delivered.

In the film, Susan Sontag questions Mailer's use of the term *lady*, in the way he introduces Diana Trilling as "foremost lady literary critic." Sontag gives him a serve: nobody would ever introduce a male writer by denoting their gender. This isn't gallantry, she explains, it is patronizing in the extreme. The crowd applauds her.

Sontag rose to prominence with the publication of her 1964 social critique *Notes On Camp* in New York's *Partisan Review*. She published a collection of her essays, *Against Interpretation*, in 1966. Sontag became a mainstay activist, continuing to support a variety of anti-war and women's movements until her death in 2004. Her numerous published works deal largely with human rights, ethics, art criticism, and philosophy.

In 1975, Sontag's essay *Fascinating Fascism* was published in the *New York Review of Books*. Here she rips through Leni Riefenstahl for cultivating a grandiose post-war image — cashing in on the Nazi mythology she helped create, while distancing herself from the party leadership, Goebbels in particular. After Riefenstahl was hired to photograph Mick and Bianca Jagger, Sontag coined the term "eroticization of fascism" — applicable as much to the art world as we have seen in the popular music world.

In justification for her work with the Nazis, Riefenstahl claimed simply to be entranced by any form of "beauty". Her later photography work focused on the human physique. Sontag notes that this draws obvious parallels with Nazi ideology — and fascism as a movement. Fascism, Sontag explains, is not simply "brutishness and terror." Fascism maintains its mass appeal through other clearly defined aspects: a strong sense of identity and belonging, the cult of beauty, idolatry of the courageous, the scorn of intellectualism, and a fetishistic view of leadership.

Chapter 13

The Crowd Mind

In Leni Riefenstahl's *Triumph of the Will,* Joseph Goebbels is seen addressing the vast throngs on the subject of propaganda. He calls it the "background music" of a strong governmental policy:

> There are times when statesmen must have the courage to do something unpopular. But their unpopular actions must be properly prepared, and must be put in the proper form, so that their people will understand. All practical politics depends on its persuasiveness. Popular support of government can only be gained by untiring propaganda that brings the broad masses knowledge and clarity. Crises must be prepared for not only politically and economically, but also psychologically. Here propaganda has its place. In a manner of speaking, it provides the background music. Such propaganda in the end miraculously makes the unpopular popular, enabling even a government's most difficult decisions to secure the resolute support of the people.

The entire purpose of Reifenstahl's film was laid out in those few sentences. The impetus for Riefenstahl was to focus on the beauty of fascism. This was 1934. The Nazis had another five years to condition Germany for what came next.

Goebbels, of course, was as close to a monster as any human has been. As Hitler's minister for propaganda he fervently prepared the mindset of the country for a course of genocidal war that led to the murder of six million Jews and the destruction of Europe. He did it using the techniques laid out above.

Goebbels closely studied the work of French sociologist/psychologist Gustave Le Bon, who outlined notions of crowd influence in his 1895 work *The Crowd: A Study of the Popular Mind.* In it, he speaks of a "magnetic influence of the crowd" that dulls individual thought and behavior and gives way to a kind of "crowd mind." He states that crowds, in a kind of contagion, provide individuals with a sense of anonymity and open them up to suggestibility. He writes: "An individual in a crowd is a grain of sand amid other grains of sand, which the wind stirs up at will." More on this later.

Not surprisingly, political leaders tend to be fascinated by this material. Along with Goebbels and the Nazis, Benito Mussolini and Vladimir Lenin are also known to have studied Le Bon's theories. It might be both alluring and disturbing to imagine that there are recipes for exercising a commanding influence over a large group of people. But for a performer, it might be fun.

Aidan Prewett: I'd like to know — when a large space is crammed full of people, like for *Depeche Mode*, is there like, an energy or an electricity in the air — was there something you could *feel?*

Chris Hegedus: Yeah. I definitely think you can feel the energy.

D.A. Pennebaker: Oh, yeah. You know, earlier on, I think in one of the other cities where they performed, he did this thing on the last song, which was really about drugs, although at the time I didn't know that was what it was about. I just thought it was a great song. But he did this thing of waving his arms back and forth, and the audience kind of picked it up. And then, I don't remember the next time, whether it happened again, but when we got to the rose bowl, he got up by himself on this high place, and he started to do it, and that whole audience — it was a hundred thousand people, all doing it, right with him. It's like — nobody told him to, there were no pieces of paper delivered saying *be sure to wave* — and the people in front couldn't tell — everybody knew that that's what they were going to do. And I thought that's such an interesting example of mass communication — because nothing was said. He just did this thing — and when you see this whole audience of — as far as the eye can see — and they're all going *just like this.* In time to the music. It really shakes you. It's a heavy thing to watch. That's why I thought you should see that film if you could.

CH: I do remember the moment when I turned around and started filming the audience. It really seemed like a sea of bodies. It took a few minutes for them to stop going cross-purpose with their waving, but once they did, it just — it was an amazing quality. And very powerful, as a cameraperson, when you film that kind of thing. But there have been other odd moments. I remember on one of the concert stops with the band, filming David kind of … go off the stage and how a performer reaches down to the audience. And he reaches down to a girl, and she passed out. You know, right when he reached out to her. That kind of power between a performer and an audience must be very strange, to have something like that happen — when you touch somebody and they pass out.

* * *

> Goebbels furthered Le Bon's theories by laying out specific techniques for influencing an entire nation, not just a crowd. But at the center of these

> phenomena is the need for a central, unifying figure. A personality with enough charisma to manipulate the crowd, to arouse the necessary excitement to push the people in front of them to nefarious ends.

Ian Anderson: I'll give you an example. A chap called Michael Bentine, who was one of the original Goons, the fathers of British surreal humour in the fifties and sixties — Michael Bentine was an oddball eccentric, funny guy, writer, actor, TV-program maker, did all sorts of stuff. He also claimed to have trained special forces in Latin America in combat hand gunning and a number of other rather nefarious pursuits. He came around to my house once — I think his guns were all locked up for safe-keeping of the general public — he got his guns out of hock and wanted somewhere to shoot them. Because I had a pistol range on my farm, he came over to shoot. So he got all his guns out, and *bang bang bang* all afternoon. And then he decided he wanted to demonstrate his powers of healing — he wanted to heal my wife's broken arm, which he attempted to do. And then he wanted to trace out the foundations of some ancient monastery in our garden, and then he decided to do some cloud-busting.

So he and his little entourage and a few other people who were around for an afternoon of drinks and whatever, set off into a field inthe middle of the farm. He decided he was going to disperse clouds, and we had to go along with it — use the power of our minds to disperse these clouds. And even people that you would think *there's no way they're going to go along with this* because they're just not those kinds of people — they were caught up with the charisma of this man. He was just a natural.... He was a snake-oil covered wagon kind of charmer. Nice guy. But he knew he had that power to take people with him and create this feeling of everybody having this raised consciousness about *we're going to do this and make something physically happen.* And he had them all believing that they were dispersing a cloud.

Well, clouds, if you watch them in the sky, do tend to sort of come and go and dissipate a bit, and solidify — if you watch a little cloud in the blue sky long enough, it doesn't just stay there forever. It'll change its shape, and sometimes disappear, or clouds will appear out of relatively nothing in the space of several minutes. But he had everybody believing this.

But I'm just one of those people who — the minute I get the feeling that someone is doing this to people — I'm away. I'm standing off at the side. And I didn't want to mess things up or make a joke of it. But my instinct was *stand to one side. Don't get caught up in this little germ* — this little bug that's going around infecting people, making them believe that under the spell of this magician, they can do things that are beyond the usual human capability. And it was harmless enough — he was having fun.

But there is a danger that they're not just having fun. That they actually do believe to some extent in their own power, that they get caught up in what they do. That's the danger. That they rather revel in the fact that they can manipulate and control people.

Even in a benign way, like dear Michael Bentine did. 'Cos he was a nice guy. But you can see how someone who is not as nice as Michael Bentine could use that power and do some pretty evil stuff. And there's always a few of those around. They're not the Robert Mugabes, they're not the Moamar Gadhaffis. They're just little soldier boys with bad blood, and able to do things. But not through real charisma and power.

AP: Could you tell us about a time when a crowd has "gotten ugly," so to speak?

IA: I don't think they've ever really got ugly with me, but I've seen it happen with some support acts. Roxy Music had a terrible time at Madison Square Garden when they opened for us probably around '75, '76, and the crowd booed them and gave them a really hard time. I mean, it wasn't ugly, but it was embarrassing and sad because I quite like Roxy Music. We were very pleased to have them come and do their first two shows in America ever, playing with us in Madison Square Garden. But the crowd hated them.

They also hated Alex Harvey, who toured with us in America. And if you've ever seen ten thousand people rise to their feet as one, and boo somebody, really badly and nastily, then you do sense this collective consciousness. But it was poor old Alex who just got them really riled up, by — I don't know what he did to upset them. It came to a head where he used the C-word at them. "You're a load of…." So yeah, that didn't help.

But no, I haven't really seen an audience get ugly with me specifically. You get a few troublemakers here or there in the audience, and sometimes it can get a little tense. It's not usually aimed at me. We had a special guest at Carnegie Hall, a violinist called Lucia Micarelli, and some drunks in the audience started to shout things at her. Which were really disrespectful to a girl, twenty-two years old, she was trying to laugh it off or smile it away, but you could see that it was deeply unpleasant. So I did have to step outside the usual restrictions and use that bit of power to shut these guys up. They actually brought in some police off the street and threw them out as they were extremely drunk and disorderly.

I've heard of it happening a lot in Glasgow at the Empire Theatre, where the crowds were ugly when English comedians would play. And it still to this day has this reputation as being the most tough crowd in the U.K. Even tougher than the Liverpool Empire…. The Glasgow Empire is the one which has this huge reputation as being an incredibly tough crowd particularly for English comedians in the sixties and sevemties. But I played there last year, and they were as good as gold. But then, I'm a Scotsman. And even though I'm from Edinburgh instead of Glasgow, they give me the benefit of the doubt. I've sensed it — you can smell some hostility in the air at the Glasgow Empire, but it's something that's about thirty years old and it was directed at Morecombe and Wise, not at me.

AP: Can you tell us a little about the Isle of Wight in 1970?

There was a lot of hostility at the Isle of Wight in 1970, but again it wasn't really within the orbit of those that you were entertaining. It was on the periphery; it was outside where some more anarchic extremist kind of stuff was going on. It was the dying embers of the hippie era and a change from rather easy-going love and peace kind of values to *if we don't get what we want, we're going to take it.* It's always been there; it's still there today. I was just reading about that TUC (Trade Union Congress) rally in the streets of London, where two or three particular groups were responsible for a lot of planned violence. They're avowed to go and smash in shop windows and cause as much madness and mayhem as they possibly can. Just because they're bad people with bad blood. They have no political or real issue. It's just they're bad people. Just people who unfortunately are a little sick. And that's what they do. And sometimes they try to give it some credibility with argument about politics or society or whatever, but they're just bad people. They're the same people you'd find at a football match, kicking the shit out of each other. There are just some bad folks out there. Call it what you want, put whatever label on it you want — they're just bad people.

So that's kind of something that's around, but I don't think audiences, as a rule, tend to exhibit that. I don't see it myself. It's only when it's aimed at somebody else, or it's in the periphery — you know, the few drunks at the back, or the few rowdies trying to get into some festival without paying. Whether it's 1970, or 1990, or 2020 … there's always going to be some of those folks there. But I don't think they represent — by any means — the majority. They are just a tiny fraction of very disagreeable folks. It's tempting to think that they were born that way, although I don't want to believe that, I like to think that all people are born equal and essentially good people, it's just *stuff happens* along the way. And if you're in the company of other people that are like that, then that infection I was talking about — that nasty virus, that nasty bug can infect you. You get caught up in something that … that you weren't born to.

I mean, Hitler … why are we talking about Hitler? It's the third time I've talked about Hitler today. I haven't talked about Hitler for about ten years, and he's come up three times today. We have to think: was he born a bad and ugly child? To me it's always fascinating to know, *what is it* ... what's the pivotal moment that sends some people this way and other people that way? Supposing the young Adolf Hitler had decided to become a priest instead of joining the army and finally getting involved in the dangerous side of politics in the thirties. He might have been a wonderful character, he could have used his power of oratory in a positive way, within an organized and benevolent church, or he might have turned into the equivalent of some god-awful gospel TV evangelist preacher, you know, rallying people in some iniquitous way to get their money to fund his Rolls Royce and his ten-bedroom home.

Are people born bad or not? I don't know. Do they have the power to raise people's expectations and hopes and bring people together in that mass kind of a way … was it just something they were born with or do they learn to do it along the way? Most of us aren't interested in going out there and trying to change people, trying to use that power. Most of us don't need to do that. We're a bit more secure in ourselves. But it's often a sign of deep insecurities in people who have to do that, to demonstrate this power. They need it for themselves because they're essentially insecure people. And again, going back to some of those people like poor Adolf Hitler, who was obviously a deeply insecure man behind it all. I mean, sexually repressed; very strange kind of weird things going on in his life that we'll never know about.

We can only guess about. He wasn't really a fulfilled and whole human being. But he did have this power to do something. But God help us, we don't want to see that happening out there on a concert stage. This is about art and entertainment. End of story.

* * *

Hitler keeps popping back up. As does the question about why people turn one way or the other — Woodstock or Altamont. This idea was also touched upon by Susan Sontag, who stated "Ten percent of any population is cruel, no matter what, and ten percent is merciful, no matter what, and the remaining eighty percent can be moved in either direction."

Crowds continue to operate in mysterious ways. We're about to hear some acute insights from modern observers with their own experience of crowd behavior.

PART THREE
Present Day

The 2011 TUC rally in London drew an estimated crowd of half a million people and was the largest union-organized rally in British history. Demonstrators were protesting public spending cuts proposed by David Cameron's Conservative-Liberal Democrat coalition government. Several "independent protesting groups," as labeled by the media, were responsible for planning violence — many shops and some banks in London's West End were vandalized and clashes ensued between police and rioters. There were sixty-six total reported injuries — thirty-one of them sustained by members of the police force. Two-hundred-and-one arrests were made.

Later that year, further rioting erupted throughout London and the wider United Kingdom in the wake of the controversial police shooting of twenty-nine-year-old Mark Duggan. Unrest continued from August 6th to 11th. Five people were killed. More than threet-housand arrests were made across England in connection with the rioting. Shops, homes, cars, and a double-decker bus were burned. Social media had been used to coordinate extensive looting efforts. By the end of the violence, it was estimated that the property damage bill was £200 million.

The ways in which crowds form and their reasons for forming maintain a similar appearance, even half a century after the Vietnam era. People come together because they're excited about something. They're either dissatisfied and pushing for change, or they're celebrating. Performers have unique insight into this phenomenon, not just because they're in front of crowds, but because art is capable of simultaneously celebrating and expressing dissatisfaction. Protest songs are prime examples, along with standup comedy. These artforms themselves would scarcely exist without deep dissatisfaction and the passion that arises from it. The need to push back against something — the excitement of a defiant act — is a powerful motivator. It's also a strong connection point for audiences. The point of dissonance can make people sit up and take notice.

Here we will speak with some leading figures in the modern entertainment world — people who have truly considered what it means to be in the public eye in the twenty-first century. They've taken note of how things operated in the past, and they know how they fit into that picture — or how to break out of it.

Chapter 14:
Paul Provenza

We're late. The taxi pulls up in the back lane of a Venice, California street. It's a beautiful area with waterways and elaborate bridges intertwined amongst the roadways. But this is an alleyway. It feels somehow exposed. The taxi driver is gruff. I think about asking him to wait until we're inside, but I reconsider. He departs quickly.

I ring the doorbell. No answer. I try again. Nothing. We're now standing in an alley with some very obviously expensive film equipment and nowhere to go. After a minute or two I ring the neighbor's doorbell and ask if we're in the right place — is this Paul Provenza's office? The neighbor doesn't know.

A car speeds toward us. Are we about to be robbed? No. It's Paul. He's very apologetic for being late. We explain that we were late too. And now we realize I've forgotten the tripods for our cameras. And our lighting kit.

"That's okay, we'll improvise," says Paul. This puts us at our ease as Paul takes ownership of this minor debacle. "When I was shooting interviews for *The Aristocrats*, I forgot to turn the sound on for Terry Gilliam. So I have two hours of glorious footage of Terry doing these wonderfully expressive gestures."

Paul made his first appearance on *The Tonight Show Starring Johnny Carson* in 1983. Since that time he has enjoyed a stellar stand-up career; co-directed *The Aristocrats* — a Sundance Grand Jury Prize-nominated documentary; authored *Satiristas* — about the nuances of the comedy world; hosted *The Green Room* for Showtime; while producing and touring with the live show *Set List: Stand Up Without A Net.* He knows comedy backwards.

We shoot outside to make the best of the light. To use as a background for the interview, Paul's office has a picturesque dumpster in the courtyard. It's that or palm trees. We choose the dumpster.

Aidan Prewett: Have you ever felt a sense of power over an audience?

Paul Provenza: Oh, absolutely. The stand-up audience relationship is very much a power-play. Very much. In fact, in *Satiristas*, in the intro, I talk about how one of the reasons comedians are worth listening to when they criticize conventional mores, or the status quo, is because we know a lot about groupthink. That's our stock-in-trade. We take x number of individuals, and get them all thinking exactly the same way, to such a degree that at some point, in unison, have an involuntary physical response. It's crazy power.

AP: Could you tell us a little more about groupthink? What's your understanding of that?

PP: Well it's very easy to manipulate an audience. And I don't necessarily mean that with its negative connotations, it's just — you get a sense as a comedian that you can turn two-, three-hundred — five-hundred, a thousand, *ten-thousand* individuals into one entity. They go from being animals to being cells in one big giant animal. We are very, very well versed in that. We're all aware of that. And the mechanics of groupthink, the instincts for groupthink, the temptations of groupthink are really powerful. I mean, it's what we do as comedians. We get out there and we take this group of individuals and we get them all on the exact same thought. It's very different from drama, or even an action-adventure movie, where you can feel *anything*. You can have any feeling. You can be really deeply moved, you can be awed, you can have any sort of reaction, and it's working. But with comedy it has to be *one very specific* reaction. And it has to happen to everybody at the same time. So how do you do that? That's groupthink. That's manipulation. And you can use that power for good or evil.

Just to get everybody's mindset — especially with comedy, a sense of humor is very individual. I mean, you can't argue with somebody if they think something is funny or not. It's like a painting. *I think it's garbage. I don't like it, its not pretty to me*, and somebody thinks *it's a masterpiece, it's beautiful, it's unbelievable*. It's about as subjective as it gets. But with comedy, with a sense of humor, it's even more intimate. Jimmy Carr talks about it as a sexual attraction. That if somebody turns you on, there's no arguing it and you can't judge it, and they turn you on or they don't. That's the same thing with a sense of humor and comedy.

So to get hundreds and hundreds of people, all in one fell swoop, to be in the same place as you are, it really is like trying to turn everybody on at the same time. So I guess there's a lot of different people with a lot of different foibles and a lot of different desires, and you've got to get them all wet. You know, it's like a crazy idea, but that's kinda what we do, is get everybody into that kind of place with this real sort of connection. Of an idea and the involuntary physical response.

It's all groupthink. There's a lot of manipulation, there's a lot of tricks of the trade. We just know how to get a whole group to just — it's like fish schooling, really. It's like when one fish turns, they all just go *right there*. We see that happening with audiences all the time. It's unbelievable. That's how one person can fuck up an entire show with a thousand people. It can change the whole dynamic, if it's the right circumstances and the right alpha. So we see it, we see groupthink when it's happening, we watch people just all kinda go off at the same time.

AP: Your film *The Aristocrats* really paints you as a scholar of comedy.

PP: I mean, I grew up on seventies comedy, which was for the most part, subversive. George Carlin had emerged, after his transition, Richard Pryor had established himself and really had crossed over from black to white, at a very particular time in race relations in America. Really, the big breakouts in comedy — Saturday Night Live was just hitting the airwaves in the seventies. National Lampoon had really done its thing and influenced a lot of people. I grew up in N.Y., so there was a lot of that kind of countercultural, subversive comedy happening and that I was steeped in in my early teens.

National Lampoon used to do live shows, and they did a famous show called Lemmings — it was a satire of Woodstock and the Woodstock generation and all, and the idea that we're all just drinking the Kool-Aid; we're all just lemmings going off the cliff. So that's the kind of comedy that I was really steeped in at a very formative age. And it's just the comedy that spoke to me. I mean, George Carlin changed my life. What George Carlin did — and I'd been a fan of his in his straight conservative days too, his straight, sort of mainstream days. Because he was great. He was whacky-silly. And then he went through his transition at the perfect time in my life, where I was like, "You know what? He gave me the permission to be wrong." He gave me the permission to go against the tide, and made me realize, I'm not the only one who feels this way. And I'm not the only one who's cheering him for saying it.

It was the equivalent of if I were a kid who was passionate about playing guitar, hearing Hendrix for the first time. Just like, "Oh, it's a different universe now." Mr. Carlin was that trigger for me. That's what I was steeped in, and all that stuff is all about just, *what are we buying in to?* It's a slightly more sophisticated interpretation of the counterculture of the sixties. So the comedy that is sort of in my DNA, is really all about questioning the status quo, and questioning prevailing moods and trends.

AP: When somebody takes your particular brand of subversion the wrong way, what's your reaction?

PP: It happens all the time. I think it comes with the territory. You're going head to head against somebody who's bought in. I don't really look at it as a negative. In fact, what's interesting now — again, I have to point to technology as being a big part of changing the form of subversion — even just subversion in comedy — the funny thing now is that you don't have to say a word. Your fans and followers will defend you for you. They'll do a much better job of it. It's really great. It really is. That's the whole point — the whole point of somebody taking it the wrong way, is when people take it the wrong way, it's kind of best not to say anything. For me — I can't stand it when comedians apologize for people being offended by their jokes. I think, "Where are your balls? Where are your balls? You're not a politician, you're not a judge, you're a comic." How many cars do you need to drive at one point, how many homes do you need to have? Seriously, you can't fucking own it and go, "It was a joke. You don't like it, don't buy my DVD." I just think it becomes a question of personal integrity. As Billy Connolly puts it in *Satiristas*: We're not in the service industry. We're not like waiters where if you don't like it you can send it back and get something different. You take what we give you, or you don't. That's the way it works.

Having said that, there are a lot of comedians who are like people who paint paintings to match your furniture. That's fine, more power to you. But there's enough of us out there who don't need it to be that. So that's part of what makes it interesting, that's part of what gives it traction. When somebody butts up against it.

An interesting story about that is Howard Stern. You have to have something to rub up against. If you don't have something to rub up against, then nobody notices and you've not been successful in subverting anything. Howard Stern is a great example. When Howard Stern was on broadcast radio, he was up against the FCC regulations all the time. He was up against the fact that anybody could tune in to his show in their car with their kids — he was up against all those realities, and it made his sophomoric sensibilities really meaningful. When he would do dopey, silly stuff — having hookers on the radio talking about their breast reductions, whatever. All that sort of stuff, it offended people, talk raunchily about something a politician has said or whatever. Typical Howard Stern-y stuff. It used to matter! It would end up in the papers. People would talk about it. It was water-cooler talk. It meant something. As soon as he went to Sirius radio, where you could say whatever you want, when's the last time you heard any news item about Howard Stern?

It used to be that whenever you were pushing something, a movie or a book, or something, you would always get a list of the top ten media outlets to get on, to publicize. And Howard Stern was always in that top ten. As soon as he went to Sirius Radio, he fell out of that top ten. Nobody cares anymore. And I think that's largely because there's nobody there to complain. So it's just masturbation at that point. If you're gonna be subversive, you've gotta piss somebody off, so that a dialogue can take place. Because you can't win the fight — and as a comedian, *Good Lord, what if I did win the fight? What if I had to actually make policy?* Put a bullet in my head right now. Comedians should not be the ones who have the answers. We just really like to ask the questions.

So what happens when people complain is, you get the chatter going, you get the dialogue going. You get people talking about the material. And people talking about the material is the most comedians can hope for in terms of affecting any change — is just to have that dialogue.

On *The Green Room*, one of the caveats of the show is that we just want to have conversations that people have *all the time*. People have these conversations every day. Every night at the pub, every morning in the carpool on the way to work. People have these conversations all the time. We put them on television and people are like, "Oh my God, did you see that? I can't believe they said that." That's so interesting. If we didn't have that obstacle, there'd be nothing interesting about *The Green Room*. I was talking with George Wallace, and George and I had been very close. I was always fascinated by George Wallace, because George is this six-foot-four black guy, big guy, big loud booming voice, and a big giant teddy bear. And he uses this physiognomy of his to be really funny and loveable. And I would see George work and I would just be — "Oh my God, look — it's such a feel-good show, everybody's so happy, and the audiences just love him, they love what he's doing." It's a great night out, to see a George Wallace show. It really is great. And you can bring your Grandmother, you can bring your teenage nephews — it's great. It's just a great show.

I once said to him, "George, I don't know how you do that. I don't know how you turn a comedy show into an uplifting, revival meeting. How do you do that?", and he just said, "That's what I like to do as a comedian, I like to make everybody — everybody's got a hard life. Everybody's life is hard, and they've worked hard and they've spent their money to come and see me, and you know what — this group of people will never be in a room together again ever. And I want to make this a special night for everybody, and I want everybody to feel good and be happy. And I do everything I can to make all those things come to pass." And it dawned on me. I said, "That's the difference between you and me. I really want everybody to have an argument on the car ride home." That to me is a great show.

* * *

Paul Provenza is following in the footsteps Lenny Bruce, a hero of 1960's counterculture and progenitor of "offensive" comedy. Bruce began his career in mainstream comedy in the late 1940's after serving in the U.S. Navy in the Second World War. By 1961, however, his unique brand of humor — based in social taboos — led to an arrest at a gig in San Francisco. Obscenity laws had been broken. Tame by today's standards, Bruce had explored the various linguistic possibilities of the word *come*. The authorities started to take an interest in Bruce, and he was arrested on five other occasions in quick succession. In 1962 he was arrested mid-performance at a folk club in Chicago. The next year he was barred from entering the United Kingdom as an "undesirable alien." In 1964 Bruce was found guilty of obscenity and sentenced to four months in a workhouse. The court received testimony and letters of support from Norman Mailer, Woody Allen, Bob Dylan, James Baldwin, and Allen Ginsberg, among others. Bruce appealed the decision but died of a heroin overdose in Los Angeles while on bail in 1966.

Half a century later, the comedy world is capable of the deepest reflective thought as well as crude insensitive humor. In the 1970's George Carlin carried on his friend's legacy with the seven words you can't say on television: *shit, piss, fuck, cunt, cocksucker, motherfucker, and tits.* When the secret tapes of the Nixon White House were released, each of these words was exonerated. They were now distinctly presidential; Richard Nixon is heard uttering nearly all of them.

After Lenny Bruce, obscenity limitations started to dissolve. People ceased to be shocked by dirty words. In the 1980's, Carlin was considered tame enough to narrate the American version of *Thomas the Tank Engine and Friends*. Comedy has never looked back.

Lenny Bruce invited the world of comedy to push the envelope and to deal with objectionable and subversive subject matter. He rallied against the uptight social attitudes of the generation that held power. He refused to appease the authorities. He remained true to his art form, and he inspired generations of entertainers and thinkers to come.

Chapter 15

The Gregory Brothers

In 2011, I saw for the first time the potential that social media has for bringing people together around an issue. It was then that my wife introduced me to *Schmoyoho*, the YouTube channel run by The Gregory Brothers. I was in stitches. Each of their two- or three-minute clips had me bent double. I felt like a child. I had to watch each clip again and again. I found myself thinking, *this is the future of satire*, but also *this is the future of political subversion.*

Each clip created by the Gregory Brothers takes a piece of found footage — often from the news — and auto-tunes the speakers' voices into song. And the songs are catchy. You may have come across them yourself. *The Double Rainbow Song, Bed Intruder Song, Can't Hug Every Cat* and *Obama Sings to the Shawties* are all theirs. They currently boast 928-million views and 3.2-million subscribers. They're hilarious, and original. Their satirical *Auto-Tune the News* style is now widely imitated and has become the template for other YouTube sensations like Bad Lip Reading. The Gregory Brothers have become part of the modern zeitgeist. When auto-tune comedy is required, they're the people to call. Even Netflix knows this — the Gregory Brothers were hired to create the opening credit sequence in *The Unbreakable Kimmy Schmidt.* At the 83rd Academy Awards, the Gregory Brothers were commissioned to create an auto-tuned comedy segment featuring some of the nominated films. This clip was subsequently Emmy-nominated for Outstanding Short-Form Picture Editing.

The Gregory Brothers work out of a large office building in Brooklyn Heights. It's an open, friendly, post-industrial space. There's a studio, a sound mixing room, offices and a huge lounge/ screening area with a ping pong table and plenty of comfortable seating. Very well equipped. YouTube revenue covers it all and provides serious income on top.

A platinum record hangs framed on the wall — celebration of a million iTunes downloads of the *Bed Intruder Song*.

Evan Gregory: "We had to pay for that."

Michael Gregory: "You'd think the record company would send them out for free, but no."

Aidan Prewett: Could you tell us a little about the process of *songification*?

Sarah Gregory: The process of songifying really is very similar to a traditional collaborative song co-write. Where you come up with melodies and lyrics that you wouldn't normally, just sitting alone in your room. You're really influenced by the give and take of the particular strengths and weaknesses of your co-writers — and in this case, your unintentional singers.

MG: We just kinda write a beat that we want to write, and then fit everybody to that. So both those end up being really interesting in different ways — ways of song-writing. 'Cos when you fit people to the beat that you've written, you really write melodies that you wouldn't have written otherwise. Because it's not what would have come into your head at first.

EG: It's like in the pop music world, there are people who are known for their voice — the quality of their voice, and not necessarily their lyrics. And in that case, we might write music to support their singing. But on the other hand, there are also people out there that are great lyricists — but don't necessarily have the vocal quality — so we'll write music in a different way to try to support them if that's the case.

AP: So was that something that has a real draw for you — to sort of subvert someone's original intention?

EG: It's not always a subversion of intent — sometimes, and I would say *most* often for us, it's even an amplification. Where, by adding music to someone's words, we can actually distill the original message and put it on a higher platform than it might even be as a spoken word.

MG: It's like, if they're making a point, why not make that point in an even more powerful way, by singing it in the key of C.

AP: Have you guys ever amplified a message that you really believed in?

SG: One example that just comes to mind instantly are some songifications we did of historical speeches. Like Martin Luther King, Jr. But also, JFK, Winston Churchill — and I think it was definitely the intention to amplify their message — I think amplify is the best way to put it. And lots of people really responded well to that. We got a lot of response to that from educators who were saying that their students were now listening to the speech in a new way, or maybe even paying attention to it for the first time — but then we also got feedback that sort of misinterpreted that, and thought that we were making light of the original message.

AP: How do you guys respond when people do take your message the wrong way?

EG: It didn't carry too much weight with us because the vast majority of people understood what we were doing. And the only possible misinterpretation of our work is from people that had seen a large body of our work that was primarily comedic — just assuming that everything else we were doing was also comedic. But we had some very straight interpretations of these pieces. When we songified historical speeches in order to emotionally support the message in that speech — it was just something we wanted to do, and we felt like it turned out really well. And we're proud of how those pieces work on a completely straight and serious level.

MG: I remember in my calculus class, my teacher was always ragging on this one girl in my class, who was always memorizing all these song lyrics, but she'd never memorize the formulas. And she'd be like, "Why are you always memorizing the lyrics, when you could be acing these tests?" and she said, "Oh, the lyrics are just so easy." So I was thinking about that with Martin Luther King. I was like, "If this stuff were a song, maybe people could remember more of the speech." I mean, that occurred to me, but I didn't know it was going to have that much of an impact. I was getting emails from teachers that were showing it to their classes. And they said it became sort of like a gateway drug for people to really want to go hear the full speech. 'Cos these were only like three-minute versions and a few highlights. So the kids wanted to go learn more about MLK, for example, and hear more of his speeches. I didn't know it was going to have that much of an educational value. It's like learning your ABC's, it's a lot harder to learn if you're just speaking them in a drone — rather than singing them to Ba Ba Blacksheep.

AP: Can we talk about the word *viral*. Obviously you guys have a really clear understanding of how that works on the internet, do you see it as going beyond the internet as well? I mean your audience to a certain extent is viral.

EG: They're all very sick.

SG: Sick, sick people.

EG: Troubled people.

AP: Is there a shared set of emotions or principles that joins your audience together?

SG: I think so. I mean, with the very basic things our audience obviously enjoys music…

MG: I think of it more of like Robin Hood's merry band than an organized army of people. It's more of a loose affiliation, you might think. But when I think of a video going viral, I don't think of it like all your fans gathering collectively around it. For example, if we get a few million views on a video, I don't necessarily consider it viral because it hasn't gone beyond our audience. For me, viral is when a video you do, or something you do, goes beyond your fan base. Like, say, even if you have a couple of million fans, it has to go beyond — like if your fans are all thirteen to twenty-five, if your fans are all thirteen to twenty-five, and all of a sudden you hear that like, moms are watching it. Like, oh, why is it on all these blogs for moms. Like — *now it has truly gone viral because it is now on a morning show.*

EG: Colloquially, the word viral is kind of, now used to just mean *online*. As in, this is an online video. But in our estimation, to really use the term viral, you're talking about the way something is spread to new areas. And it's spread person-to-person, rather than being disseminated through a system. If five million people watch a TV show, you wouldn't call that *viral.* Because it's reaching its intended audience. The first video we ever had go viral was *Auto-Tune the News #2*. It was seen by about a million people in a week. But at the time, our existing audience was only a couple of thousand people. So that was just widely disseminated in a viral fashion from person to person. Now, if we had a video that was — when our audience is about one million people, if we had a video that was seen half a million, or one million times, we couldn't really claim that that video's being shared virally. Only if it gets seen by several more times that number, would we ever say that we really hit something with that video, so that it got shared beyond our normal threshold.

SG: Our scientific definition of a viral video is when your mom in Idaho has seen it, multiple times.

EG: If the Moms are watching it. It's gone viral. But your original question was about, does our audience have some kind of collective viewpoint — or is there some way to kind of — that they identify together. And I would sort of say no to that. Our audience is primarily virtual. It's people that have found us online, and there are just wildly varying degrees within our audience of how much they connect to us. Whether they just kind of casually watch our videos and enjoy them and then leave, or whether they really want to know more about us. And they look up every one of our side projects and follow our personal projects and stuff like that.

MG: They have things they can all agree on, like they may love Katie Couric's accidental singing, or Joe Biden's. But then there are things that they're all very — they disagree on, like what musical genre's their favorite, or what video's their favorite.

SG: Whether or not to use a Mac or a PC. Or a laptop or a desktop. *Wildly* different life perspectives.

EG: Like whether or not Michael should marry them, for example. There's a lot of differing opinions out there on that. We get a lot of comments.

AP: And your response to that?

MG: *I don't know…*

EG: I mean, we're taking submissions, so...

SG: I mean, I would say that it's a happy by-product of what we do — that music sort of diffuses the subject matter a little bit. So that you can relax and kind of see it for what it is, rather than making it a very personal affront to your own opinions. But I wouldn't say that that was ever our goal — or our philosophy. I think we just really like music, and we get a tickle out of putting an apple in a vegetable bin, or a pickle in an underwear drawer. You know what I mean? It's just interesting and fun to mash things up — and that's part of where our culture is right now, it's mash-up culture. Where re-mixing and mashing up things gives old standards an interesting new approach.

EG: It is true that the addition of music can allow a new perspective on some issue. And allow analysis of that thing in a new way. For example, in our work, take the case of Newt Gingrich criticizing portable electronic spa funding. That might just kind of flit by in the public consciousness — we tried to capture it in song, and then, upon repeat viewings, new subtleties arise from this music, and you're able to really analyze this issue with a new level-headed take. Similarly, if you were at the club, and there was a young woman there that you might want to make love to, you might be flustered by this issue. You might be torn emotionally and not sure how to approach it. But then if Usher's *I Want To Make Love In This Club* were to come on, it would allow you to attack this issue in a new way. It would give you perspective on how to approach it level-headedly — with a level-headed sense — and how you could approach this young woman, and have a meeting of the minds on how you could kind of get over this obstacle.

AP: My very last question is: With the internet and all the conveniences that we have today, do you think that the current generation is less politically involved or aware, than perhaps previous generations may have been?

MG: I don't know if our generation is less politically involved because I haven't been alive for very long. But when you look at footage from the sixties, and everybody just rising up and kinda changing things, we definitely don't have that. But that was kind of unprecedented at the time.

EG: But it's also not true to say that kids today don't know anything and that the conveniences of the internet are taking away from their awareness. In contrast, having access to information and seeing political videos or just current events, kind of being shared on YouTube or other platforms, helps kids be connected to what's going on currently. Whether they are burgeoning tea-partiers, or Wall Street Occupiers, it allows them to stay connected and understand what's going on.

SG: I think it's probably the same — I think there's more access to information than ever before, obviously, but the challenge is the same as it was in any generation — *is there a desire to know?* And I think there have been times in our country's history where the desire to have that information and to analyze it and to compare it with all sorts of other sources of information has been much greater because the need has been much greater to know those things, and to be involved politically. And then there are times when people are pretty comfortable with their state and they don't necessarily desire to access the information as readily. So if our generation is any less interested in politics, it's certainly not because you don't have access to it. It's just, complacency.

AP: Can I just add one last thing onto that — do you think that this convenient society does breed complacency, to a degree?

EG: I think — my short answer is no. But to expand on that a little bit, I think a society with more conveniences allows for a wider range of outcomes in people's lives. And so, on one side of the spectrum, you have more complacent individuals who are happier to take advantage of modern conveniences and not get involved in issues or current events, or connect with other people socially. And on the other end of the spectrum, you have people who take advantage of the tools that are online and in the information age to consume more information, to learn more. And also, to react more. You can share through social media — whether or not people see your contributions — you could be on Twitter and YouTube and Facebook and so-on and so-forth, to kind of contribute to the discussion. And so I think there's a widening of the spectrum of how people can or cannot be involved.

SG: Totally. We get a lot of comments from our fans that are like, "Thank goodness there's *Auto-Tune The News* because it's the only way I hear about the news."

EG: "I learned so much!"

* * *

Historically, mass entertainment has been pervasive, one-sided; without recourse for the consumer. In these ways, mass entertainment follows the playbook as set down by Goebbels. It has a huge influence on societal modes and orders. In the subversive form employed by the Gregory Brothers, it becomes a kind of *anti-propaganda*. The songification process highlights the absurdities of the political messages we receive today.

But the viral nature of the online world can be subversive in other ways. The internet now provides a platform for the spread of misinformation in ways we never expected — least of all the notion of the online echo chamber. Online social connection has also become a daunting political force.

Subversion for comedy is one thing; genuine political subversion — well, that's something else.

Chapter 16

Ted Leo

The Gregory Brothers are taking part in a live "Rejection" show in Brooklyn. The premise is that established artists are invited to perform previously rejected material that they still enjoy. We tag along. It's a fun idea, and we hear a bunch of completely un-commercial ideas explored in front of a live audience. Some material lands, and as expected, some bombs. But it's a safe space.

Also on the bill is Ted Leo. Ted is presenting segments from a rock opera musical that he penned about the 1954 CIA involvement in the Guatemalan banana trade and political coup. He takes the stage inside a full-sized banana suit. As un-commercial as it sounds, the songs are catchy. And the story turns out to be strangely moving. We're hooked. We invite Ted to take part in the documentary. I wanted to hear more about the Banana Wars, which were previously unknown to me. But I also wanted to know more about Ted.

Front man for Ted Leo and the Pharmacists, his music is usually focused toward the punk and post-punk genres. His career began in New York with the band Citizens Arrest. Through the nineties Leo was part of the bands Chisel, Puzzlehead, and Sin-Eaters, before forming the Pharmacists in 1999. Six studio albums followed.

Ted arrives at our hotel a few days later.

Aidan Prewett: We really enjoyed your set the other night, it was really interesting because — does it seem strange to you that that's the only music that we know you for?

Ted Leo: A little bit! I mean, it doesn't seem strange — it seems strange that *that* specifically is the only thing you know me for — it doesn't seem strange that you don't know who I am. That's very ... more often than not, that's the case. But the fact that that particular — 'cos that's literally the only time that's ever been performed, and probably the only time it will be. So it is a little bit strange, yeah.

AP: I think we really stumbled across something special there, and we're definitely going to check out your other stuff.

TL: Thanks. That makes me feel really good about it. Because it was — it was definitely nerve-wracking to think about that stuff after it had been sitting dormant for six years or whatever.

AP: In a normal set, do you usually tell stories in between songs?

TL: I do. I talk a lot on-stage, much to the chagrin of my bandmates. I know when I've gone too long when the drummer starts shuffling around. But yeah, I do. And obviously there was backstory to that particular batch of songs that — it was part of the act that night, that I needed to tell. I do write a lot of somewhat serious songs, and more so in the past, I would spend time discussing them. These days, I'm less interested in — I'm more interested in letting the songs speak for themselves and the simple fact that I have a lot of songs that I want to play every night, and only a certain allotted time to do it. I'm talking less and less these days. If I'm understanding what you're asking, based on what I know about the film, I definitely have traditionally used the stage as a way to *talk* as well as play music.

AP: Do you find that speaking to an audience makes them connect with you more easily?

TL: I think it really depends on the context. Oftentimes it depends on the personality of the performer, and personalities in the audience as well. I very rarely have ever — I have done — but very rarely have I ever straight, like *ranted* about something on stage. But there are definitely times when things have been going on that I feel compelled to address beyond letting the songs speak for themselves, and have spoken about. In the midst of doing that, it really depends on the situation. I've felt crowds — I've started to lose crowds because of that, and I've felt crowds become more unified, in communion with us on the stage because of that.

AP: What kind of issues would you discuss?

TL: Well, the big one obviously is the last fifteen years — the past fifteen years of the ridiculous war that we've been going through in the states, and all of the surrounding and successive issues that have grown out of that. And throughout the past decade, there have been many times when a particular politician, or person in the administration or whatever, has said something that's stuck in my craw in such a way that, in the midst of getting to play a song that I know is going to be relevant to this — I'll feel compelled to get it off my chest. It's also not an infrequent thing that I myself, or with my band will be playing a show that actually has some relevance to a particular issue. Whether it's a benefit for something local, or something organized by a larger group — I do think that personally it's important to acknowledge whatever that kind of meta-issue is, and not just treat the music as the entertainment portion of the evening.

AP: So you see it as two very separate things?

TL: No, I don't actually. I actually see them as working hand-in-hand and would prefer to *not* separate them. I'm never someone who will say that all art has to be immediately political. I think that the world would be a much drearier place without some of the basic love songs that have enhanced my life, throughout it. But at the same time I take even stronger issue with people who feel that art should be kept out of politics or music, or that politics should be kept out of art. And specifically music, which often seems to draw out the *shut up and sing* type of comments. But for me — and this probably has something to do with having grown up from a very young age with the world of punk as my biggest influence, and something that I've participated in since I was a little kid — in that sense, it doesn't seem at all strange to have these things connected at the root. But also, I just think personally, who I am and what I do and why I do it when I sit down with a pencil to begin trying to write lyrics for the music I'm working on — It's rarely something that I have to consciously say, "What's bugging me that I need to address?" All of the issues of life — including the love song stuff — there's no separation between any of that, unless you want there to be, in my opinion.

AP: From what I'm hearing, it sounds like it's just natural for you to take these kind of issues to task. It's not like a duty that you feel responsible for, it's just something that you *have* to do?

TL: Right. That's definitely the case. In the broadest sense of how I at least perceive myself as a musician, it does not feel like a duty. That's not to say that there aren't times when I feel either duty-bound to address something specific, or that I feel that it's been a while since I've written a song that has tapped that vein in a serious enough way. And sometimes I do push myself in that direction, for better or for worse. Sometimes definitely for worse, as far as songwriting craft goes.

AP: Were you involved in Occupy at all?

TL: Yes, I went down to Zuccotti Park a couple of times. A really cool thing was, just via one tweet on Twitter, I'd say *hey, check out our tour dates — if you're occupying in your town, let me know and I'll come by.* And I was able to hook up with people around different towns around the South doing that. Either to stop by and do a song, or to invite people down to the show to talk or leaflet or whatever. It was cool.

AP: So what kind of reactions did you get when you were — did you speak to crowds at the occupy places?

TL: A couple of places I performed. And I wouldn't say much in those cases — somebody else would say ... I'd say some small things and play some songs. But in that particular situation, I'm actually more humbled and hold a great respect for the people actually doing the occupying. I wouldn't presume to speak too much to them. So in that case I would prefer to just play some songs.

AP: And the audience reaction was obviously very pleasant.

TL: Yeah, for the most part. There were definitely some shows of my own.... Toward the end of November 2011, I did a show in Boston where I was actually opening for someone else. I had been down to Occupy Boston earlier in the day, and just mentioning that from stage drew a smattering of boos. But for the most part, people that I've encountered in my — I hesitate to call it a bubble — but in my world, people have been appreciative of it.

AP: In terms of subversion, we've mainly been talking to people about protesting and using that in their art in terms of taking something — like the Gregory Brothers — taking something and changing the meaning of it. But listening to you the other night, speaking and singing about the Banana Republic — that was really fascinating from the point of view that that's actual, political, *dangerous* subversion. I'd love to hear you give us an overview of what happened.

TL: Well, I mean, you can frame it as just another classic case of unfettered capitalism and the money-to-power structure resulting ultimately in the very chilling effects on humans in Guatemala that created this situation that led myself and the guy who I was originally working on the play with into the story. Which was, that this woman named Jennifer Harbury — a Harvard-schooled lawyer, was documenting human rights abuses in Guatemala — fell in love with a Guatemalan who was a commandant in the actual front, fighting against the oppressive government at that time. He subsequently disappeared, and she spent the next decade trying to get his remains back. Which led to exposure of CIA collusion going back half a century in Guatemala, requiring our president Bill Clinton at the time to issue a formal apology for being involved in this, etc., etc. But it really goes back to just how crazy things can get when you threaten business in the world. It started with one guy. One guy with a banana cart in New Orleans, who made enough money selling almost-overripe bananas, which he would buy for cheap off ships, to people around town at a slight profit, that he could actually grow his business that he actually purchased land in Honduras, started his own company, bought out the Boston Fruit company, which became the United Fruit Company. With all of this massive money power at his back — because United Fruit Company had like a thousand ships sailing the globe selling bananas — he was able to overthrow the government in Honduras to put his guy in power, and get our government to essentially overthrow the recently democratically elected, and decidedly *not communist* government in Guatemala, who sought only some simple land reforms, overthrown as well. Which resulted in half a century of murder and torture, and destruction. And that's the story.

AP: For the sake of bananas.

TL: For the sake of bananas. Well, for the sake of the money that the bananas brought it.

AP: For me, it sounded so reminiscent of the stories of the cocaine industry, coming from something natural — the coca plant or the banana plant, and just creating … although the effects of a banana upon the human condition is slightly different, to that of cocaine….

TL: A little more salubrious.

AP: That, to me, seems even more poignant than the cocaine wars and all that stuff, because that is about cocaine, but this is *just money*. This is not to do with changing the human condition or any of that kind of stuff, it's just for the sake of the fact that these bananas are making money, and *we want to be making that money*. And that scares me, a lot.

TL: Yes. It's tantamount to slavery. I think the closest analogue to what living in a banana republic would have been like in the twentieth century, would be what miners have gone through, having their entire lives revolve around the company-owned town, run by the company-owned police force, and having to buy their goods in the company-owned store, and earning nothing for their back-breaking work. And year after year, safety conditions are ignored, and people die, all because of the fact that they can't stop the flow of the coal, just like they couldn't stop the flow of the bananas, because giant industries would collapse, and rich people would be slightly less rich.

AP: So the protagonist in the Banana Republic story was called Sam?

TL: Yeah, the one guy who had the banana cart in New Orleans, his name was Sam Zemurray. He was Moldovan, which was at that point called Bessarabia. He was Jewish — there was a pogrom, and his family left in the late nineteenth century. First they settled in Mobile, Alabama, and then moved to New Orleans. And he was just one of those guys who had a vision that the banana trade could be really big. I guess it wasn't at that time. I mean, bananas were being shipped from Central America to North America. But it just wasn't that big a deal. There are some crazy statistics, which I can't quote for you right now, the amount that led to, with all of his success in promoting the banana.

He wasn't just a smart businessman with a vision and a violent streak. He actually hired social psychologists like Edward Bernays to help him sell the banana to the world. To sell it as a thing that everyone should be eating. And he then used Edward Bernays again to sell the fact that the Arbenz government in Guatemala needed to be toppled, as we were looking at every potential red scare in the hemisphere, and wondering if that regime needed to be toppled. His use of propaganda, both in business and in war — which I guess was part of his business at that point, was really amazing. It's too easy to look at that as just a little side-track in the story, but it's actually a really interesting part of the story. And one wonders how many other times in one's life one has been manipulated by propaganda like that, you know?

So Sam Murray grew his business enough that he was able to buy some land in Honduras, and when Manuel Bunia was the president. When he was defeated and sent into exile, he managed to find Bonia, and with a couple of mercenaries, literally two I think, were able to go back, overthrow the government, reinstall Bonia, who then eventually gave Sam *carte blanche* to run the country as one big plantation for his bananas. And hence the "Banana Republic" — the whole idea and the phrase Banana Republic was born.

AP: How much do you know about the CIA involvement with that coup?

TL: Quite a bit. I think I knew more at one point, when I was in the thick of writing it, than I do now. The CIA, as I remember, they managed to get a new ambassador put into Guatemala at the time, who was essentially *their guy*. And there was an official operation, called Operation PB Success, that involved a couple of bomber planes dropping some bombs on the coast.... Part of the idea was that they got involved here in the states, in propagandizing the idea that this was a communist government that had just been elected in Guatemala, which it wasn't, by any stretch of the imagination. And on the ground, in Guatemala, they got involved in intelligence during the overthrow, and in actively fomenting the overthrow. And in trying to goad the Guatemalans into shooting at our airplanes, etc., etc. And then subsequently, over the course of the next fifty years, they were involved, if not directly complicit, in the actual maintaining of torture sites and jails in Guatemala. There were people who were trained in the school of the Americas who the Guatemalan army and government, which was the same thing at that point, were using. And Jennifer Harbury speaks often in her stories from the personal knowledge of seeing American operatives in these Guatemalan prisons, and in the actual rooms with people.

AP: Who was the male love interest in the story?

TL: Yeah, his name was Efraine Bamaca Velasquez, and he went by the name Everardo. And he was a commander on the front. The love story — it's actually pretty touching. She couldn't stay there continuously and would have to leave the country. They would have to meet at safe houses over the border in Mexico just to see each other. But yeah, eventually he disappeared. They knew that he had been captured. And the idea of being disappeared means that nobody can ever find out what happened to you. Like in Argentina and other places where you hear about the disappeared. People know — it's not that they just disappeared off the streets. Sometimes that happened. Sometimes you know that this person has been jailed, and *then* they disappear. You know, all records are refused. She went through every diplomatic channel that she could. She eventually staged a number of hunger strikes both in Guatemala and here in the states. Eventually, she did find a couple of people in the U.S. Congress…

Going back to United Fruit…. When the CIA operation PB Success was authorized by Congress, there's another statistic that I'm going to misquote, in an exact way. The impact of it is relatively the same: something to the effect of fifteen of the twenty people on the voting committee had either personal or family ties to the United Fruit Company through their investments. Fifty years later, forty years later going to the Congress and one woman saying, "I fell in love with this rebel commander who was disappeared, and I wasn't to get his remains back…." I mean, why would you even think that anyone would listen to you at all, in the U.S. congress? But they did find a few people who listened. And they started some poking around, and kinda went to the wall for her. One congressman in particular, Richard Nuccio, took up her case as his cause. They managed to open up an investigation of the files, and they did — as things eventually settled into some kind of stasis in Guatemala and the civil war died down, they were able to eventually get the records of what happened to him, and find his remains, which were stored in some kind of vault.

AP: Do you know the Boomtown Rats song *Banana Republic?*

TL: I don't, no.

AP: It's actually about Ireland, but they were relating it to the oppressive government in the seventies … and apparently it took on — because Bob Geldof does a very similar thing to you, actually, at his shows, where he will really go into some detail in explaining what the song is about. It's something that I was really switched on by. And he was saying that his song *Banana Republic* is about Ireland, but people in Germany thought he was singing about Germany, and so it was a number one hit in Germany. In like '79, I think it was. So that was fascinating, but now I know where the term Banana Republic actually comes from.

* * *

The 1954 Guatemala conflict was to become a decisive moment for one Dr. Ernesto Rafael Guevara de la Serna. Che Guevara — as he is better known — was present in Guatemala during the CIA-backed coup to depose President Jacobo Árbenz Guzmán. Guevara briefly fought with the pro-Arbenz forces and cites this conflict as definitive in his decision to pursue a revolutionary path.

Guevara had just completed his Bachelor of Medicine at the University of Buenos Aires and decided to travel throughout South America to get some perspective on how best to provide assistance to the most poverty-stricken areas. Almost by chance, he ended up in Guatemala just as the Árbenz government was violently ousted; the Castillo Armas dictatorship was installed. In Mexico City the following year, Guevara met with Cuban exile Fidel Castro. He decided that he would devote the next stage of his life to Cuba.

In 1956, Guevara rose from guerrilla medic to become Castro's second-in-command. Their group of revolutionaries landed in Cuba and began a three-year march across the island, recruiting sympathizers and gaining the trust of local villagers. Guevara's brilliance as a military strategist led to guerrilla victories against the much larger Cuban forces and eventually led to the overthrow of the Batista regime. Castro came next. Guevara stayed in Cuba long enough to forge a strong relationship with the U.S.S.R., and played a major role in negotiating the delivery of Russian nuclear weapons to Cuba in 1962.

Guevara's relationship with Castro began to fray and he left Cuba to continue to export the revolution to the world. In 1965, he was a key organizer in the Congo, then in 1967 he went to Bolivia. While in Bolivia, he was captured and summarily executed. Fidel Castro called for three days of mourning across Cuba. One million Cubans descended upon Havana's Plaza de la Revolución to hear the eulogy delivered by Castro. Che Guevara became a martyr for revolutionaries around the world.

* * *

U.S. involvement in South America is emblematic of the arrogance of a post-war nation intoxicated with its newfound power — and terrified of losing it. The cold war pitched the U.S. against the U.S.S.R. and both superpowers made considerable efforts to leverage power in other nations around the world. Thus the Cold War ran as an undercurrent to human existence throughout the post-war era. Existentialism itself enjoyed a major resurgence at this time. As creators of the A-Bomb, we suddenly had reasons to question our own existence as a species on the planet. *Why are we here, if only to annihilate ourselves and everything around us?*

A key proponent of the existentialist movement was Jean-Paul Sartre. His most influential work, *Being and Nothingness*, was written during the German occupation of France and published in 1943. Its central tenet is that *existence precedes essence* — we exist first, and only then do we come to try to make sense of things, by way of science, religion, political ideologies, philosophies, and other means. Another key element of Sartre's writing is the idea that perception is a negative process — deciphering what things *are* by first deciphering what they *are not*. He calls this process *nihilating* — creating nothingness as a means of perceptual distinction.

This is a highly reductive take on Sartre, but it's clear why he became the poster boy for existentialism. The post-war generation, under threat of nuclear annihilation, was starting to experiment with the idea that *being is nothing*.

Earlier, in 1939, Sartre was conscripted into the French army as a meteorologist. His unit was captured in 1940 and he spent nine months in a POW camp. He somehow arranged his release in 1941 and he returned to Parisian life during the occupation. He came to idolize those involved with the resistance and contributed several writings to underground papers.

Sartre observed: "Man is condemned to be free; once thrown into the world, he is responsible for everything he does." He explains that people are generally terrified of having the responsibility to bring meaning to their own life. He goes on to say that oftentimes, people push back against the weight of this freedom by embracing authoritarian ideals. The lure of fascism lies within. He applied this theory specifically to those who chose to collaborate with the German occupation of France.

Also during the war, Sartre met his lifelong partner Simone de Beauvoir, author of *The Second Sex* (1949) and a key influence on the women's movement. In 1960 the pair were invited to Cuba to meet with recently-installed President Fidel Castro and his lieutenant Che Guevara. Sartre spent long hours with both men, noting his genuine affection for Guevara: "He is not only an intellectual, but also the most complete human being of our age."

The players at the center of the Cuban Missile Crisis were students of existentialism, too.

In 1964, Sartre was awarded the Nobel Prize in Literature, despite his attempts to refuse it. In the riots of May 1968 he took to the streets of Paris in solidarity with student protestors and was arrested for civil disobedience. President Charles de Gaulle issued an official pardon, stating, "You don't arrest Voltaire." When

Sartre died in 1980, fifty thousand Parisians marched in solidarity with his cortège.

Existence precedes essence — by nature of our existence, we try to frame the world to make some kind of sense of it. For some, the world makes sense through the application of science, religion, or political action. For others, the world makes sense through chords, melody, and song lyrics.

Chapter 17

Jann Klose

Our time in New York is an eccentric blend of Old Guard and New School. The city is so iconic, so well established, so familiar. Immense, crowded, and strangely comfortable. The discovery of the Gregory Brothers and Ted Leo has turned us on to new sounds and ideas in a clean segue from the Dylan-esque feeling of D.A. Pennebaker's offices and the sentimentality of a Cavett interview.

It's snowing outside. From our hotel window we can see the expanse of Fifth Avenue leading up to Central Park. The hotel is still taking good care of us. The cameras are set; we're ready for our next interview. He's coming to us. We've found that a hotel near the Park gives interview subjects a little more incentive to travel.

We wanted to explore a contemporary perspective on the audience phenomenon. Jann Klose is a singer/songwriter and one of the acute observers of performance artistry. He provides a telling interview on the subject. Has the music world changed that much since Woodstock? We're about to find out.

Klose is a natural performer with a distinctive, emotional, and powerful voice. Known for his perceptive observations of the world around him; he is a student of the philosophy of music. He makes sense of the world through music. His lyrics are introspective, and we're about to find out that his reflective nature makes him an excellent subject for interview.

Jann Klose spent his formative years in Germany, South Africa, and Kenya. He fell in love with the United States while on a high school exchange, and currently resides and bases his operations in the Bronx. He racks up around one hundred live performances annually, and frequently tours to Germany and South Africa. He features heavily in the film *Greetings From Tim Buckley* (Focus/Tribeca) as the singing voice of Tim Buckley.

In 2016 he released the album *Stereopticon* in collaboration with Jeff Buckley guitarist Gary Lucas. His new album *In Tandem* has recently hit shelves via SONY/The Orchard.

Aidan Prewett: As a performer, do you feel a sense of power when you step out onto a stage?

Jann Klose: I don't know if power is the right word for it. I mean, it's an experience for me of wanting to draw an audience in to what I'm doing. Drawing them into the emotion that I'm going through. And the more that happens, the more I feel like everything sort of becomes a channel — like I become that. I become sort of just a part of a bigger picture, rather than just me on stage playing a song for somebody. I feel like, I want to draw the audience in, and have them be just as much a part of it as the bass player is, in a sense. Or the drummer, or other musicians on-stage. There's a feeling of satisfaction that comes out of that. A feeling of being really in the moment, and really experiencing every second as a reality that constantly changes, but that has a — there's a line that kind of flows through that. It doesn't always work that way, for various reasons — like when you have a bad show, or something's gone wrong, you have technical problems. But when it does, when you have that kind of connection with the audience, you really feel like the room is listening. And you're listening to them. It's extraordinary. Nothing really feels better. It's a really great feeling.

AP: Would you say that it's — when that occurs, it's like a unification? That everybody becomes....

JK: Sort of, I mean, at least to me it is. I really enjoy that feeling of unity. It's great. And I don't know how much it has to do with power for me. I mean, that sort of scares me. I feel like, what I'm doing and what's coming out of me is happening because I've lived, and I've listened to a lot of music and because I've tried to get better at what I'm doing, and because I've struggled with it. I feel like who I am comes out in that moment. So it's not because — I'm not doing it to feel power over the audience. I mean, in a way I'd rather them have power over me. But sort of giving them what they need. Everyone gets a fair share of entertainment, if you want to look at it that way.

AP: Could you tell us about the experience of growing up in Germany?

JK: Well, I was born in Germany and then, as a one-year-old, we moved to Kenya. And my brother was born in Nairobi, which is where we lived. And as a four or five-year-old we moved to Johannesburg, South Africa. And all the time speaking German at home, and speaking English when we would leave the house. So I grew up bi-lingual because of that.

We moved back to Germany, and I went through the German curriculum. And as far as growing up in Germany, the first thing, or one of the first things you learn about German history is the holocaust, with the Nazis leading up to the Second World War and so on and so forth. Eventually you come to that subject. And the way we were exposed to it — other than what we already saw on television growing up — was by sending an entire seventh-grade class off to see a movie about the holocaust, with documentary footage from the death camps. So you have this kind of thing built into your subconscious. Growing up, this is what you learn.

It can be very intimidating talking about it because it's such a horrible, horrible part of German history. But what I like to have people remember — or have myself remember, really — is that there's a lot more to German history than just the holocaust and the Second World War and the First World War. There's an entire culture that has a lot of other aspects that it has built up over centuries and millennia.

AP: Were you in South Africa during apartheid?

JK: Yeah. We left just as it got out of hand. Which I didn't find out until we were back in Germany and I watched the German news. Because the South African news didn't show you what was going on.

AP: Did you see any crowd behavior when you were there?

JK: No, I was too young. I was ten when we left there, so it was … we were so sheltered. When we traveled, we went to the coast or on safari, or … we'd experience it like a cultural Africa, but not what was going on sub-culturally. Which at that point wasn't even sub-culturally anymore. So I was really sheltered from that, and too young to really understand it, I think.

AP: You obviously have a clear understanding now.

JK: Oh yeah. I mean, I had a better understanding of it after we moved back to Germany, and I watched the news, and you could see what was going on. And you were like, *wait a second … we were just there! Why didn't we* — and then, even as a child, you connect the dots — or I connected the dots and realized that what I was seeing was trying to get me to believe that there was nothing going on. Which was what the media was doing in South Africa — clearly, because they were controlled by the whites.

AP: That's fascinating to even consider, 'cos Australia is completely sheltered, in the sense that it's an island, and it's quite removed from —

JK: A *big* island.

AP: That's it. It's frustrating to see the way that politics is going lately. I wonder if this kind of isolation has something to do with it.

JK: It's fear-based. It's fear of change. It's like a lot of what's going on in America right now. Because we have a very divided country — we have a country that in part is ready to leave the America of the past behind. And to sort of forge a new, very different path. And you have a more conservative America that is so disenchanted with the ways things have gone over the last decade, that they want to return to … like *really* go back, like *way* back, and just make everything the way it was. But that's what happens when you have discomfort, or when you have — when you're going through a recession or large changes in an economy, then there's two ways to go. There's, "Let's continue this change," or "Let's go back." And a lot of people, I think, will go with the way back, because it's easy and it's comfortable and it's something they know. They don't know what's going to happen. You never know. So it's a big issue right now. It's an election year, and it's being covered like — it seems to me like never before. Mainly because of the internet, I think. More and more, we have access to so much different information.

AP: Do you think that people today are less *or more* likely to stand up for something they believe in?

JK: You know, I thought they were less likely to do so. Until Occupy Wall Street started. And I realized, *Oh — okay! There's still a pulse on the left.* We certainly knew there was a pulse on the right, that developed with the tea party and so forth, but when Occupy started I was like — *good. We need this — as a balance, on the other side.* I think we need as much of that as possible — if we want to keep calling ourselves a democracy.

AP: Do you think that that's probably necessary for a democracy — to have people who take authority and forcefully sort of push themselves against it?

JK: Well, forcefully pushing against something — I think if you do it by questioning it, I think that's the best way to do it. You have to be careful not to get too emotional about it, because people will be on the defensive if they feel attacked. Anyone will. But if you point out the realities, and give information to the public that way, on a larger level, then you have something that you can stand on. And I'm — that's what we have to do. On both sides — and in the middle. I mean, if we stop doing that, then we can just switch off.

AP: As an independent artist, you have an audience that — you have a specific audience. Could you tell us about how you relate to your audience?

JK: Well, because I'm independent and because the growth that we've seen, with my band, and the people I'm working with — it's been very step-by-step. I used to just — get to know every single one of my fans. It was just a few people, and then it became more and more. So now that there's — I can't meet everybody anymore, but I still really want to, and I really enjoy that personal relationship with the fans, at shows. It's just been something that I've found to be something very normal. Because I want to know what they like about what I do, so I can do more of it. So yeah, it's personal to me. I'm lucky — I have very loyal fans. They will — they'll be there no matter what.

AP: How do you see the future of the music industry?

JK: Sometimes you just have to stop thinking about it because it's just so crazy right now. You literally still don't know where it's all going to end up going, but we were just lamenting the fact that it's so difficult now. Even though in some ways it's become easier, I think. I mean, I've never known the music business to be anything else than kind of what it is now. 'Cos when I started, the CD was on a steep decline, the internet was already in full force, or was beginning to really take off. Now, we're at a point where it's becoming "okay" to convict people for file sharing. It's beginning this new phase. And I'm sort of concerned with how that's going to play out. Because now it's — if it gets this stigma, I don't quite know how that's all going to play out.

I always thought music was there to be shared. But I also think that it's important that artists get paid. 'Cos everyone has to eat, and we have to make records, and it costs money to do so. And it costs money to travel, and it costs a *lot* of money. Whatever people think. I'm a big advocate for people to pay for music that they love. I don't think there's anything wrong with that. Yes, if you want to get it for free — sure. But I actually saw this video that Kid Rock did — he did this video, and it went viral online. He was talking about how "Well, if you're going to steal music from people that are rich and successful, then why don't you start stealing cars from Toyota? They're rich and successful. Why not just steal everything?" And I thought that that kind of brought home the point that it's not okay to do it just because you *think* there is all this money. There isn't — that's the reason that there isn't all this money anymore, in music.

* * *

Jann Klose points out the utopian dream of music: it's the ultimate climactic group experience. An escape, yes, but deeply focused at the same time. With an audience that becomes a part of the band itself, there is a blurring of the division between commander and commanded. If the groups are *one*, it's not clear who is leading and who is following. An ostensibly leaderless group is subject to the push-and-pull of popular opinion; of changing public discourse. Within the herd mentality, there are many subtleties in the variety of factors that can draw influence. This brings us back to the concept of *groupthink*.

Chapter 18

Groupthink

Over the years the concept of *groupthink* has evolved into two distinct definitions. The word itself was first defined in a 1972 study by Yale psychologist Irving Janis. Janis studied small group decision-making in government cabinets and corporate boardrooms. His findings indicated that decisions become less rational in group situations, especially when the group places a high value on finding a consensus. More on this later.

A second definition, evolved through its use in the media, has taken the word *groupthink* to mean the prevailing assumptions and attitudes of a particular time; the general discourse of a crowd, an audience, or an entire nation.

The second definition of groupthink is visible in many aspects of society; the prevailing notions in group discourse can be seen as having major political implications in everything from the lead-up to the First World War to more recent elections around the world. The Second World War was rife with examples, from Goebbels' propaganda studies and dissertations to the attack on Pearl Harbor.

Groupthink was a common topic of discussion during our interviews. In order to bring the relevant remarks together into a focused treatment of the theme, the following section has been assembled and curated from a number of separate conversations.

Paul Provenza: What's interesting. — a modern version of that is really 9/11. That was a game-changer in many ways. It's a moment, that really when you look at any aspect of culture in America, that's a point where things have to be addressed differently in some way, shape, or form. Which I felt became obvious to everybody far later than Doug Stanhope was talking about it, or than John Stewart had been talking about it. Or than Bill Maher had been talking about it. We all saw exactly how this was going to play out, and what this was going to cost us, and who was going to profit from it. And we're outside watching the audience follow this groupthink down that road, because we see how it happens, and we know how susceptible large numbers of people are to it.

The flip side of that is the Arab Spring — look at what happened in Egypt, and look at all that sort of stuff. As much as a champion as I am for fighting for freedom and all, what's the first problem you have once you win? It's, "Okay, well who's going to fill that power vacuum?" And do the groupthink. Whose groupthink is going to be the one that gets traction. It's ubiquitous. And if you're a comic with any sort of thoughtfulness about yourself, you see it. It's part of what we do. That's the great irony. That's what I was saying is that it's worth listening to what thoughtful comedians have to say. It's worth more than listening to any politician or any newscaster, or any authority, because we know how this shit works. We traffic in the same goods, shall we say.

Groupthink as described above does have a certain weight to it. But other situations involving groupthink must be more benign — and even fun.

Aidan Prewett: I'd like to know — when there's groupthink happening in a large space, crammed full of people for *Depeche Mode* — is there like, an energy or an electricity in the air — was there something you could *feel?*

Chris Hegedus: Yeah. I definitely think you can feel the energy.

D.A. Pennebaker: Oh, yeah. You know, earlier on, I think in one of the other cities where they performed, he did this thing on the last song, which was really about drugs, although at the time I didn't know that was what it was about. I just thought it was a great song. But he did this thing of waving his arms back and forth, and the audience kind of picked it up. And then, I don't remember the next time, whether it happened again, but when we got to the rose bowl, he got up by himself on this high place, and he started to do it, and that whole audience — it was a hundred thousand people, all doing it, right with him. It's like — nobody told him to, there were no pieces of paper delivered saying *be sure to wave* — and the people in front couldn't tell — everybody knew that that's what they were going to do. And I thought that's such an interesting example of mass communication — because nothing was said. He just did this thing — and when you see this whole audience of — as far as the eye can see — and they're all going *just like this.* In time to the music. It really shakes you. It's a heavy thing to watch. That's why I thought you should see that film if you could.

CH: I do remember the moment when I turned around and started filming the audience. It really seemed like a sea of bodies. It took a few minutes for them to stop going cross-purpose with their waving, but when they did, it just — it was an amazing quality. And very powerful, as a cameraperson, when you film that kind of thing. But there have been other odd moments. I remember on one of the concert stops with the band, filming David kind of … go off the stage and how a performer reaches down to the audience. And he reaches down to a girl, and she passed out. You know, right when he reached out to her. That kind of power between a performer and an audience must be very strange, to have something like that happen — when you touch somebody and they pass out.

AP: When you're in front of an audience, do you see them as a group of individuals or as some kind of collective?

TL: At various times throughout a show, I think that the audience can meld into a collective identity, from my point of view — while at the same time, remaining individuals. That's the kind of ebb and flow that has probably more to do with where I'm at, in the midst of performing, than what's actually going on in the crowd. Although they obviously feed off each other. If I'm lost in the moment, then I'm lost in the moment, and everything is one collective moment. If I step out of that, then I tend to see individual elements interacting more.

AP: Have you ever been caught up in some kind of collective thing where you've found yourself doing something, or have a thought process that you wouldn't normally have?

Ted Leo: I have, I think, found myself caught up in a mob mentality, for lack of a better term. But I can honestly say, I'm really just talking about little kid stuff. Like getting — you know, I was a much more fearful and frail child until I got to high school, thanyou might think if you knew me now [Laughs]. Certainly the rush of being swept up in whoever was being cool at the moment, which often engendered being mean, or violent, or something stupid at the moment, I was not immune to. But I think it's been pretty rare — honestly I can't.... If I'm involved in a big group activity for most of the x amount of years of my adult life, it's usually something that I'm pretty well already behind. Or am able to be skeptical about in the moment if I feel that I need to be. Without tooting my own horn.

AP: So is there, therefore, a danger that people might be susceptible to falling under the spell, so to speak, of a charismatic performer?

TL: I suppose so — this is a tough question for me to answer because it requires me to draw a distinction between myself and behaviors that I would, I suppose, condemn. But yeah, there is a danger. There's certainly a danger. I can put it in a real innocuous context: people just becoming too big a *fan* of the music of somebody. That can often just take over someone's identity just for a short time. And creep the artist out a little bit. And that's a real benign thing, but obviously that can happen. I'm sure that at every single rally that I've ever been to, where I'm feeling good about myself for being able to be in my right mind about it all, there are probably people who aren't in their right mind about it all. At those marches and rallies, you always see people who are very much a part of your movement, and have to remain a part of your movement, but who *in the moment* do seem a little swept up in the energy of it, to the extent that it can be a little off-putting, where you feel that dialogue might actually shut down.

The groupthink displayed in a small crowd will often mirror that of a large crowd. If you look at the micro, you see the macro.

Dale Bell: You look at the Occupy movement, in the very first days in NYC, which is where it began with a small group on Wall Street. You saw a group of people trying to — as it's depicted in the *Woodstock* film in the mud underneath that bar — people are chanting and using bongo drums and, on Wall Street, there are people who are trying to go beneath the barricade that's been put up there. And sliding, as they do. I saw this and I said, "My God, this is a clone of Woodstock." Absolutely the same thing. You look at people commenting on the inauguration of Obama, and people looking out and seeing hundreds of thousands of people and saying, "This is Woodstock — convocation, if you will, without the mud." There it was, on January 20th, and it was freezing. But there were hundreds of thousands of people who never thought they would ever be in this place at one time. And there they are.

You look at what went on in the Arab Spring. What goes on in Tunisia — one person immolating themselves, and a whole country getting behind that kind of a deed, and saying *we want to turn our people out.* That is called sticking it to the man. That is what happened in Egypt, that is what is in the process of happening throughout the Middle East. Hopefully it will go and drift down into Africa. These are significant events. Can Woodstock be *the cause* of all of these? Not directly, of course. But indirectly, subconsciously and/or consciously — yeah, I think we've probably got some strings and some balloons out there. This is a film that has been seen around the world, and it represents a hell of a lot of really great values. And I hope that Arab Spring and Global Spring is one of the values that we represent.

* * *

National and international discourse is a major factor in the court of public opinion. As the Watergate scandal unfolded between 1972–1974, television broadcasts brought the minutiae of the proceedings home for amateur analysis. In November 1973, President Richard Nixon badly needed to sway public opinion. His strategy? A gigantic press conference and the words "I'm not a crook."

Chapter 19

Subversive Politics

At the height of the Watergate scandal, the American public learned of a comprehensive audio recording system in the White House. This system was responsible for keeping an exact record of conversations between the president and his staff. As part of the Watergate investigation, the House Judiciary Committee subpoenaed the tapes, but Nixon refused to release them, citing executive privilege. Nixon ordered the firing of a successive chain of people involved in the Committee; several of his staff, including his Attorney General, resigned in protest rather than carrying out the order.

In the landmark 1974 Supreme Court case *United States v. Nixon*, the court found that the courts are not compelled to honor claims of executive privilege. They ordered Nixon to release the tapes. On what became known as the "smoking gun" tape, recorded six days after the break-in, Nixon is heard discussing plans for a cover-up. This constituted evidence of a conspiracy to obstruct the course of justice. The tape was made public on August 5, 1974, triggering enormous public outcry and creating an opportunity for impeachment. Nixon announced his resignation on Thursday, August 8, to be effective at noon the following day.

As an influential and potentially dangerous person-of-interest, Dick Cavett is mentioned twenty-six times in the Nixon tapes. He is joined there by John Lennon, Jane Fonda, Carol Channing, Steve McQueen, Paul Newman, and Barbra Streisand. In total, there were over five hundred names on Nixon's "Enemy List" — political dissidents to be put through whatever political ringer was readily available.

Dick Cavett: It's like the beginning of a crime novel. I get in the back of a car at L.A. Airport, and the guy who's picking me up opens a laptop. On the screen is Richard Nixon and H.R. Haldeman. It was a still image. But the sound: it's from the Nixon tapes. And there's *my name* in the dialogue.

> *Richard Nixon: What the hell is Cavett?*
>
> *Haldeman: Oh Christ he's, he's…*
>
> *Nixon: He's terrible?*
>
> *Haldeman: He's impossible. He loads every program. We've complained bitterly about the Cavett Shows.*

But the best line of all is right at the end. It's only a few minutes … and it's a strange feeling to have the most powerful man in the world saying about you:

> *Nixon: Well, is there any way we can screw him? That's what I mean, there must be ways.*

He came up with something. I found out years later — when two of my former staff members had happened to bring up the subject of being audited the same year — and then found out that other staff members had. Mr. Nixon had in his favorite way of doing things — illegally — frequently used the IRS to punish people. And he decided, I guess, the way to get at me was to audit my staff — and me. But I didn't know he'd done it to the staff. And he hurt some people. Not for the first time in his life.

There were a couple of other things. The Nixon administration *forced* a guest onto my show once, to counteract talk against the Supersonic Transport, which had taken place on earlier shows. And they put this guy on and he said his piece, and then I said, "well I certainly hope the SSD is defeated, but thank you for being here." They didn't like that — I was supposed to play the game. And then with John Kerry, they placed and coached a right-winger to come on and debate him. And Kerry was much more successful than the other guy was.

I sent interview requests to the offices of every member of the U.S. Congress. I promptly received a barrage of polite rejections. Some I tried to push to do a pre-record interview, but nothing came through. I figured my pitch was in the wrong direction. No politician wants to talk about Nixon. No politician wants to talk about commanding power. But documentary filmmakers do.

Aidan Prewett: You guys have worked with quite a few politicians over the years — is there anybody in particular who stands out as having a strong command over their audience?

Chris Hegedus: One of the people who we did do a film about, who ended up being a politician — although he wasn't exactly a politician when we began filming him — was Al Franken. Who has subsequently become a senator. But he was at a point where he was kind of changing over from his comedy SNL persona into writing books and really wanting to change things and talk about the way that politics was going. And we decided to follow him when he had just put out his latest book, which was kind of bashing Bush and Fox News and the right-wing establishment. And the audiences for Al were really interesting, because they were looking for somebody to kind of give them answers.

It was at a point in this country where a lot of different comedic and television figures like Jon Stewart — and Al's one of them — were starting to be looked at for political news. And one of the great things about Al is that he's a really powerful speaker, and he can also make people laugh. And the power of being able to tell jokes while you're delivering a serious message is an amazing skill, and not very many politicians can do that. So he was unique in that way, and it was interesting to watch audiences for that reason, because they loved coming to hear him, because they knew they were going to get something besides some political knowledge; they knew they were going to get entertained.

D.A. Pennebaker: And he could talk off-script. I mean — he didn't need a script at all. Clinton could do that, and Obama could do that. And Kennedy could do that.

AP: Did you meet Kennedy?

DAP: Oh yeah, many times. But I could see he was so different from Bobby that he was never going to be your best friend, at least not in that role. But he was always very well disposed toward me. And occasionally I filmed him doing things that he knew I wasn't going to release. Like the morning that his mother-in-law called him up and was balling him out because the cook had just quit. It was a big story in the *Times*. He was saying, "Yes Mrs. Auchincloss, no Mrs. Auchincloss…" and I was filming him and he was kinda laughing at my filming him. It didn't bother him. He had a very strong sense of what we were doing, as opposed to what the nightly news was doing. And he kind of knew that anything he did [for our cameras] would be historical — would not efface him the next day on the television. And that made a difference of how he looked at what we were doing.

AP: But Bobby was different?

DAP: Well, Bobby was more of a friend, yeah. I knew Bobby pretty well. And I did several films with him.

AP: Did either of the brothers ever say anything to you that's really stuck with you?

DAP: Well yeah, sort of. They'd say funny things — like Jack would show me the holes in the floor of the Oval Office. He said, "*D'you know what they are?*" and I said no, and he said, "*That's where Eisenhower had his golf shoes.*" There were these little holes all through this cork-ish floor.

Bobby would say things that were really heartfelt sometimes. I always — I don't know, it made me have such a strong feeling about him. When the two Black kids were trying to get into Tuscaloosa [University of Alabama], and he said that they shouldn't put them down there where they can get yelled at by the governor just because politically it would be a good thing. He said they shouldn't have to listen to that kind of stuff. And that's the way he kind of thought. I liked that about him, that he was — he thought about people all the way through.

The terrible events of June 1968 sealed a presidential victory for Richard Nixon. He finally took office eight years after losing the election to John F. Kennedy in 1960. Nixon won the republican nomination over Mitt Romney's father and took over the Vietnam War from Lyndon Johnson. It was under Johnson and Nixon that the protest era really began — drawing crowds larger than authorities had had to deal with in the past. This era brought with it a more creative style of protest.

Paul Provenza: Paul Krassner and Abbie Hoffman and Jerry Rubin were the original Yippies. They were basically agit-prop satire. They were very politicized, but their methodology was satire. You know, moments like they threw dollar bills out onto the floor of the New York Stock Exchange, creating massive havoc. They're the ones who organized everyone around the Pentagon, holding hands and trying to Levitate the Pentagon.

They ran a pig for president in '68, on an independent ticket. They were very, very comically subversive. And Abbie Hoffman himself actually invented the sound bite. He very consciously said: *Look, there's seven-and-a-half or eight minutes of film in every news camera, and they're only going to lead off a story if you give them a nice ten-second thing that's going to hook everybody in. So let's do that as much as we can.* And he did it by creating really funny ideas and moments. He looked at how the media was playing and said, *how do we subvert it?* August, 1968. Chicago. Confrontation breaks into violence between long-haired Vietnam protesters and riot police outside the Democratic National Convention. The brutal imagery — truncheons, head wounds — caused television stations to turn away from their live coverage of President Johnson inside the convention.

Suddenly the national spotlight was firmly on the anti-war movement — and the political authority was not happy about it. Charges of conspiracy to incite violence were brought against seven of the protest organizers — who included two of the founding Yippies, Abbie Hoffman and Jerry Ruben. After their acquittal, months later, they found themselves on national television again, on one of the few programs with enough political clout — and enough of an iconic host — to allow guests to voice opposition to the war.

Dick Cavett: The network panicked when I had the Chicago Seven on at the height of Vietnam and all that stuff, of course. And almost didn't air the show. But Jerry Ruben said, "Cavett, you've got to use your medium to do politics — politics is one of the most important things you can do with your life." And I said, "politics bores my ass off."

That might have been a censorship problem if I had said it to the late Spiro Agnew. But they left it in in the bold way the networks sometimes have. We didn't always have the same opinion, but as the Great Unindicted Co-Conspirator from Yorba Linda liked to say: "That is your right."

I've always hoped I could sit there with Nixon when he reminded me that I had a right to my opinion. So I could say "You're kidding! I mean, what? When did that start? Boy, I'm going to use that. I have a right? Oh, thank you. Can you put that down in writing for me, Mister, uh, Nixon, is it?"

As history repeats itself, we've been coming together to protest ever since.

Ted Leo: I've been on so many marches over the course of my life. And some of them have seemed so huge and so powerful — how could this be ignored? But of course, because it's a march and a rally, it lasts for at most two days — in two days it's gone. And the media can stop talking about it. The actual occupying aspect of the occupy movement — it's pretty amazing in how well it was able to maintain itself. And how well it forced the issue to remain in the media, and thus the public eye.

Joe McDonald: Just a little spark of something — in this case, some people going to Wall Street and setting up an encampment. Just *Boom.* Caught on. I mean it's one thing to advertise something and try to cram it down people's throats — but obviously it was time for something to happen.

TL: Just via one tweet where I said *Hey, check out our tour dates and if you're Occupying in your town, let me know and I'll come down and check it out.* I was able to hook up with people in different towns around the South doing that. To stop by to do a song, or to invite people down to the show to talk or leaflet or whatever.

JM: You can't dream these things up. People just sort of create them collectively. It's a funny human thing that happens ... which I'm not — I'm not really a religious person but there is a spiritual something that happens. And in the sixties I was always surprised that something would happen in America and then *boom* — within twenty-four hours in France, in Germany. I mean, it was happening. So there are these moments. It almost seems like science fiction, in a way.

The leaderless nature of a protest must be disconcerting for establishment figures who use their persona as a tool to gain control. So it makes sense that one of the first moves of a frightened government is to clamp down on a crowd's ability to protest and spread their message. And if strict congregation laws don't hold the people back, the next logical step is to put up a wall.

The Berlin Wall — pieces of it — are on display in Washington. In 1963, John F. Kennedy delivered one of his most famous speeches outside the wall….

JFK: "As a free man, I take pride in the words: *Ich bin ein Berliner.*"

There's a common misconception that he used some bad German grammar with an interesting double-meaning. The theory is that the crowd heard the President say *I am a jelly doughnut.*

Kennedy was there to console a crowd of 120,000 West Berliners who were isolated within their own city. Separated from friends and family just a hundred meters away. Separated from the rest of West Germany by two-hundred kilometers. Kennedy's speech was broadcast over loudspeakers to be audible to those on the other side. The East Berliners were facing an even more difficult existence.

As has been witnessed throughout history, totalitarian political figures seem to use walls as a kind of dam for people. The more despotic politicians also seem to relish heavy restrictions on the freedom of the press and broadcasters — and those who create or publish satire are often the first to be locked away.

PP: You know the famous quote by Peter Cooke, who said, "Satire? Oh yeah, remember how the Weimar Cabaret stopped Hitler?" You know, so does it really have any effect? Yeah, it does. It's been going on forever. It's just kinda keeping the flame alive.

Standup comedy actually works with all the hallmarks of Gene Sharp who wrote *From Dictatorship to Democracy* — and is kind of a handbook for non-violent revolution. He says you don't bring down a government. A government is this big slab on top of *everything*. And it's held up by pillars. And you don't go after the huge slab — you take away the pillars. And one of the ways he says you do that is: the police. The military.

When you're in a confrontational situation with, literally, the enforcer of the institution — when you're literally face-to-face with the cops, the military — they're *us*. They're the ninety-nine percent. They're not running things. They are closer to us than anything else. So instead of putting your most fierce warriors out in front there, you put the old ladies and the little kids out in front. So that they relate. So that they see the humanity that this is all about. And their positions as authority figures and as enforcers now have to go through their moral filter. So you're putting them in a position to make the correct moral choice.

Standup comedy does that. Standup comedy is the mother and the child who are out in front going, *Hi, come on in, we're going to have a nice time here today. We hope we're all going to have fun*. He talks about taking the pillars away. You don't have to win the revolution; you just have to keep inviting people to it. And that's what stand-up comedy does. It doesn't actually change anything. But it does get a lot of people who are not sure about what's going on, to sit and think about it a little bit more. It just kind of spreads the means, if you will.

Stand-up comedy is all about taking the values that matter, and communicating them in a way that people will respond to. And that's what comedy does. Comedy takes these really challenging or difficult ideas and makes them palatable.

JM: I became quite disenchanted with the political movements of the sixties because they had an agenda — an end result. And there were winners and losers. I liked to work with the Vietnam veterans who were trying to stop the war. But there were a lot of dialectic, complicated, philosophical agendas, you know. When the Occupy movement happened a few years back, it was very similar to the early sixties in that they were leaderless. I'm sure there were internal struggles and people trying to take over, but people were essentially just getting together and seeing what could happen. Of course, there is the element of the police coming in and busting up the camp, but maybe that added a sporting atmosphere, you know?

They came together with a common spirit, which is, they're unhappy with what's going on. And when they come together, people have a lot of different backgrounds and things, sharing in the same way that people came together at Woodstock, and they looked around and said, *Oh wow, we have things in common.* We have things in common. They're discovering things that they didn't know before. And they're brought together out of a need to be together and to try to bring about change. I don't know where things are going now. But it's interesting, the breaking down of traditions, and in this case the traditional way of doing politics and change. With just a spark....

* * *

The hippie counterculture was formed in part as a response to the existential threat of nuclear war that proved to be terrifyingly real in the early 1960's. In 1961 the Kennedy administration approved a CIA plan to launch an invasion force against Cuba, which had been under Castro's increasingly communist control since 1959. The CIA set up the operation and trained Cuban exiles in Guatemala. The prevailing notion among the Kennedy staff pointed toward a weak military force and unstable government in Cuba, despite intelligence that indicated the presence of Che Guevara's heavily-armed militia training camps. Any dissent in the room was quickly stifled — the early Kennedy government's priority was to work quickly and establish a consensus.

On April 17, 1961 the invasion force of 1,400 landed at the Bay of Pigs and quickly overran the small beachside town of Playa Girón. Two-hundred-thousand Cuban militia soon came to their aid. Within three days, the invasion force surrendered to the Cuban Revolutionary Armed Forces. The world quickly learned of the CIA's involvement in the attempted coup, establishing international sympathies for Castro and strengthening bonds between Cuba and the U.S.S.R. This became a key moment in the Cold War.

The Cuban Missile Crisis followed in October 1962. Over thirteen days, the genuine possibility of thermonuclear war was delivered to living rooms around the globe through the magic of live television. The world stood on a precipice as the United States negotiated with the U.S.S.R. in an attempt to remove Soviet nuclear warheads from Cuba, ninety miles off the coast of Florida. The missiles had been installed in Cuba at Castro's request, to deter any future Bay of Pigs-style invasion. This time around, Kennedy brought in a variety of experts and encouraged his staff to question all findings in their separate departments. The resulting negotiations proved successful, and the missiles were removed on the proviso that Kennedy stay out of Cuba, and remove U.S. warheads from Turkey. But for those thirteen days, the world was very much aware of what was at stake.

The American embarrassment at the Bay of Pigs was used as a key example of committee groupthink in Irving Janis's Victims of Groupthink: A Psychological Study of Foreign Policy Decisions and Fiascoes (1972). This original definition of groupthink speaks to the errors made in group decision-making, largely by emphasis on group consensus and minimization of conflict. Janis states that small group decision-making is often hindered by insufficient testing, analysis, and evaluation of ideas.

PART FOUR
Psychology

One of the reasons I was excited to tackle these themes in a book was that the film *A Venue for the End of the World* focused exclusively on performers. There was no scope within the time constraints to speak with academics in the field of crowd study. So I was thrilled to hear that a number of prominent experts were interested in assisting with the project.

The crux of this project comes down to *why do crowds go one way or another? Can the modes and orders used by the Nazis also be put to benevolent use*? Here we uncover some answers. Many of them are surprising.

Chapter 20

Dr. Justin Clemens

Dr. Justin Clemens has published extensively on psychoanalysis, contemporary European philosophy, and contemporary Australian art and literature. He was founding secretary of the Lacan Circle of Melbourne (2004–2009), and was chief art critic for *The Monthly* (2004–2009). He is currently senior lecturer in the School of Culture and Communication at the University of Melbourne. His paper *Man is a Swarm Animal* (2013) was of key interest in my research of crowd behavior. In Dr. Clemens's research, he has dealt extensively with the work of Freud.

By the time of Freud's death in 1939, he had escaped the Nazis' annexation of Austria and was living in exile in Britain. His books were often burned in Hitler's Reich. During the near forty-year span in which his findings were published, Freud had fathered the concept of psychoanalysis and forever changed the way we view human nature, from personality development to dream analysis, to the makeup of our psyche. He was nominated for thirteen Nobel prizes; he never won. Hollywood recognized the power of his theories and in 1925, Samuel Goldwyn requested that he consult for MGM on the psychological power of cinema. Of course Freud turned him down. Through the twentieth century, Freud continued to be a touchstone for psychology; however, his ethics are often called into question. I was fascinated to hear more about a Freudian concept: *Schwärmerei* — a human "swarming" behavior involving a kind of fanaticism, rapture, or ecstasy.

Aidan Prewett: Can we talk about Freud's perspective on the crowd? I was so interested to hear of the term *Schwärmerei.*

Justin Clemens: One of the things that I think that gets lost is that Freud had a pretty strong theory of how human beings are forced to come together in groups in weird ways. If you think about animals of all kinds, particularly mammals, they all bunch up in different ways. So you have flocks and swarms and packs and so on. But the problem for Freud is that with humans, there are radical different forms of human groups. We're so varied in the way that we form groups that there seems to be something weird going on, right? Human beings must have this incredible variability in them as part of their nature. So you have to find some way of explaining how people form into groups, within all of this variability.

Freud looks into a whole series of things and, of course, it's all about sex. Sex, and the fact that we're children for a long, long time. Some animals are born ready to leave home, like guinea pigs. And others, like humans, you stay at home with your mom and dad now, or with your family, until you're there *forever.*

That *forever* is the time that you're being trained to do something, and that training is not just education — it's culture and knowledge and, actually, your relationship to the other sex. How are we going to breed? How are we going to have institutions? How are you going to meet? How are you going to fuck? How are you going to bring up your kids? And so on. These are big problems for all human societies, and every human society is a kind of version of its vision about that. And the problem for Freud is, even though we are kind of sex-mad killers — which I think is obvious when you look around the world today — they're also sex-mad killers who deny being sex-mad killers, right? It's that self-denial that's so crucial to Freud's explanation. "We're all sex-mad killers but we can't admit it." That's a form of repression. So we have to lie to ourselves constantly in order to have anything to do with anyone else even though we're still — in our heads at least — and unconsciously, madly fucking and killing everyone else. That's the situation that he's interested in. It's very interesting because he, rather than many other theories prior to Freud, which just assume humans are naturally like this, Freud wants to say, "No, there's a real problem and an indetermination in humans and that indetermination is where sex and politics hits at the same time and why humans are such a weird species on earth." And it's about the problem of forming groups.

AP: In *Man is a Swarm Animal*, there's this concept that you touch on that maybe perversion has something to do with it all. The depth of perversion may have something to do with egotism?

JC: Freud has a number of different explanations, but the thing that he does want to mark is that we're a biological species, but, because of this indetermination, this kind of non-programming, this lack of programming that's in humans, born mute and helpless and completely dependent for donkey's years, you really are subject to your family and your society in a way that other animals just aren't.

So he said that this indetermination of humans has to be linked to what he calls in children their *polymorphous perversity*. Little kids, they stick fingers up their nose, in other people's eyeballs, they eat shit they shouldn't eat. Their libidinal impulses go every which way. There's something a bit undirected or unfashioned about humans, and that's why there's so much training for humans as we grow up; whether it's toilet training, or school, or how to act, etiquette in public, and so on. And that training is very, very hard to push onto kids, and you have to constantly repeat and belabor, and hit it, and hit it, and hit it again until, after a couple of years, maybe, a kid will poo in the right place, right?

But that's part of group formation for Freud. That's part of the development of our ego, where our ego developed out of this structure of both dependency and bullying and so on.... We then have to direct and guide ourselves around the world using this silly little ego, which is then constantly menaced on all sides by its repressed desires, by the persecutory nature of some laws we've had to uptake in order to be who we are, and just by the everyday happenstance of the world being inimical or indifferent to what we want to do.

Our consciousness ... we're constantly at threat from ourselves and from other people, and it's those people who plug into that in different ways who can sway us into different group formations. And so we see these kind of political demigods. Some people are political geniuses at speaking to hundreds of thousands of completely different people with almost nothing in common. All of a sudden, some figure will be able to coordinate them through their speech, through their gesture, through some incredible political power.

But that power is also, to come back to a great myth, an Orphic power, which is the power of the rock 'n roll god, who just plays music so amazingly that people who have nothing in common start to be coordinated, start to coordinate themselves around that beautiful voice, incredible guitar, or just fancy attitude. And so you do have something very close between the political demigod and the poetical or musical rock star. And I think there are things that Freud would be very interested in.... *What is it that these great figures of demagoguery or rock are able to do to address themselves towards humans?* It must go far beyond our consciousness.

AP: If you look at a cult leader, somebody like Charles Manson or Jim Jones, or one of these people — they seem quite able to tap into this unconsciousness, as well. Do you have any thoughts about how they might do that?

JC: Well, it's pretty interesting. I mean, I think to Freud that possibility is always present for almost all human beings. So it's not just a few dupes or a few unlucky people in the wrong place at the wrong time who can become subject to the force of cult leaders. Particularly, the really terrifying guys, Manson and Jones, David Koresh of the Branch Davidian.... These charismatic figures were able to just totally control and dominate groups.

But Freud ... there must be something in all of us, at least in the very indetermination. Because we could have been something other than we are. That polymorphous perversity, which is infantile, but hard-wired — even if our lives are settled and well ordered, they're always susceptible, very deep down, to looking for a leader figure, for a parent. Someone on whom we're still dependent. And a very wide range of events can shake us from our normal complacency. At particular times of life you're particularly susceptible. As a little kid where you're totally dependent, or when you're an adolescent — where you've got this shock of hormones ... *Bang!* You can't control what's happening to you, and there are people around who'll pick up on that, whether it's the cult leader, or, in fact, the socially acceptable form of the pop or rock star.

AP: The other thing that really sparked my interest is where you spoke about Freud talking about telepathy as a concept. I think, in terms of a mass crowd situation, that's really the root of what I'm trying to investigate.

JC: I would say that Freud was very interested in that. One key term for Freud is identification. He wants to say, *Humans are definitely part of the natural world. The idea that we think we're special is lunacy.* If we are special, what makes us special? At the same time, insects move in this incredible coordinated way.... I mean, Freud was before all the pheromones and a whole lot of twentieth century science gave us answers around chemical trails, about the way in which insects can respond to these sorts of cues. But he's still interested in *How the hell can you have hundreds of thousands of insects all working together in a coordinated way?* Like in an anthill, for instance? It's like telepathy.

So what Freud was interested in about telepathy is *how is it that it seems that people in a crowd can communicate with each other* — even though they're totally different, they may have just come together, they've never met before, no one really knows what's happening. But there is a kind of, I guess one would say now, pheromones or some other thing also.

A whole load of things come together for Freud to think, *Well, there must be something like an unconscious telepathy going on.*

It is a bit occult, as well ... most of our daily lives are pretty occult (i.e. unconscious identifications of determining what we do with relations to other people). We don't really *know* it. Under certain extreme or stressful situations like the formation of crowds, for instance, then this really primal thing comes out. It leads to a kind of perverse identification and a suppression of the ego, actually, at this point, you know? You're just moving as if you were part of a dark, violent, great, much greater mass, and the whole crowd sits as one organism, which is often said, and, I guess, you're underlining in your film a bit.

AP: Absolutely. And the concept of hypnotic suppression, I suppose, ties in with that perfectly.

JC: Exactly. I mean, human beings — always, even with the domination of our ego — we're very, very close to some extreme sort of behavior. Even the phrase *hypnotic suppression*: other people are doing things to us by weird hypnosis, magic, telepathy, so to speak, all the time. And, look, *music* is a kind of telepathy, right? As one of my friends says, who's played in a lot of bands, "Even as a musician, how is it that we're all working in time together? We're hearing and we're playing and we haven't yet rehearsed this, but we must all know something about what to do...?" You know what I'm saying, right?

AP: Absolutely.

JC: There's something mysterious about it and that's ... I mean, you may as well use the word telepathy. It's reasonable, but it's also more hypnotic suppression, as well. There's also something violent about it. Let's not forget that even in this ecstatic communion with the rock god, there's something Dionysian where you might wake up having ripped off someone's arm or slapped someone. You're pretty close to some violence.

AP: What would Freud have thought of Woodstock?

JC: The image of psychoanalysis is someone lying on a couch with a bearded guy sitting behind them going, "Ja, tell me about your mother." So it's a very individual practice. It's just about *you*, and your absolute singularity. You have to talk and talk and talk for years in order for all that to come out. At the same time, Freud is always wanting to say that there's no individual without others. It's your unconscious identifications and relationships to these other people, that is really at stake in your unconscious. So every individual is already a kind of multiplicity of ancient and unconscious identifications.

In *Group Psychology*, Freud talks about how, after a piano performance, all the women cluster around the performer — in a *schwärmeristic* way. He already has a definite image of what that looks like, that *you're all together in your love for this one leader-figure*. So Freud is very aware of that phenomenon. The crowds that you've focused on here, the size of them are unprecedented. These huge festivals all over the world — of which Woodstock is the very emblem — the size of it is incredible. The mechanisms of that scale — I don't think Freud would be surprised, but he may have been a bit shocked by the scale.

AP: These mechanisms — what mechanisms can be exploited in these large-scale crowd systems?

JC: Freud picks up on the work of an extremely odd and yet influential — not always in a good way — theorist, in terms of crowds of the nineteenth century, called Gustave Le Bon. Le Bon was originally a doctor; he gets into anthropology. He's exceptionally racist, and a theorist of post-Darwin, racial evolution — in a quite disgusting way. But he also writes a book on the psychology of the crowd, in which he tries to give what he thought of as scientific explanation of how crowds form. One of the things that Le Bon had seen was the great crowds of the Paris Commune of 1871, after the French lost to the Prussians in the war.

In the *spaces* of crowds, architecture and cities are very important. The thing about Woodstock is that you get a massive crowd in the countryside, which is very interesting and rare because crowds mainly start in the city. Baron Haussmann had very famously destroyed medieval Paris in the mid-nineteenth century and rebuilt it with the wide boulevards that we know today. Part of the reason for those wide boulevards was not only for nice people to go walking so that they could be painted by impressionists, but if there was any civic trouble, cannons could be wheeled into position and it would be very difficult for a mob to protect themselves in those open boulevards. So even the city planning of the nineteenth century has the fear of the crowd in it. One of the things the commune did was develop a whole series of new forms of urban guerrilla fighting, and they managed to re-barricade, or create new kinds of giant barricades and ways of fighting in the city, as a way of taking back the streets. Le Bon saw this and he went berserk. He hated it; he was very reactionary. But it did inspire him to think about these sorts of mobs.

He gives three main reasons where he talks about the alteration of psychology of individuals in crowds.

1. The sheer number of people — the individual develops, paradoxically, a sense of invincibility. And individual, even though they're nothing in the crowd, and could be destroyed immediately, somehow develops a sense of invincibility.

2. Le Bon calls it a kind of contagion. One person gets excited, another gets excited. Mao in China used to have this famous statement, "*One becomes two, two becomes four, four becomes eight*," about the production of revolutionaries. But a similar principle holds for Le Bon.

3. The hypnotic suppression of ego.

These became very influential ideas all over Europe in the twentieth century. All sorts of different people are influenced by Le Bon's work. But Freud himself starts to think about a new theory of identification, which is *we can identify with other people in all sorts of ways*. Freud is very clear that the peculiar thing about when we identify with people is that sometimes it's an imaginative appropriation or takeover of their power. So even unconsciously, even imaginatively, we model ourselves on other people. And sometimes we copy people, not because imitation is the sincerest form of flattery, but that imitation is an attempt at a hostile takeover of the power of the other. So one of the things that Freud starts to develop is these mechanisms of identification after reading Le Bon and a lot of other anthropological stuff. He wants to say that *these mobile traits can be picked up*, they have been translated as *unary traits*.

A unary trait, in principle, can be almost anything. Some people are masters of it — the rock stars, the tyrants — but sometimes it can be quite accidental and contingent. For example, he talks about a girl at a boarding school who receives a letter and bursts into tears. All the other girls in the school are wondering *is it a breakup letter, has something terrible happened*; they all burst into tears too. Freud says that it's the tears that are important. They're not identifying with the girl, they don't feel sorry for her; they might *think* they feel sorry for her. What in fact they've been captured by is this kind of weird physical hysteria. That's Freud thinking about contagion as a form of unconscious imaginary identification. Sometimes when people cough in a meeting, and then everyone else starts coughing. You start mirroring some of the other gestures in a kind of mimetic way. You mentioned this in your film with the mosh pit — where you were thinking *aren't these people embarrassed moving their arms around like this?* only to find that you yourself had been taken over by this weird spontaneous trait that seems to transmit itself across all sorts of diverse bodies in order to unify them in a very odd way.

You were really affected. An effect that that's physical, but also you're thinking *don't they feel shame? Oh, I am part of the thing feeling shame*. You've been bonded together by the rhythm, by the gesture, by the sound, by the situation, but also by the shame. Embarrassment or humiliation can be one of the key emotions of crowds.

AP: I believe Goebbels studied Le Bon quite intensely.

JC: This is one of the things about Le Bon. He was very influential because of his absolutely revolting "race science". This was very appealing to the worst elements of European demagoguery, of the early twentieth century in particular. And part of the problem is that at the same time, Le Bon says some very interesting and incisive things. And those things can be very clearly listed. Any good manager, like Hitler's propagandists were, knows how to instrumentalize them. So it's the managerializing of Le Bon's observed phenomena. And Goebbels is one of the guys who says *what things do we need to do?* This is where Albert Speer and Leni Reifenstahl come in. It comes back to the problem of urban spaces, but also of the design of spaces to force crowds, or to induce crowds, or to suggest to crowds, to channel them one way or another, to organize them around particular points, whether focal or disperse. These are all part of Hitler, Goebbels, Speer, the entire panoply of goons. They're very attentive to the special managerial design particularities of crowd unification. And Goebbels in particular would take cues from many different places. Hollywood cinema, Busby Berkeley's Girls — the careful aestheticization and orchestration of diverse bodies into a compelling image or picture or structure. Riefenstahl is obviously right on to that.

AP: In a generational kind of way, all these parents who fought World War Two are watching their kids grow their hair long and suddenly they're off to Woodstock. Was there some kind of generational trauma that these generations were facing?

JC: One of the things that I took from your film was the differences in all of these situations. You made this point around Vietnam in particular — and Woodstock — about the nature of anti-authoritarianism as opposed to the authoritarian crowds of the classic dictator or the leader.

When you have a master or a leader, there's always another master somewhere fighting them off or trying to contest them. The masters of other people can look pretty annoying to you, if not contemptible, irrelevant, reprehensible. I think about Beatlemania, where people were just horrified — *What the hell is going on?* These four guys with weird floppy haircuts. Or with Elvis, Jimi Hendrix, or any of the other rock stars. The disgust and terror that people have that others are caught up. And you don't understand it yourself, it's almost incomprehensible.

But there's also another thing that you talk about — there's also a technological thing. New technologies that were previously not there, for example the television. Yes, we have radio in the twentieth century, yes we have film. Two great inventions of around 1900. But post-war it's all about TV. It brings people together and it disposes them quite differently. And it establishes different sorts of relationships between host, camera, audience. So, rather than just generational, there's also a technological transformation.

AP: I was interested to hear that you've written about the concept of *antiphilosophy*. Could you tell me a little bit about that?

JC: I read a lot of philosophy and psychoanalysis. Some of the people I was reading, like the French psychoanalyst Jacques Lacan, almost explicitly calls himself an antiphilosopher at various points. And I was thinking, well, *what does this mean?* For Lacan as a psychoanalyst, he thinks to Freud, he thinks of a number of other quite strange conceptual characters like Søren Kierkegaard — also an antiphilosopher of this time. What they see in philosophy is always an attempt — precisely — to legitimate the return of the tyrant, or the return of the *master*. Lacon himself says philosophy is a master's discourse. Why? He says that we can take observed phenomena — paradigmatically, the labor of slaves. We, the philosopher, turn that into clear and organizable propositions for you, and therefore we can use that knowledge to better exploit the slave. In a thumbnail, that's what Lacan says about philosophy, and why he says psychoanalysis is against all forms of mastery, and that antiphilosophy is one way to characterize it. Because you're *anti* the extraction of knowledge from slaves in order to turn that into a managerial tool of productivity. Or as Goebbels does, to take a theory of the crowd and turn it into an actual intervention into the crowd. That's not what psychoanalysis does. Even though I'm very interested in lots of theories and forms of thinking, I do like that as an orientation toward what I want to do. It's anti-philosophical in that way. I'm not extracting knowledge from anyone in order to better exploit people. I see our job as the opposite.

* * *

The master/leader concept is key to most crowd scenarios. It is also key to the extraction of knowledge from human subjects. One example of this is the Stanford Prison Experiment, led by researcher Philip Zimbardo. This became a hugely controversial clinical study into the human capacity for violence.

In August 1971, Zimbardo set up a detailed mock prison at Stanford University. Twenty-four vetted applicants were selected and split into two factions: prisoners and guards. The experiment was expected to run twenty-four hours a day for seven to fourteen days. It was abandoned on the sixth day when psychological abuses from the guards became overwhelming. In his report, Zimbardo concluded that the roles expected of participants, and reinforced through uniforms and prison bars, led participants to become dangerously absorbed in their new roles. Experimenters reported that approximately one-third of the guards exhibited genuine sadistic tendencies.

Much criticism has been leveled at Zimbardo for the experiment's dubious ethics and the psychological trauma endured by participants. The controversial research raised more questions than answers. What power is contained in mere roles, rules, symbols, group identity, and situational validation? How easily can people be led to engage in deeply antisocial behavior?

Chapter 21

Professor Leon Mann, AO

Ten years prior to the Stanford Prison Experiment, the 1961–1964 Stanley Milgram Experiment was a study of human capacity for violence as it relates to obedience to authority figures. The study was inspired by the trial of Nazi fugitive Adolf Eichmann, who pleaded the *just following orders* line. The experiment simulated an environment in which an authority figure exerted pressure on a research subject to inflict pain upon another subject. The findings were disturbing: sixty-five percent of participants followed their orders through to completion — delivering what they may have believed to be a lethal electric shock. Milgram's ethics have been questioned and debated ever since. His method was unique and controversial:

The experimenter would lead subjects into a room where they were given the role of a "teacher," while another subject, really an actor, was the "learner." A word association quiz was delivered to the learner. Upon a wrong answer, the experimenter would instruct the teacher to administer what they believed to be real electric shocks to the learner in increasingly higher voltage. In some of these experiments, the "learner," acting convincingly, would explain that they suffered from a heart condition, especially when the shocks increased significantly.

Eerily, Milgram's findings echoed Eichmann's sentiments: vast numbers of ordinary people could very quickly be manipulated into undertaking truly awful deeds at the encouragement of an authority figure.

Professor Leon Mann, AO is director of the Research Leadership Program at the University of Melbourne. He completed his PhD at Yale University in 1965 and took up an assistant professorship at Harvard University. During his time in the United States, Mann worked closely with Irving Janis and Stanley Milgram, dealing largely with studies of group psychology. Janis was, of course, the progenitor of *groupthink*, while Milgram's Obedience Study is still as relevant, and terrifying, as it was in 1961.

Leon Mann is best known for his pioneering scholarship on decision-making and particularly for his book *Decision making: A psychological analysis of conflict, choice and commitment*, co-authored with Professor Irving Janis. Unusually for its time, the book approached personal decision-making not as an exercise in utilitarian calculation but as a conflict-laden process frequently bound up in emotion, doubt, avoidance, rationalization, and social pressures.

Professor Mann's more than 130 research publications include major contributions to the study of attitudes, aggression in crowds, queue behavior, cross-cultural psychology, team and organizational leadership.

Aidan Prewett: I'm fascinated to hear that you worked with Stanley Milgram. I'd love to know — what was his character? What was he like as a person?

Leon Mann: He was charming. He was an intellectual too. He loved European civilization and culture. He spent time in Paris. He did the stuff on the psychology of the city, so he knew all about cities and how you map them. My first publication was with Stanley Milgram. It was the Lost Letter Technique. We dropped letters around places at night, you know, friends of the Nazi Party, friends of the Communist Party, medical research associates with post office boxes — and we looked at the return rate of these lost letters. So, it was a two-page article, but the lost letter technique actually had quite a lot of impact. It's interesting because it shows you that the return rate was say, what you'd call a standard letter, like medical research associates is about seventy-five percent, eighty percent You know, some of these get blown away. But, the friends of the Communist Party and friends of the Nazi Party — twenty-five percent. With some people looking inside and saying, "Good on you," and some people saying, "You bastards. What are you trying to do? What are you up to?"

Milgram was an intellectual. He died far too young. He was a bit too hot to handle at Yale because of the obedience studies that sort of pushed the boundaries of what's ethical. He genuinely wanted to take a look at *what was the after effect.* There have been people who have been sort of jumping on him because they reckon that he misinterpreted some of his findings and that the people that he claimed had been thoroughly debriefed and were not scarred by it, had actually been scarred for life by being a participant in these studies, and knowing what they could be pushed to do.

I subsequently did a — not a full Milgram study — an experiment when I was at the University of Sydney in which we used a blood pressure cuff, and I was faking my monitor for a thing as the way in which you as the teacher would say instruct someone to get a little bit more pressure on the pump to sort of let him know — let the student know that he made a mistake here. So, they weren't screaming, "Bloody hell. I've got a heart condition.

I'm going to die. I'm going to die." They'd say, "Ouch," and that sort of stuff.

The point about that, which was very gratifying is that even once they found a more innocuous kind of device for "teaching" someone, our Australian sample of students at the University of Sydney were far less obedient. It was about thirty percent,whereas the Milgram thing was about sixty-eight percent

That too was contested. Was Milgram kind of pumping it up, et cetera. I don't believe so. You know, you can actually look at the films. You can sort of see it. Was he a bit sloppy? I don't know. May have been a bit, but he certainly was highly motivated, a true intellectual. We'd correspond a lot after I came back to Australia, and it was tragic that he passed away, you know, so early. He had a couple of heart attacks, and I think the third one was his last one. He must have been not quite fifty. But, a brilliant mind and someone who, in his short life, actually made quite a contribution.

AP: Am I right in the understanding that *groupthink* in its clinical definition is somewhat different from the way it's commonly used in the media?

LM: This is the academic aspect of it and so there's quite a literature in which these concepts exist. You know, *what produces it?* Irving Janis and I wrote a book together on decision-making, which there's a whole chapter on it with the illustrative case example of what happened with Pearl Harbor and Admiral Kimmel's complacency, you know. "We're gonna be okay and we don't have to worry about the enemy, they're incompetent, we're gonna prevail." And people not speaking up and being heard. Janis is talking about a failure of, kind of, rational, careful, vigilant decision-making rather than, you know, mob hysteria.

Then there's that kind of mob thing and there is the dressing of the panoply of staging and loud music and crowd warmed up and the response. "Who do we want?", kind of stuff. The cadences, if you like, of whipping up a crowd.

I saw *Bohemian Rhapsody* recently, and I thought, *by God, there's a lot of fascism in the way in which he moved a crowd.*

AP: Isn't there?!

LM: You know, the strut? The sort of arrogant strut across the stage and the whipping up people, et cetera, et cetera. So there certainly are tropes which are there. I thought *this is so, kind of suffused with some knowledge in how you use crowd psychology in order to get a sort of a crowd thoroughly emotional and thoroughly worked up.*

I mean the descendant of all this stuff is Phillip Zimbardo in his deindividuation series — the Stanford prison studies. He a very neat model; it was the loss of individuality that sort of submergence in a kind of a crowd. So it's not so much you get a *crowd mind*, but you become uninhibited. And the factors that go with it include, obviously, the arousal that comes with close proximity to a number of people, duration. You're hanging around there, you're standing. There's heat, especially if you're looking at a warm day. The size of the crowd is hugely important.

A crowd of twenty doesn't really deliver, but a crowd of say two thousand, and you could start looking at.... So crowd size is a very important factor. Part of it is just the noise that's being put up, but also it's the press of people against people, the distance between the performer and the people who are there. And they're craning and looking and they're up on a big stage. They have to put up big screens in order to get it across. I think you can see a parallel, that you could draw it. Nüremberg and the big emblems and the big what not. And that idea say, there's a whole lot of stuff in which the performers strut their stuff including synchronized movement, you know, whipping up a crowd.

I thought, for example, the way in which — getting back to Queen, that Queen concert at Wembley — there was a kind of a pattern of … a riff before it. "*Boom Boom Clap. Boom Boom Clap.*" And then of course, the *We Will Rock You* and getting them to respond to it. So it really is very calculated. These buggers have read their social psychology.

But with Zimbardo, you know where he picked it up? He actually picked up a lot of it after he went to Brazil to the *Carnival* in Rio. The Samba bands are going up and down the streets and he actually talks about it and some of the most disinhibited behavior. The Rio marching bands and the display and the women who are semi-naked and the guys who are thrusting around and they're up on a pedestal and the whole lot. It's like a movie. And movement's very important in all this. Zimbardo said the best murders occur in Brazil at the time because the inhibition comes off, and then people are partying, people have been watching this sort of sexual display — and sex goes with violence. I mean, that's what Sigmund Freud had to say.

But groupthink is worthy of a separate study and this only converges with the mass hysteria thing to some extent if you think about the leader effect — where you've got a kind of charismatic or pushy leader.

But, as I say, what's the decision that's being made? At the end of the day it's not whether you take on the Japanese or invade Cuba in the swamp, but whether you are going to decide to follow the leader or not. I don't think that's a group decision, it's essentially a situation in which some people are against it, sort of horrified that they don't speak out because there are *mind guards*, like bodyguards saying *don't do it, you support the leader.*

AP: In your research, I found it quite fascinating — I'd love to hear about the difference between a crowd that is formed under the auspices of a leader, as opposed to one that has formed more organically. Would you be able to speak about that a little bit, in terms of how those crowds would differ?

LM: Stanley Milgram wrote a kind of taxonomy of crowds and misbehavior. So I overlapped with him. He taught me sexual psychology, as did Irving Janis. It's interesting. I was a student at Yale in the 'sixties. It was just after the war, fifteen years after the war and we were still trying to come to grips with what happened. A lot of social psychology is influenced by it.

But Milgram has done the classification of differences between types of crowds. So, bystander crowds, baiting crowds. I've done a study on baiting crowds. Actually, I've just published a couple of things late last year and this year, on baiting crowds online.

AP: Ooh. Yeah, that's a whole extra dynamic again.

LM: It is a very interesting dynamic in which they're not in physical proximity with each other. So of a crowd, of an online crowd, of maybe five hundred, or one thousand, or two hundred watching someone who is threatening to top himself. But, that too has got elements of baiting, and also, happily, people who sort of say *don't do it*, which is an interesting phenomenon.

But getting back to Janis's interest in this *groupthink* thing stemmed from a class paper that his daughter was doing at school on the Bay of Pigs. Charlotte, his daughter, was showing him what she was writing and he said, "Gee, look at all this." Kennedy was there. Everyone loved him in that group. Bobby was saying *you've got to support my bro*. There is a decision to be made about how you have to handle the Cubans and Fidel. Eisenhower had said *you can't be soft on Comms*, so we've inherited that. We can get in there and do it, and they were being urged by the joint chiefs of staff to go in and handle the Cubans, and they did very little thinking through the consequences or the options and so on, and he thought this was classic. He started to pull out case materials. He was terrific at looking at case materials, really good at it. In the end, he wrote a book with about eighteen different cases of groupthink, and anti-groupthink — groups that made wise decisions based upon good stuff.

When he and I wrote our book together, we integrated that into a chapter and also a separate chapter in a separate book. It's been recognized as an alternative way of thinking about what happens when policy making goes awry. We've got our fans who write supporting stuff and think it's wonderful, and others who say it *ain't the whole story*. That doesn't bother me. There are other things.

But, what can I say about it? It had huge influence. He wrote a piece for the *New York Times* about it. There was groupthink. It's appeared in, you know, popular, or sort of semi-popular, semi-serious science journals. It's got entries all over the place. Not that he coined the term itself. I mean, it's assumed that he coined it, but it was before his time.

But, the groupthink hypothesis has been bastardized to some extent, mainly by journals. *The Australian* in particular will say, you know, *this mindless bunch of people, et cetera, or climate change groupthinkers … they get on the bandwagon and then they lose their brain. There's great science showing that climate change is not real.* All that kind of bullshit.

So groupthink gets bastardized as a concept. In that case, there's something to be said about that, how an interesting concept has been transfigured into something else. But, as an explanation for either popular opinion, which you think is fairly mindless, or for groups that make crappy decisions, there are obviously very different factors. A leader is important. I think that's right, but you have to question. I've been on a bit of a ramble here, but you asked the question about spontaneous crowds versus a leader.

AP: Yeah, the person made leader by the crowd, versus somebody who is persuading the crowd, I suppose.

LM: The first example out of that is the way in which a Trump, or a Hitler, or one of a number of other people, *boy* they play them around the world. You can have a look at Maduro, and he's always there with his mob behind him, and, you know, everyone's got a mob behind them when they make a statement. You know, [Australian Prime Minister] Scott Morrison can't go anywhere and speak alone. He's got a bunch of assenters behind him, nodding their heads in approval. It's all crap. So, that's the leader-produced kind of display of authority and *who I am* with all these symbols and emblems which go behind it, buses, caravans, posters.

Then there is: *how does a leader spontaneously come out of a crowd?* It would be like someone at a baiting crowd, and this is a crowd that's not kind of organized to stand at the foot of a building where someone is threatening to leap off the sixth floor. But, someone half-jokingly cries or calls out, "Why don't you jump, you mug?" Out of: *I've been hanging here for an hour and a half. He's putting on this sort of show and he's playing us for fools. Yeah, why don't you jump, you mug?* So, it gets picked up.

A leader? Well, it's a *trigger* in that sense of the word. Are there crowds where someone emerges out of a revolution and they're there on the streets, at the Bastille, or in Paris in May 1968? Probably not. I think you find that most of the sort of crowds, even though they may look as if they're not being led, if that's the case, have in fact been led. There was an announcement made, "We will meet at such and such a place." Crowds go with mass movements or social movements.

That's one of the things that Milgram talks about. If a crowd is going to do what it does effectively, it's usually pretty well organized and it's probably very savvy in that it's thought through what it wants to do. How much violence, how much it wants to provoke, how much it wants a reaction from the cops. It's always very useful if you're on the very left wing of politics to get a few martyrs to be beaten up — then you can say the cops are brutal. It's all part of the, if you like, the armament. It's part of the apparatus of all this. Or — that *we want to show that we're peaceful.* So, the kids' rallies on Friday will be very peaceful. They're not out there kicking cops. They're there to show that they care. Hopefully no one hits *them* in response.

So I think it's very rare that you get literally someone who emerges out of the crowd and becomes the leader.

AP: In terms of Woodstock, I mean, speaking to Chip Monck, who ended up making lots of crowd announcements, "The brown acid that's circulating is not specifically too good." That's what popped into my mind — is somebody who, out of necessity, needed to sort of come to the microphone. But, maybe that's not the same thing.

LM: Yeah look, it might be that, I think that maybe you're picking up on phenomena that I hadn't sort of responded to, and that is that Woodstock lasted what for three days?

AP: Three and a half, yeah.

LM: Three and a half, as against the sort of thing that I was thinking about, like the rally goes down the street or you get a demo in the park or you get a baiting crowd, or you get a Trump rally, or a Nüremberg Rally, which goes on for probably five hours. But, you're going into day two, day three, and there are people who are seeing opportunities and who need to take some sort of charge, and they spontaneously, or at least they — and maybe that's what's going on there, when you're thinking about the role of a Chip Monck. It's organized. It's captive. They're away from the city, and there is that opportunity.

I'll put it this way, there are many aspects of leadership. I think that what you're picking up here, leadership is distributed. When you look at Hitler, for example, he is the figurehead. But, there were a whole lot of these people at a Nüremberg Rally, one after the other, that get up and start screaming and ranting. So, they're part of the warm up act, and they are giving the messages and getting it all. So, a useful thing for you to keep parked, as you get your notes together, is that modern leadership theory doesn't talk so much about the leader. I mean, that's a kind of, the leader kind of mythos. Quite often leadership is distributed. It bounces around. We might have our figurehead, but it will be a team effort, a leadership team effort, which is really working with this. If the leader is too arrogant, I mean the examples where you really, like something was just hugely dysfunctional, destructive, goes to the leader types who are working in cults, and that's a good one. That's Jonestown.

That is, you know, truly crazy bastards who were getting their followers to suicide, but that is a whole different story. So, that is into psycho-social psychopathology of people who are bit by bit seduced into doing things and the power of the cult. But it's not what you'd call mainstream stuff.

AP: One of the things in my notes, from what you wrote about — the analogy of George Orwell shooting an elephant while stationed in Burma. I just went, Oh, wow. What an incredible act to feel that the crowd is expecting this of me. So, was that a fear that he had, that they crowd would turn on him if he didn't?

LM: Who knows? It must have been a very young Orwell. And a very kind of, *this is the power of the norm.* I never underestimate how a kind of, a standard of behavior is set up very easily by a group, by the majority sort of saying, "This is the proper behavior and you will kind of follow it." But, this sort of normative thing can be informative. Information comes out of the crowd a bit. *This is the way we do things here.* We've got, you know, an elephant that's running amok and mucking up the fields and they are enemies. I was in Sri Lanka recently and they've got — the elephants are their enemies there. They're trampling down the crops, et cetera.

Then, you've got the social pressure of *total disapproval if you don't do what we expect you to do*, and you don't want to be thrown out. But afterwards, Orwell didn't quite know why he had done it. With the gun, he was kind of looking at what was happening with this rampaging elephant and he popped it, and he probably would never have done it again.

You think about jury behavior in groups where people go along with the majority. For me, a very powerful thing is the concept of the runaway norm. *I can top this.* It's the, "Yeah, I can massacre. I can do one more." That's the scary stuff about what's going on now. It gets worse and worse. It's pointed out, I think, that a kind of demarcation between what is hate speech and what is freedom of expression is cut very blurry.

So, there's a slippage going on, and I call that a sort of a norm, which is shifting. What's going on with both sides of politics is you get a polarization. Norms that push you to the left, or norms that push you to the right or norms that push you to sort of accepting speech of a certain kind, are starting to move. You can scream at people, abuse people, troll people, all that sort of stuff is happening. Very scary stuff. And that's a social influence type thing about it. It's going on all the time. People are saying things and it's acceptable.

AP: You were at Harvard when all the student riots were happening? Did that reach Harvard?

LM: Yeah, actually it did indeed. They took over the Students for a Democratic Society and, aided by a couple of faculty in my school of Social Sciences, marched in and took over the building for about a week, and eventually the police pulled them out. But, you know, the big fist was drawn at Harvard for the first time.

It was disruptive. It was the Vietnam War, which was worrying them a lot. It played upon our minds, the faculty. But I was there during that, and the Haight-Ashbury stuff and the Civil Rights movements. But that was already at Yale. That was already, we were just doing that in '62, '64. Some of my colleagues were writing about it, about the peace movement and various tactics that were being used, so it influenced me and some of my thinking about why crowd behavior, collective behavior, was already a topic of study.

AP: Was there a moment during any of these sort of riots that's stuck with you, that would sort of illustrate what it was like to be there?

LM: Detroit was one which was really in our face. The Detroit race riot, and Watts — really because it was shown live on television and you could see cops trying to handle it. One guy, who is very good at it, is my colleague at the time, Gary Marx.

Gary was doing stuff in which he got some support from the U.S. government to sort of analyze the riots and what had happened in terms of, sociological terms, et cetera. But, you know, we were very much aware of those riots. We were camped on the east coast, and we're away from it all, but television was showing it all the time and Detroit isn't all that far.

I wrote a piece and actually it's not mentioned in the stuff that I sent you called "Crowd Counting," and the effect of estimates of crowd and how that has got a secondary impact on the way in which you, the reader, think about the importance of crowd behavior and crowd activity. The theme is pretty simple, that whenever you see estimates of crowd size at a rally, I read ten thousand kids or ten thousand protestors turned up on Spring

Street on Friday. But they reckon that the police probably gave a bigger estimate.

Here is a good way of actually getting close to what would be the truth: look at whether it was a dense crowd, a sparse crowd or a loose crowd. That is the kind of proximity of individual to individual. If you had a helicopter shot of it all, and you could very quickly say well, it's a rectangular shape, Spring Street between Collins Street and back down to Flinders Street, and maybe it spilled out. There might have been twenty thousand. It might have been five. We don't know.

But you read this and you could see rival claims, depending upon what the newspapers — the *New York Times*, the *Washington Post*, or the Southern newspapers — if it was pro-war, the Southern papers, the estimate of the protest crowd was very low; if it was anti-war, the estimate of the crowd at the rally was very high. The rule of thumb was, take what the police estimate was, double it if you were anti-war, and half it if you were pro-war. Because there was a fight going on, a contest about how popular or less-than-popular were these movements. So there is a politics of what is the crowd.

* * *

Rioting and mob violence seem to be a product of the *runaway norm* — the same phenomenon that led to George Orwell's reported shooting of an aggressive elephant at the behest of a crowd in Burma in the 1920's.

Orwell's first job as a writer was a critique of censorship in England, published in 1928 by *Progrès Civique*, a French communist paper. Prior to this he had been an assistant district superintendent of the Imperial Police in Burma, at that time still a province of British India. His first novel, the semi-autobiographical *Burmese Days* was published in 1934 and included the piece *Shooting An*

Elephant. The first-person narration carries a palpable sense of guilt, but it is still unclear as to whether the story is based on a factual occurrence. The incident is used in the book as a powerful metaphor for British colonialism — the destruction of self that is experienced by an oppressor. The narrator closes the piece wondering whether the crowds of onlookers knew that the shooting was carried out "solely to avoid looking a fool."

During the Second World War, Orwell worked for the BBC, writing and producing radio broadcasts for their Eastern Services division. This material was produced in support of the war effort, in some instances as a direct attempt to counter Nazi propaganda. At this time, Orwell also began writing for New York's *Partisan Review*, which later brought Susan Sontag critical acclaim.

George Orwell died of tuberculosis in 1950. His book *1984* was published the year prior. In it, he provided us the ultimate cautionary tale — and a new blueprint for totalitarianism and propaganda.

Chapter 22

Professor John Frow

In 1890, French criminologist and sociologist Gabriel Tarde published *Laws of Imitation*; one of the first attempts to codify propaganda techniques. Tarde states that people are quick to copy what they see in others — peers, their superiors, and mass media representations. This work was carried on by Gustave Le Bon, and later, by Elias Canetti in *Crowds and Power.* This dissertation is mainly concerned with Canetti's experiences in Germany prior to his escape to England in 1938. Canetti won the Nobel Prize in Literature in 1981. He died in 1994.

Canetti lists four main traits of a crowd: it always wants to grow; there is equality within; the crowd loves density; the crowd needs a direction. He also demarcates types of crowd based on its prevailing emotion: flight crowds, formed by threat of danger; prohibition crowds, formed by refusal; reversal crowds, formed by desired social change; feast crowds, formed by abundance.

A final category is perhaps the most unsettling. Baiting crowds are formed with reference to a clearly attainable goal. Canetti writes: "The goal is known and clearly marked, and is also near. This crowd is out for killing and it knows whom it wants to kill. It heads for this goal with unique determination and cannot be cheated of it.... A murder shared with many others, which is not only safe and permitted, but indeed recommended, is irresistible to the great majority of men."

Professor of English at the University of Sydney, John Frow works in the areas of literary theory, narrative theory, intellectual property law, and cultural studies. Frow was a founding member of the *Australian Journal of Cultural Studies*, among a wide variety of other publications including his latest book, *Character and Person* (2014).

Aidan Prewett: Where might our understanding of crowds come from?

John Frow: In terms of crowds, the person I've been most strongly influenced by is Elias Canetti, who wrote a book called *Crowds and Power*. He was a central European intellectual, writing in the 1930's, 1940's, 1950's — *Crowds and Power* was published in 1960. He was an anthropologist among other things. He thought really interestingly about crowds in terms of their amplification of the self, in terms of survival mechanisms. He was particularly interested in the way crowds were used in Nazi Germany as a psychological mechanism for drawing people into actions that they wouldn't undertake as individuals, but that they would get drawn into once they become a part of a crowd.

AP: Could you describe the difference between individual psychology and group psychology?

JF: People will do things in crowds that they won't do as individuals. They'll lynch someone, for example. As individuals they might find this behavior morally repugnant. That moral *block* disappears when they are integrated into a lynch mob; they'll take violent action of one kind or another in a way that wouldn't be thinkable to them as individuals. Crowds break down inhibitions, they work through a kind of mimetic psychology. They spread a kind of contagion amongst the members of the crowd, by breaking down the barriers to the individual self by absorbing individual selves into something much larger and something that has a different kind of *will* than the individual has.

AP: That's such a fascinating concept, that a group might become its own entity, and have its own will.

JF: It's still a pretty mysterious process. I don't know that we have any particularly good explanation of how that transformation of the will works. The crowd is obviously more than the sum of its individual parts. It doesn't reflect the will of each individual that goes into it. Rather, it transforms individual wills into something that has its own autonomous motor. And clearly what crowds can do is unleash actions which are not restrained by traditional moral constraints. It simply works to disinhibit the will of individuals. Where the decision-making power of crowds comes from, we don't know any more than we know how the decision-making powers of a colony of ants operates. We know that ants act in unison, as a colony, they make decisions as a colony, in a way that doesn't depend on the will of any one individual ant. Crowds seem to have that kind of peculiar autonomy of the group.

AP: A crowd that has a moral block that is lifted when in the crowd, does that return again and is there a sense of shame on the part of the people who were in that situation?

JF: I think that's a fairly typical reaction, that people will undertake actions that they will then — when the crowd dissolves — be ashamed of. Because their individual self separates off from that mass. Their normal moral operations start to be effective again. Yes, it's quite typical that people will be ashamed or deny the actions that they took as part of a crowd. Although there may also be a sort of afterglow, an emotional high that survives the formation and dissolution of the crowd.

The analogy of the rock concert that John Castles employs in *Big Stars* (2007) is probably not a bad one. We know that in a rock concert your own personality may get absorbed into the personality of the crowd. You feel an emotional involvement that, if you were sitting separately, blocked-off from everybody else, you might not feel. And you get the same kind of emotional high that can survive the concert, continuing as a kind of afterglow.

AP: In terms of actually getting a crowd to experience this phenomenon, of having their moral block removed, do you know of any techniques that a leader or a performer might use?

JF: Clearly there are ways in which a charismatic speaker, like a charismatic performer, can use a public performance, a public speech, to whip a crowd up into an emotional state that has the characteristics of the *crowd will.* There's that process of mutual amplification, mutual reinforcement, mutual feedback that goes on. There are well-known rhetorical techniques for developing the emotions of a crowd. Often they can involve defining the crowd against an *other* of some kind: identifying a common enemy and unifying the crowd against that common enemy. So Nazi rallies typically, on the one hand, talked about the unity of the German people, and on the other, identified enemies like the Jews. This was a way of unifying the crowd and bringing the crowd into an emotional state, that gives the crowd a will of its own that's reflected backwards and forwards from the will of the charismatic speaker.

AP: Is there a difference between what propaganda seeks to achieve, and what happens in a crowd?

JF: Well propaganda doesn't necessarily bring about the mass unifying aspects that the behavior of a crowd does. The Nazis certainly managed to deploy propaganda, in particular through new technologies like radio, but also the mass broadcast microphone. They were able to create mass audiences for propaganda.

Propaganda has been around forever, but they had ways of deploying propaganda that were novel in the twentieth century.

AP: And we're seeing this with new technology again at the moment.

JF: One of the things about social media is that they are *narrowcast.* They differentiate their audience. They put people into a crowd-like situation which can be incredibly intense in those ideologically concentrated chat rooms, in ways that are not dissimilar to crowd behavior at all. They cut off external reality, they cut off forms of reality-checking, so that people are driven to quite emotionally intense forms of belief — and eventually behavior.

AP: Could we hear a little about your time at Cornell University in the early seventies? What was it like to be a student in that era?

JF: It was an exciting time. When I got to Cornell in '71, the previous year, the Black students had taken over the administration buildings, they'd gone through underground tunnels armed with shotguns. They were scary, and they were very serious. People were still talking about that when I arrived. And then I was involved in another occupation of the administration buildings, and I was involved in the mass moratorium marches in New York, as I had been in Australia, but the one in New York that I remember had at least a million people there, so to be a part of something like that was pretty amazing.

AP: With the moratorium, is there a moment that's really vividly stuck with you?

JF: Not particularly; I've been on a number of those mass demonstrations. They're similar in the intensity of the emotion that they generate. Just that sense of being a part of something *huge*, being a part of an historical movement. Which can be deceptive — I was part of a million-strong march in London against the Iraq war in

2002. We filled the whole of central London. It was clear to us that we were an overwhelming force. But it didn't work, the Blair government went ahead with its participation in the invasion of Iraq, despite that overwhelming presence of an opposition movement. There's something enormously exciting about mass demonstrations, but they can also be very frustrating and I suppose I'm more skeptical about them than I used to be.

AP: Back at Cornell, were you one of the occupiers of the administration building?

JF: No, I wasn't. I was part of the movement of occupation, but because I was on a student visa, I didn't physically occupy the buildings. I was part of the support groups that brought in food and rallied outside. But I was a bit cautious, because I didn't want to be expelled from the country.

AP: Can you illustrate a little about what that felt like, to be a part of such a strong student movement?

JF: I was at the Australian National University in '68, and we were caught up in the worldwide student movement. We had the same mass rallies on campus, teach-ins, demonstrations … we were faithful imitators of what was happening in France. It was an incredibly exciting time because we had a clear and strong sense that we could change the world. It was the moment of Vietnam, we were all passionately opposed to the war, and there'd been countless demonstrations against the war. There was just a sense that we were on the right side of history — that history was changing inexorably.

AP: I've looked at be-ins, and love-ins — what is a teach-in?

JF: Teach-ins were student-organized classes rather than conventional classes. Someone would lead a class on *The Thought of Che Guevara* or *The Thought of Mao Tse-Tung*. We'd read those texts, or we'd at least listen and try to learn about those things. There were people giving classes about all sorts of things. I remember somebody who'd been to Palestine, and who had changed from being a strong supporter of Israel to recognizing the way in which the occupation was oppressing Palestinians. That sort of thing was enlightening for someone like me who came from a fairly apolitical background. So I was radicalized by the Vietnam War, and radicalized by these processes of self-education, that were part of '68.

AP: When you say radicalized, to me that word implies some kind of *action* beyond the norm — do you feel like you were swept up in anything *radical*?

JF: No, my radicalization was an intellectual radicalization. I never joined political parties — I was always very wary of political parties. But lots of my contemporaries did become Trotskyists or Maoists. After I left the ANU in '68, I went to live in Buenos Aires in 1970. Again, that was a very radicalizing moment for me, because my friends there were all left Peronists. There was a military coup the year I was there. So I was deeply caught up in South American politics, which were quite radical. These were third world politics; much more radical than anything I'd experienced in the West. Then, during the time I was at Cornell, I did a year's exchange to Heidelberg. That was in '73–'74, and just before I got there the Baader-Meinhof people, the Red Army Faction, had been active. Heidelberg was the center of their activities. But as I said, I was always an observer rather than a participant in these radical politics.

AP: What happened in Buenos Aires?

JF: Living through a military coup in Buenos Aires was scary because there were soldiers with machine guns on every corner. It was made clear to me and my wife whom I married that year, we were teaching in an English-language school — it was made clear to us that we were considered to be agents of the Kremlin, and that if we didn't leave at the end of the year, things would not go well for us. So we left. This was the South America of Che Guevara. He'd recently died — he was a presence in Buenos Aires. Many of my friends who were Left-Peronists — some of them were among the Disappeared in the dirty war of the later seventies.

Che Guevara was an enormous presence for all leftists in South America, and in the United States. I traveled through South America as far as Guatemala in '71, and most of the countries that I traveled through were governed by right-wing dictatorships supported by the United States. So there was a clear polarization. It was clear that the United States was the imperialist enemy. The line was so much clearer then. Cuba was unambiguously a beacon for people on the left. Whereas I think we've learned since then that Cuba was in some ways incredibly progressive, in other ways incredibly repressive — if you were homosexual, or if you were a political dissident, Cuba was not a good place to be.

AP: Is there a moment for you that stuck out as being illustrative of this period in South America?

JF: Well, one day we were on a bus in Bolivia and we got talking to a person who was, as it turned out, a CIA agent. There were CIA agents operating all throughout Latin America, almost out in the open, in the places where they could be.

AP: What can one say to a CIA agent in Bolivia?

JF: He was surprisingly frank about America's role in propping up dictatorships and hunting out leftists. He was unapologetic about it, but actually a really nice guy. Intelligent, well-read.

AP: And you were comfortable to voice your disdain for what was happening?

JF: Yeah. It was an open and frank discussion, of a very peculiar kind.

AP: Did he justify what the CIA was doing?

JF: Yes, he had a rationale for it — to do with maintaining order and — in his view — building democracies. Paradoxical to us, given the kinds of governments that they propped up. He talked about the construction of the Pan-American highway, the aid money that America poured into South America. For him, there was an ultimate benevolent purpose for the American presence in South America. And of course, resisting what he saw as totalitarian governments. For him, Cuba was morally equivalent to the Soviet Union.

AP: Is it possible that he had been subjected to any kind of propaganda — or brainwashing?

JF: I wouldn't call it brainwashing. He had an ideological perspective. He was well-read; he'd thought through his decision. I'm not arrogant enough to think that anybody who doesn't agree with me has been brainwashed or a victim of propaganda. People work out their positions; they work them out on the basis of their experience in life, the people they talk to, the books they read, the way they see the world, the models available to them. My own way of seeing the world is very much shaped by my own experience. It would have been very different if I hadn't lived in South America, or had all of the experiences that I had.

* * *

The terms *group mind, crowd will,* and *groupthink* were coined under the heavy influence of the Orwellian dialect that includes *doublethink, doublespeak*, and *thought police.* Elias Canetti's work *Crowds and Power* was published in 1960 and was very much a part of the literary world inspired by Orwell's canon. With an

Orwellian concept of propaganda in mind, we can appreciate these words from Canetti:

"Today everyone takes part in public executions through the newspapers. Like everything else, however, it is more comfortable than it was. We sit peacefully at home and, out of a hundred details, can choose those to linger over which offer a special thrill."

Chapter 23

Professor Louise Hitchcock

In his literary criticism of Charles Dickens, George Orwell states "All art is propaganda." If this is true, even the earliest cave paintings are trying to win you over. A highly notable early example of propaganda is the Behistun Inscription (circa 522 BC): an engraved rock carving in Iran. The inscription, in three languages, lists fine details of the victories of Darius the Great of Persia. It includes hundreds of lines of text in each language — Old Persian, Elamite, Babylonian. Darius wanted *everyone* to know how great he was. The benefit for modern society is that this extensive inscription has been used to decipher all three of these ancient languages.

Egotism and propaganda often go hand-in-hand. Julius Caesar ensured that every Roman coin had his face on it. Ramses II erected giant statues of himself throughout ancient Egypt. Emperor Vespasian ordered the construction of the Colosseum in a strategic move to win over the mass populace of Rome.

In ancient Crete and other islands of the Mediterranean, the Minoan civilization sprang up as the first advanced ancient civilization in Europe. This society flourished between 2700 BCE and 1450 BCE, leaving behind evidence of its language and scripture, artworks, social structures, and elaborate palaces. The Minoan civilization is named after the mythical King Minos, whose minotaur is said to have lived in a labyrinth in Knossos, the Minoan capital.

One of the world's foremost experts in ancient Minoan society is Professor Louise Hitchcock. Professor Hitchcock has undertaken extensive archaeological work in the Mediterranean with fieldwork in Crete, Greece, Egypt, Syria, Israel, and California. She is author of more than seventy articles on archaeology, identity, piracy, globalization, architecture, and gender in the East Mediterranean. Professor Hitchcock is based at the Centre for Classics and Archaeology at the University of Melbourne.

I wanted to get a sense of the underlying historical human condition as it relates to crowds. What would Woodstock look like in 1200 BCE?

Aidan Prewett: Could you describe the earliest evidence of crowd scenes that you've come across?

Louise Hitchcock: I would say that the biggest evidence we have for crowd scenes in my area — there are some frescoes that come from the Minoan palace at Knossos. It wasn't really a palace, more like a palace-temple. It shows a group of women dancing in a public court, and then it shows large numbers of male and female onlookers. Another painting associated — is what might be the area within the palace that goes around the central court, with crowd scenes looking on. But what they're looking at, we don't really know.

AP: And what kind of leader would exist in this society — do we know?

LH: We don't really know. We have their writing systems — undeciphered. These paintings date to about 1700 BCE, but the courts that seem to be depicted in them go back earlier, at least to 2000 BCE. We don't know what kind of leaders they had. There's a lot of speculation — you hear legends about King Minos and the minotaur, but they're classical Greek myths of this era. When you go around and visit Minoan buildings, you see a lot of rooms with benches. Writing would have been a very exclusive activity; limited to a small number of scribes and administrators who probably also functioned as priests because it's shrouded in a bit of religious mystery. I suspect there was some sort of corporate group leadership, because of all these benched rooms. We do have a throne room at Knossos, but it's through that the throne was used for smaller ritual performances, where perhaps a woman sat on the throne. Also, I've interpreted that room as a shrine for the inventor Daedalus who's associated with the labyrinth which is seen as the Minoan palaces themselves, in their maze-like layout.

AP: Are there any rituals that relate to the minotaur, the labyrinth…?

LH: Well, labyrinth is actually a Minoan word, and it comes down into Mycenaean Greek. The heyday of the Mycenaeans is about fifteenth century until the twelfth century BCE. And they borrowed the Minoan writing system and used it to write their own language, which is an early form of Greek. There's a tablet that mentions offerings to the Lady of the Labyrinth, so a goddess of the labyrinth.

The Minoans and the Mycenaeans, and the Egyptians as well…. Not so much crowd scenes, but what you do have is a lot of evidence for ritual processions with people carrying offerings. And you see this depicted in Egyptian tomb paintings. You start to see courts that would accommodate large crowds in ancient Egypt later than you do in Crete. More like in the temple at Luxor and in the later temples of Akhenaten. And then the courts gradually becomes smaller and smaller. So you have an area that would be very exclusive. And you also see large crowd accommodations in the palaces of ancient Mesopotamia, which go back between 3000 and 2000 — well, they continue all the way up to about 600 BCE.

And we do have texts that we can read in Mesopotamia and also in Egypt that talk about professions where they take the statue of the deity, and they carry it to another city, maybe on a boat, or they carry it in a procession. And sometimes they even take these statues of deities to visit other deities, and statues, both in Mesopotamian culture and Egyptian culture, they were thought to be kind of living images in that they were.... We have evidence for breath of life ceremonies just like are performed on the Egyptian king after they're dead.

And sometimes when these city states in Mesopotamia went to war, they would actually kidnap the divine statues of the city they conquered and carry them off to their city.

AP: Wow. So obviously, yeah, at that time these symbolic statues, or whatever they may be, definitely had an actual link with the deities. And so that's almost like a kidnap of an actual leader.

LH: Yes, exactly.

AP: Amazing. And so when they did take these statues and things and would parade them through the streets, I suppose that sounds.... The crowds that would gather, would they, do you know anything about the size of these crowds that might gather?

LH: It's hard to do these kinds of demographic estimates. It could vary depending on how tightly the crowds were gathered. In Crete but also in Egypt, they have large windows, which our modern archeologists call *windows of appearance* where a leader or a monarch or prominent person might appear. And then the crowd below would look at them. They would gather and look at them. And it's thought that these leaders would manipulate rituals connected with the harvest and also with production and trade, use these aspects of wealth provision to manipulate people, to manipulate the populace.

AP: I'm assuming that these windows of appearance would function to whip the crowd into a frenzy much like ... I'm sure that Mussolini and Hitler, in the footage that Leni Riefenstahl took of Hitler in appearing at the window of the hotel in Nüremberg in the big square. I wonder if the windows of appearance — is that the earliest known reference of that? Is that an Egyptian invention?

LH: Yes, and it's possible that they said something. We don't really know. All we can do is speculate beyond that. But the thing is if these people were important enough, it would get people into a frenzy probably just to be observing them, and maybe they make a gesture or something like that.

AP: And if they were to, let's say in Egypt, but if they were to address a crowd, what kinds of things would they talk about, do you think?

LH: I am not an Egyptologist; I really don't know. Possibly about the harvest, possibly about the other gods because the Egyptian King was considered a living god. The term "pharoah" is actually late. It doesn't come into use until the eighteenth dynasty. And it's simply one of the titles. It means great house.

You might refer to the American president as the White House or the British prime minister as Ten Downing Street or the Australian PM as Kirribilli House. It's simply one of the titles of the king. And the king had a number of tight royal titles.

But the thing is, the main function of the Egyptian king was to ensure that the Nile flooded on a yearly basis because without the flooding of the Nile, there wouldn't be a harvest. And this is why the Egyptians did quite a lot to develop astronomy and understanding the movements of the stars and the calendar and the seasons. Because if the king couldn't correctly predict the flooding of the Nile, they could actually be killed and taken down and replaced.

AP: Wow. That would be kind of a crowd situation, like a coup where ... Is there evidence of that occurring with any specific king?

LH: Not really, no. People speculate a lot about Tutankhamen because he died so young that he might have met with foul play, but they know from examining his body that he was in very poor health. And we also know of usurpers like Hatshepsut who was a female king. She had to be a king ... she assumed the identity of a male because the king had to be male. The king was Horus. And when the king died, then the king became Osiris, whose son became Horus. And she was the wife of Thutmose III, and when Thutmose III died, she was what they would call a regent for Thutmose the fourth. He was too young to rule. And she sort of usurped power and ran the Egyptian state with one of her ministers. And then when Thutmose the fourth became older, he was able to assume power and depose her. But we don't really know exactly what happened.

AP: And looking at more Aegean archeology, is there any parallel in terms of the leaders and any of these, or of this kind of coup situation?

LH: We don't even know whether there was a king or whether there was a group of people. I suspect it was a group of people. We know with the Mycenaeans that there was a king because we have the title. He was called a Wanax, and he ruled from his palace, and there are about half a dozen Mycenaean palaces and they would have each had their own king. And this was what we would call a city state. It would be like as if Melbourne instead of a mayor had a king and Sydney had a king and Canberra had a king. And each was ruler and they had interrelations because they spoke the same language and followed the same religion and things like that. But the problem is when the Mycenaeans borrowed the Minoan script, they used it only for record keeping. And these would be like temporary records that they keep for a year or so and then they'd throw them away. It's like how you don't keep your tax returns any longer than you have to. And so they don't really record events. They record transactions.

AP: In between these different communities that had their own rules and their own leaders and things like this, I'm so interested to find out about the idea of spreading a message, for a leader to communicate to their people in that time. Is there any evidence of how that was done?

LH: Yeah, and it wasn't always communicating to the people. Sometimes they were communicating.... You have to think as the first era of globalization in that the Mediterranean was like a network and it was quicker to travel by ship than by land. And so the coastal cities and the island cities were very tightly interconnected. And Crete was very poor in raw materials; no copper, no tin, which is needed to make bronze, no gold, no ivory. So they would have to get these things from Anatolia or Egypt or the Levant or Cyprus, or maybe even as far as Sardinia. And so they would have to have something to trade. And what you had was a lot of diplomatic gift giving to relax tensions. There was a style of art during this period called the international style where things were made in a style — small objects like a cup or an ivory bowl.

AP: I'm now thinking of stuff like the Great Wall of China and they would have a network of towers with flames if they had a warning of invasion or whatever —

LH: I'll tell you something about walls. Walls do not do such a great job of keeping people out. The Minoans didn't fortify, but they probably had a powerful navy. The Mycenaeans did fortify, and at the end of the Bronze Age, around 1200 BCE, when you have a Mediterranean-wide collapse, the walls get breached. What walls do is advertise the power of the king, and a lot of archeologists now are talking about these fortification walls as being demonstrations of the power of the king and their ability to harness resources. And it's even been suggested that there was a performative act in having laborers drag these huge blocks of stone through the countryside where people would see it in order to erect these monumental structures.

AP: So it's an ego thing. It's a leader leaving their mark, which we're seeing obviously in America today.

LH: But that's not new. It keeps repeating itself. Napoleon conquered Egypt because Alexander the Great had, and he wanted to be seen as the new Alexander the Great. So it's like not just competing with your contemporary leaders, but with past history. It's also interesting where people aim their message. Like, for example, Trump aims his message at middle of America, the part of the country that really doesn't travel very much. He's addressing a particular audience, and they're always addressing different audiences.

AP: I'm obviously thinking a lot about what makes these people just desire and really so psychologically need to, I don't know, almost deify themselves in this way? Do you have any insight into why on earth a person would need that?

LH: I really don't know. There was a Roman general Sulla who ... you had a period at the end of the Roman republic that was called social wars. I'm not an expert on this era, but I know that Sulla put down all the rebellions, conquered Rome and then he retired. And that was unusual, because usually these people don't retire. They continue on like the Caesars did and assume power.

I think it also happens with people feeding their egos. It's like the Roman leaders, the generals didn't originally deify themselves. And every time there was a rebellion in Greece after the Alexandrian empire fell apart, they would call the Romans to help put it down. And eventually the Romans just decided to take over. But every time the Roman generals held a Greek city state, they would be deified and worshipped as gods.

And you have to think that maybe that plays into their ego. And I actually did my BA in political science, and one of my professors said, "On the shoulders of every freedom fighter is a head itching for a crown." So I think there's always this idea that maybe you don't like things as they are and you change it, but then you decide you're the one who can make it right.

AP: I'd like to touch on the early religions at this point because in terms of a group, a city group, as you mentioned, that would have a king, would you classify them as cults? Would they center around this individual who's a leader?

LH: You might have some focus on the individual as a leader, but you also had deities, and we don't know so much about the Minoan deities although people argue that they worshipped a great goddess. We know that the Mycenaean Greeks, again, these are the people who lived on the Greek mainland from 1500 to about 1200 BCE, they had a wide range of deities and some of them had the names of what became the later classical deities. We have the name for Athena, Demeter, Zeus, a sort of king-god and in Mesopotamia too, you have a warrior goddess, you have a love goddess, a goddess of death, a god of freshwater, a god of saltwater, a king god, a mother goddess. It's like you have the whole political system mirrored in this plethora of deities.

And you would also have deities that were hybrid creatures that embodied supernatural features like sphinxes and the genie and composite animals. And you would also have intersex deities. There's a god of the Nile, Hapi, who had a beard and had breasts. And then you have the famous Hermaphroditus in later classical Greece who had breasts and a penis. In ancient times when everything revolved around fertility, if you had a person that embodied both male and female reproductive symbols, that made them particularly powerful.

AP: Another question in terms of these deities is like, how did they gain a foothold? How were they promoted amongst the people and then how was that then spread to other groups of people living around the area?

LH: We know that each city in Mesopotamia had what you call a titular deity. That is the main deity of the city. And then you would have other temples around for more minor deities, but each city had its city deity. I've hypothesized for Crete based on the different features of the Minoan palaces, but we don't really know for sure. But it was the same thing in Egypt, and again, as I mentioned, some of the times, the statue of the city's main deity would be taken to visit another one or brought out and paraded around during certain festivals.

There's a really famous story, a myth about how Athena in early time becomes the titular or main city deity of Athens. They say that she competed with Poseidon to be the city deity of Athens, and they had a contest. Whoever gave the best gift to the city would win. So Athena gives the city an olive tree, and Poseidon gives them a pool of water, and the olive tree is useful. You get food from it. You get oil from it. Olive oil was a very valuable commodity.

The pool that Poseidon gives is a pool of saltwater because he's the god of the sea. And so that wasn't valuable at all. And this is how Athena came to be the main city deity of Athens. These types of stories — just like the Adam and Eve story in the Bible — before you had science to explain your origin, you used mythology to try to create an understanding of your past.

AP: Humanity is still doing that and thousands of years of.... It's such a fascinating thought to imagine that Christianity has been doing that for two thousand plus years. And of course there are other religions that are older again.

LH: And a lot of the symbols of Christianity appropriate pagan symbols and pagan tropes. For example, the death and resurrection of Jesus. There's a story in ancient Mesopotamia about the main goddess of love in ancient Mesopotamia. Her name is initially Inanna. And then when it becomes Akkadian, she's known as Ishtar, and she goes to the underworld to visit her sister who rules the underworld. Her sister's name is Ereshkigal. Ereshkigal makes her prisoner and doesn't let her leave.

And there's a god of wisdom, Enki, who rescues her. But to be rescued, she has to send a substitute. So she sends her lover. This story is used to understand the idea of death and resurrection is used to understand agriculture and the harvest, because the land is dead for part of the year. Then you plant and then things rise out of the ground and then it dies again. And you have the same myths in Greece with the story of Demeter and Persephone.

AP: We spoke right at the start of this conversation about in the large open spaces that have been uncovered that we know that were there for crowds, potentially large rituals. Could you speak a little about what those rituals would have been about or theorize what they might've been about?

LH: All we can do is speculate, but they could be about the harvest, the successful planting season, agricultural season. They could have been mass marriages. We don't really know for sure. They could be about watching ecstatic dancing where the divine realm is summoned and then a message is given to the crowd.

All we can do is — base this on is art and what we know about. And also people went on.... Different deities being in different cities, people went in on pilgrimages. For example, the big temple at Luxor in Egypt was the temple of the god Amun, and people would go there for.... He was the king god and people would make pilgrimages there, and it could just be to keep his cult happy, to propitiate it.

And also the dead Egyptian kings were meant to have cult activity in perpetuity and they owned plantations. They own lands that you would have a whole economy spring up around maintaining the cult of the dead king. But who this really benefited would be the priestly class.

AP: In terms of mass gatherings from ancient times, I think to the Aztecs with their golden style pyramids, and unfortunately my image of this is formed by the movie Apocalypto with human sacrifices in front of huge crowds.

LH: I don't really know much about those cultures, but often it was a way ... it wasn't just a sacrifice. It had both a religious and a political motive in that if you sacrificed your enemy and then drank his blood, you would acquire his power.

AP: What a symbol.

LH: We have something similar in Crete, although it's not human sacrifice, but they would carve these elaborate stone cups in the shape of a head of a bull and it's thought they were used only once because all the breakage patterns show that they were smashed at the nose. So it's thought that they would be used for some sort of a drinking ceremony and then they would be ritually smashed and the leaders would obtain the power of the bull. So it's the same sort of thing, conquering a powerful enemy, conquering a powerful animal.

* * *

In Ancient Greek mythology, the Minotaur (literally translated as Minos Bull) is a terrifying, murderous creature with the body of a man and the head and tail of a bull — the offspring of an unnatural union between the king's wife and a semi-divine bull. King Minos housed the Minotaur at the center of an enormous labyrinth under his palace. He would use the labyrinth and the Minotaur as his primary method of human sacrifice — periodically sending groups of unwilling young Athenians into the labyrinth to their deaths.

Theseus, son of the king of Athens, volunteered to face the Minotaur in an attempt to slay the beast and put a stop to this ritual slaughter. When Theseus arrived in Crete, the Minoan Princess Ariadne fell madly in love with him and devised a plan for his escape. She provided him with a ball of thread, which he tied to the entrance of the labyrinth and used to retrace his steps after decapitating the Minotaur in a fierce battle.

King Minos's labyrinth is a classic symbol in Jungian psychology. Dr. Carl Jung stated on several occasions that the labyrinth is an archetype common to all of humanity as part of the collective unconscious. In *Man and His Symbols* (1964), Jung writes: "In all cultures, the labyrinth has the meaning of an entangling and confusing representation of the world." The labyrinth is a universal symbol of hopelessness and dread.

Jung also used the labyrinth as a metaphor for analytical psychology: the patient must enter the vast maze of their unconscious self to slay the monster that lives at its very center. The patient's symptoms provide the analyst with an "Ariadne thread," to guide them both into the labyrinth and back out again.

PART FIVE

Conclusion: The Ariadne Thread

As we wind our way toward this labyrinth's exit, we will follow each of the major threads of this book toward some conclusions. Here we uncover some further truths relating to crowds, power, anti-authoritarianism, and human nature. Some of these stories become truly Dionysian in nature. We will, of course, enlist the help of some old friends.

Dr Carl Jung died in 1961, leaving behind a prodigious body of work to be published posthumously — some are still awaiting publication. Jung was an early protégé of Sigmund Freud, and the two men famously clashed, not least over the nature of *libido.* Jung felt that personal development relied on a variety of factors, and that libido alone was not the primary motivator. While Jung went on to father analytical psychology, Freud continued with his own baby, psychoanalysis.

A key tenet of analytical psychology is the concept of the *collective unconscious.* It's important to draw a distinction here: Jung's *collective unconsciousness* deals with instincts and symbols common to all humanity, buried in the unconscious of every human being.

Collective consciousness relates to a crowd or a societal group, in terms of a prevailing feeling or attitude.

Jung's theory is still controversial, as there is no verifiable scientific evidence available to prove its existence. It has remained an important psychological idea since Jung first wrote about it in his 1916 essay *The Structure of the Unconscious*. The essay is in part a repudiation of Freud's "personal unconscious" in favor of an unconscious populated by archetypes. "These primordial images belong to the basic stock of the unconscious psyche and cannot be explained as personal acquisitions," he writes.

In 1936, Jung delivered a lecture in London, *The Concept of the Collective Unconscious*, where he stated, "In addition to our immediate consciousness, which is of a thoroughly personal nature and which we believe to be the only empirical psyche, there exists a second psychic system of a collective, universal, and impersonal nature, which is identical in all individuals. This collective unconscious does not develop individually but is inherited. It consists of pre-existent forms, the archetypes, which can only become conscious secondarily."

He goes on to state that an individual's *persona* comes about as the result of individuation — moving beyond the collective unconsciousness into their mature selves. He defines persona as focusing upon the small portion of the collective psyche that an individual identifies with.

This forms the basis of his theory of duality, in which the human psyche is in perpetual conflict between the collective unconscious and the immediate consciousness. In his 1933 work *Modern Man in Search of a Soul*, Jung writes: "Every good quality has its bad side, and nothing that is good can come into the world without directly producing a corresponding evil. This is a painful fact."

Chapter 24:

The Power of the Crowd

In a 1936 lecture in London, Jung said, "Can we not see how a whole nation is reviving an archaic symbol, yes, even archaic religious forms, and how this mass emotion is influencing and revolutionizing the life of the individual in a catastrophic manner?" He states that people are easily targeted with the fascist brand of political manipulation; it plays upon the collective unconscious. Jung identified the seething throngs for Hitler and Mussolini as a kind of mass psychoses, comparable to demonic possession: the social dynamic of mob and leader provided a channel for the uncritical reception of unconscious symbolism.

Aidan Prewett: So the curtains open and you as an audience member become a part of the crowd at that point?

Chip Monck: Part of the spectacle. You then may join the crowd later. But you're probably all individually sucked in by the same thing. Either the immenseness of this, or perhaps the beauty of that, or the color of this or the intensity of that, or whatever it is — that's one of the things that's supposed to unify you at a theatrical experience. You're supposed to all get very excited.

Which allows you to have purchased a ticket at horrendous value. Then I guess you become a unit.

But basically you do become a unit — when you watch something that's absolutely *well produced*, there is a draw power to it, that — you may walk away with a different opinion, after the fact, but during the fact, you're all sucked in. So maybe that's the unity. But that's what it's supposed to be. That's what designers are paid for.

AP: Is this different in a small venue?

CM: Well, at the Village Gate there was intimacy. At the Gaslight, there was even more. I think that only sat about fifty. The other clubs in the area were the Vanguard which maybe sat a hundred, and the Blue Note which had only Jazz, which couldn't have held any more than seventy-five. All of them were intimate, small rooms, where you would find a person by the name of Mabel Mercer sitting in an armchair upstairs. A huge woman, well beyond Odetta's size, and she would be singing to maybe twenty-five people. And her repertoire would have been an easy one thousand songs. A capella. No instrumental coverage, nothing. That audience never left you. After that sort of intimacy.

Dale Bell: What was going on at Woodstock was something really unique. People respected other people. People knew that they had to get along. John Morris was talking about it. Chip Monck was talking about it. Max Yasgur was talking about it. The musicians were talking about it. Even though there was music that some might label "subversive" — I wouldn't. But this was not the intent. The intent was to wrest peace from music. To force us to listen to the lyrics and come together around common culture. And not to be necessarily opposed to each other, but to demonstrate that our culture was positive. That our culture really represented something that we could be proud of. And we who made the film kept saying to ourselves night after night after night as we were in the editing room, "Let's not denigrate — let us build up what's happening."

So that you have these wonderful pieces that we found, that were documentary pieces, that really supported all of the music. I think the only time that I really got alarmed, and I remember it vividly, I think it was on Saturday night — was when Sly and the Family Stone kept doing this, "Let's take it higher higher higher," and that to me was the most kind of alarming bit of crowd demagoguery that occurred. Everything else was enormously peaceful I think.

I don't think there was a sort of mass hysteria of any kind. I know that Thelma Schoonmaker said in her piece in my book that she was scared. And yes, you could be on the stage and you'd be looking at the music — and there were a lot of people on the stage — and you could turn around 180 degrees and you could look out and be terrified. But as soon as you got rid of this notion of *they're not going to come surging over the top of the fence* — except one-by-one — you can kind of handle that, if that occurs. And there are a couple of shots of naked guys climbing over the fence. I mean, we see bare rumps doing that. There was nothing that was really alarming about what was going on. Everybody was mired in the mud or mired in some kind of drug — except those of us who were making the film. And the whole sense was *we'd better be good.* Because otherwise Max Yasgur would not say what he was going to say, on Sunday.

AP: Does a performer like Mick Jagger acknowledge the sense of power — of being the focal point for that many people?

CM: Oh sure. *Lives* for it. Look — there isn't a performer in the world, for all intents and purposes, that doesn't have the same illness. It's the insecurity. It's the requirement of approval. It's the absolute necessity to be accepted and applauded, and *loved* by their audience in its entirety. And that's why they do it. They're good at it because they need it. But beyond that … all performers are practically the same. They may address it slightly differently. They may address you slightly differently. They may be a little warmer, a little easier to work with, something like that. It's like, the difference of working with David Lee Roth, Jagger — well that's about that edge of the sword, and then you go back to Mark Bolan and Alvin Lee, and possibly Dave Mason, and you get into the desire to make everything work so well that they just become clay in your hands, and they're absolutely delighted to have any suggestion that might make it better.

AP: Did you feel that kind of power when you were giving announcements at Woodstock?

CM: No. That wasn't a thing of power at all. That was simply an informational digestive system.

AP: But surely you acknowledge that if you had said something in a different way or said something completely oppressive....

CM: Or nonsensical, or stupid, or....

AP: Then things could have happened very differently, surely.

CM: Well yeah, but ... if you take something like that on, or if you're placed in a position of that, you have a responsibility, and you have a responsibility to get anybody who's in trouble, or in strife, *out* of it. Because you've been told to. Or asked to. Or taken in upon yourself. And then there are others who use that platform for other purposes. Here's 456,000 people, I'm going to make myself an absolute idiot, or I'm going to annoy this band to the degree that I'm going to be beaten by them. Or I'm going to hand out pamphlets that are subversive to the whole activity that we so much enjoy at this time because nobody's really gotten nasty yet.

AP: What do you think would have happened if Michael Lang had given the microphone to Abbie Hoffman instead of you?

CM: Abbie would have gotten tired earlier than I did, because he works on a different intensity. I don't know Abbie. I've seen him a couple of times, I've met him — I've said hello. I had nothing to talk to him about. I really don't — it's not my style. I'm not a go with the flow individual at all. San Francisco *let it flow jack* is the worst thing I could possibly hear. Which is only second to *design by committee.* Which I find particularly painful, because what it does is it softens all the edges. All that hard edge is gone. And the hard edge, and that sort of stuff — is almost, most of the time, the thing that makes it work. "Wow. Look at that." Instead of "Oh God, three more acts to go? Why couldn't he have just written two?"

AP: Do you have to push boundaries to get the hard edge?

CM: Sure you do. Do what you're told not to do. If you feel strongly enough about the fact that this is needed in this instance, in order to make whatever you're doing *better*, then it's probably a good idea to do it, and suffer the consequences later. If your head's in the right place, if you have any idea of balance, and you know your craft, I doubt you're going to be wounded.

AP: There was an instance that I read about, where there was tear gas used....

CM: Yeah, Denver. Here's the second day of a festival, and everybody wants to get in, and there's not enough tickets, or they don't have tickets, or something like that. So they're starting to put pressure against the fences. The cops are outside in the parking lot — they're trying to cool this out and push it as far away as they possibly can. And every now and then, somebody think that there's a better way of doing it, whether it's mace, tear gas, billy club, or just shoot the audience. So they decided that tear gas was a good idea. And the wind shifted. And in it comes, into the stadium, 'cos we're only using chain-link. It's not a hard wall. With a hard wall, it would have gone into an updraft and gone away.

So in comes this shit, and everybody's really packed in rows, without freedom to move, obscuring one-another's vision. So the thing to do was, *well, let's see how we're going to protect these kids.* "Okay. It's been a warm day and you all have water. So, take the water and pour it right down your back. Make sure that it's completely wet. If it's a t-shirt, even better. Don't pour the water on the ground, pour the water on you. Make sure that the back of your shirt is totally soaked. Now grab the back of your shirt, pull it over the top of your head like this, and lie down on the grass and put your nose in the turf. Do a David Crosby. Hit the dust." And it worked. I didn't know what else to do.

AP: So you just grabbed the microphone.

CM: I think I was emceeing anyway. I thought that might work. It seemed to. Or, it gave everybody enough to do, and enough mud to deal with, or enough discomfort, or whatever, in order to take their mind off that somebody had just gassed them. We could have done whirligigs. "Let's do Stevie Nicks's all around the field. It'll go away because you can flap your wings and it'll all go up."

AP: So you felt a responsibility to protect them?

CM: Of course you do. On behalf of the promoter that hired you to do the job. And because they're in strife. So there's got to be something you can do. You can't just stand there and say, "Well, I think this'll pass through," or "This too shall pass," or something even more Shakespearean. I mean, you could do like I do in Boston, when the Stones were arrested in Providence when their private jet landed first. The Boston Garden was one of those old wonderful buildings that creaked. It was just gorgeous. So, after the Frisbees came out and the beach balls and they amused themselves for a certain period of time, I said, "Okay, sit down. I'm going to read you a very current book." I sat there and read them the entire book of Jonathan Livingston's *Seagull.* And I said, "Isn't that fun? I thought that was a real neat story."

And Kevin White, the mayor, is in trouble because his city is on fire. And he's got to pull all the security out of the Garden. They're going to have to take care of themselves. And he needs every cop he can possibly find. So as the boos start, I threw the book out into the audience and said, Shut the fuck up. And it got absolutely quiet.

I said, "I would like to introduce you to your mayor. You may have met him before, his name is Kevin White. Ladies and Gentlemen, the mayor of Boston."

Boo.

"Fuck off and shut up. He's your mayor, and you're going to listen to him, okay. Just try and have some — try and yank just a little bit of politeness. Something. Do something nice for once instead of being an idiot."

So Kevin White comes on and says, "Ladies and Gentlemen, it's my distinct concern, as I must pull all the police and security from this building. You're on your own."

The crowd goes, "Yeeeeaaaahhh. We can do anything we want to!"

And I said, "Don't tear it down, we still need it."

The mayor was kinda having fun with it, because he was getting into it — that he actually could turn it around, or he could be serious, or he could have some fun:

"So, I'm taking all the security. The merchandise, the food, the things you need, the toilet cleaners — I'm sorry but there'll be no authority here whatsoever." And then it got kinda quiet. And he said, "Thanks very much — I'm very sorry. Because they are there to help you as well as to hinder you, I suppose." And — "I gotta go. My city's on fire."

That was his last note. And he walked out. And then we waited about another hour, rather peacefully — quietly. We didn't have an opening act, I don't think. And then the Stones rolled in, in their usual blissful format. And the show started.

* * *

In March 1964, Melody Maker published an article about the libidinous nature of the Rolling Stones. Entitled *Would You Let Your Sister Go With A Stone?*, it detailed how the band had fallen out of favor with parents. The article drew serious attention and predated the band's first American tour. The Stones decided to cultivate this image. They became proponents of a generational shift; the poster boys of a culture war.

Chapter 25

A Culture War

In Germany, the Baby Boomer generation is known simply as the '68ers: the generation that defined itself in 1968 by taking to the streets and wresting their identity from the clutches of their parents. Parents who may have supported the Nazi party, who had fought in the Second World War, and who had ushered in a time of cultural impoverishment. The riots in Germany were of a different ideology to their French counterparts. And in the United States, the many riots throughout 1968 were centered around more uniquely American issues.

Dale Bell: I think it was a culture war. A war that we were involved in almost unwittingly. People in authority were not necessarily there for good reasons or because they knew more about the subject than anybody else. And what we were doing in making *Woodstock* was pushing a totally different envelope on a whole array of different kinds of people all over the country. And people who were in authority wanted to take advantage of us.

It's the same thing that I was talking about in terms of the impact of *Woodstock* on society in later years. People in authority wanted to glom onto us and to be like the eels and porpoises on sharks. They just wanted to hold on to us and let us be their presence in the world. On the other hand, they also wanted to fight us and try to suppress us.

John Morris: I think that's very true, I think if you had a Woodstock today, I don't think any of us would be particularly more adult than we were mentally at that point. But I think in the political climate, you'd be torn apart by the republican right wing, editorially and the rest of it. One thing that sums up the editorial bent was Arthur Sulzberger, who was the editor of the *New York Times*. He wrote an editorial which ran on the Monday, the day after the festival was over, tearing it apart. "Mindless, hippie, drug, dirty. . . ." Up and up and up. Now half of his news staff, some of whom consequently won Pulitzers, were all driving back from Woodstock. Somebody called from the office and read them the editorial. And they were inflamed. They drove to the *Times* building, walked upstairs, barged into Sulzberger's office, and resigned.

They said basically, "Screw you, we're outta here, that's one-hundred percent wrong." And Sulzberger, who's not a stupid man, and was not a complete right-wing idiot, said: "Well, tell me what the truth is." So they just pored it out over a couple of hours. And in the Wednesday paper, you see one of the rarest things in the world. And that is the *New York Times* publicly reversing, taking away, a previously written editorial. And the editorial that was written on that day, on the Wednesday, summed it up; it reported on the good things. And these guys kept their job. A wrong was corrected. It's not about *sticking it to the man*. It's about getting what you need and what you want, without hurting anybody, if it's possible.

Aidan Prewett: Abbie Hoffman seemed to be pushing a culture war at Woodstock.

JM: Well Abbie had come up to the site before the festival. We had dealt with the Yippies at the Fillmore East — and Abbie was looking for his cut, his piece — for his people, his movement. And he kept getting rebuffed and rebuffed and rebuffed. And finally, when the festival actually started, he took a look at it, and he worked for two days in the trip tents, where they took people who were high and out of control. He spent two days in there working with them and trying to bring people down, and trying to calm them, make them feel better, send them back. Bringing food to people and doing all sorts of stuff. The total antithesis of what everybody thought of Abbie Hoffman. And then finally, being Abbie, he went "No, I've had enough of this." And dropped a bunch of acid. He was really mellow, and somehow got himself up on the stage. And suddenly Mike Lang and I realized Abbie's standing next to us. And the next thing we know, Abbie is charging at Peter Townshend — The Who were on — charging at Peter Townshend's mic. And he was saying "You gotta free John Sinclair," who was a member of a band who was in Detroit or something —

Jeanne Field: He was in the White Panthers.

JM: Townshend just saw somebody grab his mic. No political connotations or anything, but you don't go grab Peter Townshend's mic. So he came down with his guitar on Abbie's shoulder and knocked him to the ground. Pete's a hell of a lot bigger than Abbie was. Abbie hit the ground, came up, went down to the film platform, went over the film platform, went over the fence and went the length of the field, and went back to New York. And that was the end of that.

When he was on the run — it turned out he was living in upstate New York — I made contact with him. I don't remember how I did it. I had lunch with Abbie Hoffman in P.J. Clark's. Which is an establishment-ish writer and director's bar. Right in the middle of it all, when the FBI was looking for him and everything else —

JF: He had plastic surgery, didn't he?

JM: Not that much, I knew him half a block away.

John Binder: He was still Abbie.

JM: And we had a great time, we talked about it and he explained to me what he did when he hit the ground, and on the way out. But that's the only visible example of violence at Woodstock, since you didn't punch him.

JB: I was close. I mean, I do have an ironic note about *peace and love* at Woodstock. In the middle of the performances one night, Abbie and his side gang kids were milling around behind the stage. Some of them were kind of tough kids. And Abbie was being left out of the show. Somewhere in the middle of this, I was walking backstage in the gravel, and these guys were all in a little coven talking about what they were going to do, so I just joined them. It was too dark to notice who I was.

They were going to rip off our equipment, they kept referring to it as Warner Bros. equipment. So I grabbed a guy on our crew, who was a big strong mountaineer, Charlie Groesbeck — and Fred Underhill — and I said, "Man, we gotta do something about this."

So we follow these guys over, and they're already in our van. One bigger kid had one of those thousand-mill lenses, very expensive. We confronted them and Groesbeck grabbed something from one of the guys, and Abbie and I started arguing about it. This other fella wouldn't let me have this very expensive lens. I said our equipment wasn't insured, it was rented on our back, not Warner Bros'. It got pretty tense. I was losing my temper, and this guy probably would have beat me up. We were about to get into it and Abbie realized that it had gone past his sense of humor. And he turned and looked at me and said, "Are you going to be the first person to throw a punch at Woodstock?" I said nope. Abbie told the kid to give me the lens back, and that was that. True story.

Abbie Hoffman originally had plans to distribute pamphlets arguing for festival patrons to rush the stage and tear it down. John Morris and Michael Lang caught wind of this and managed to convince him to instead create pamphlets advising patrons of the available emergency services.

Chip Monck: Abbie was one of those sorts of folk who could really behave in a destructive manner. If you're going to organize something, I would imagine it would be a good idea to organize in a way that benefits something rather than destroy it. What does that mean? You distribute pamphlets saying *Rush The Stage* — there's no more stage, no more music. There's obviously going to be injuries. There's a huge power pole at the back of the stage, which luckily was there, because when the stage slid slightly down the hill in the mud, as the towers for lighting were also moving down at the same speed, it hit against the power pole and stopped. There was a huge transformer on there. And we came in with something like 23,000 volts. Right, sure. Perfect idea. Good thinking.

Abbie Hoffman and the Yippies straddled the worlds of politics and comedy in sometimes-dangerous ways. Over that last fifty years, these worlds have drifted closer together, often unintentionally.

AP: Is there a line between subversion for comedy and subversion for more political means?

Sarah Gregory: The line is: subversion in comedy is funnier than subversion in politics.

Michael Gregory: Sometimes subverting in a political forum, or a political forum, can be unexpected, and so it's … it might make headlines more, and I guess sometimes people expect you to subvert in a comedic forum. Like when Stephen Colbert is interviewed by some house subcommittee, it's like all over the place because it's meant to be very serious and boring. But all of a sudden he just lights it up.

Evan Gregory: What I would say, is there's not so much a line between comedy subversion and some kind of political subversion. The realm of subversion and twisting of messages is rather a map of many Venn diagrams, with large overlapping circles. And there's a big overlap between the circles of comedy and politics. And sometimes people in the politics circle don't realize they're also in the comedy circle.

SG: I guess there's an interesting difference — or interesting similarities, rather. Because there are some politicians that want to just maintain the status quo, and there are some politicians that want to subvert and change things. And there are some comedians that just talk about the status quo, like, "Oh, can you believe it when my husband doesn't do the dishes."

EG: "Have you seen this airplane food?"

Sarah Gregory: And then there's comedians who like to blur the line a little bit more, and use their microphone as a little bit of a way to challenge people's social norms. I mean, it's the same goal, to basically comment on our current state of affairs, but you can do so in either aggressive ways, or ways that just maintain.

EG: Like, "So the other day, Barack Obama was eating his airplane food, see?" See what I did there?

SG: He doesn't eat airplane food, silly!

AP: I guess, what I'm trying to get at is: Now that you're really well established, do you set out to convey any kind of message ... or are you just trying to be funny?

SG: One message that we're confident communicating is that the majority of things that are spoken would be better sung.

MG: And — it is possible to turn the world into an accidental opera. No longer impossible.

SG: No longer impossible. We're living in the future.

EG: That's a principle that we've long espoused, and we're continuing to try to get that message out there. I don't think that having a message and creating comedy are mutually exclusive, so we try to sprinkle a little bit into a lot of our pieces — from both worlds. But a lot of times we like to let people or issues speak or sing, if you will, for themselves. And by kind of showcasing the inherent message. Then people can find the inherent humor, or surprising message in it that they didn't know was there all along.

> *Think For Yourself, Question Authority* was a slogan made famous by Timothy Leary in the late sixties. Leary died in 1996, but his ethos continues to influence and inspire comedians and nonconformists. Leary was a Harvard University clinical psychologist who became a counterculture icon after being fired from Harvard over an ethics scandal involving LSD and psilocybin testing. He continued to advocate for controlled use of psychedelics throughout his life. President Richard Nixon once described Leary as "The most dangerous man in America." Leary was all about questioning authority, and sticking it to the man.
>
> Leary's other famous slogan was *Turn On, Tune In, Drop Out.* These words were immortalized in his speech on February 1967 at a "human be-in" of thirty

> thousand hippies at San Francisco's Golden Gate Park. Hippie gatherings were gaining momentum.

DB: At Woodstock, we had a different message than those people in authority wanted to hear. So, whether it was, "sticking it to the man," or whether it was really standing up for what we really believed in, and what we were in the process of implementing — I would go with the latter, rather than with the former. We found our strength, we became *adults*, as a result of making this film. Even though we were adults to begin with when we conceived of the film. And we were errant in many instances, as all adults have to learn a little bit along the way.

When we found the Port-o-San man [Woodstock's portable loo cleaner], he said, "I'm so proud of these people up here. I've got a son who is here at Woodstock and I also have a son who is fighting in Vietnam." We had to remember at the time, that as many people who were at Woodstock, were equal to the many people who were slogging through the jungles of Vietnam. There were half a million young men — mostly men, very few women — who were fighting a war that we did not believe in. And we did not want to display that kind of vengeance or anything against authority even though all of us were standing opposed to the political authority that was in front of us. This was a very peaceful manifestation. A positive demonstration constructive criticism, not subversiveness.

> The importance of Woodstock as a cultural event was highlighted and reinforced by the release and subsequent re-releases of the film. This sustained exposure provided a lesson in publicity for future generations — particularly for those who saw parallels in their own anti-war movements.

Ted Leo: I've been on *so many marches* over the course of my life. And some of them have seemed so huge and powerful — again, thinking specifically back to the beginning of the war in Iraq under George W. Bush during his first term — the *massive* protests that went on in D.C. and New York. I was at, I don't think it's an exaggeration to say, most of them. And some of them were so beautiful and so huge, it seemed — *how could this be ignored?* And of course, because it's a march, and a rally, it lasts for *at most* two days. And in two days, it's gone. And two days after that, the media can stop talking about it, and you're left with everything intact, as it was before you began that march.

The actual *occupying* aspect of the Occupy movement — it's just pretty amazing in how well it was able to maintain itself, and how well it forced the issue to stay in the media, and thus the public eye. And how it enabled people — at every single one that I was at — whether it was in Boston or Raleigh, North Carolina. Of course, while I was there, somebody would drive by and go "Get a job!". If they did it just while I was there, that means it's happening all day. And aside from the fact that sometimes it would be after working hours, so that's a kind of ridiculous thing to yell at somebody when it's past 5:00 p.m. — a lot of people gave up their schooling or jobs or whatever to do this. Or managed to somehow wrangle it that they can continue to occupy these spaces so that the people who *do* have stricter jobs can be a part of it. The unions showed their support here in New York and came down, when they could. On weekends, evenings. Especially when the weather was considerably better, there were nights when it would swell massively at 7:00 p.m. And it's fantastic that that's able to happen. It was a place to go *when you could go there.*

JB: This tension of gathering … the establishment was nervous *then* because of the war, because the war was so unpopular. The establishment *now* is nervous because of *everything.* And this next generation, whenever they get together, they have to mace them or something.

AP: Did Woodstock, as a protest, have any effect on the Vietnam war?

JM: Not in the slightest. The Vietnam War had started, was on — was a political maneuver of the government. I think what Woodstock — I think *influenced*, rather than changed — it made more public the attitude of an awful lot of people. Michael Wadleigh and Marty Scorsese and Thelma Schoonmaker and everybody else orchestrated it in a certain direction; preserved the positive things. There weren't many negative things about it, and they didn't gloss over bad stuff, 'cos there wasn't any bad stuff. But the other thing was that they understood the music and were fans and enjoyed it. And that was infused into the movie. So it's a music film. I see it much more in social terms than I do in affecting something. The war went on, it ended when it ended. I don't think we — I'd love to claim that we made it end earlier. I don't think so.

AP: Do you feel that you're being subversive?

TL: Subversive... I don't. Or if I am, I feel like it's because of the nature of the oppositions in society that are drawn between viewpoints, and how the power structure enforces those viewpoints. I feel like I am — first and foremost — creating art, and secondarily, but not too far secondarily, participating in a dialogue. And oftentimes, in my world, that dialogue can become a little bit of a communal monologue, if you know what I'm saying? It can be a little bit more about community catharsis than actually specifically challenging that power structure itself.

I'm under no illusions that the secretary of defense is going to hear something that I wrote and immediately — "Stop all the wars!" I know that's not going to happen. But I almost put more value on — and I know this is platitudinous — the multiple ripple effects that happen when something hits you in your life in a way that either energizes you or helps you maintain the energy that you have going, or aids you through a tough time in your life or helps you re-think an issue. And from all of those little audience moments, things are carried out that may or may not have an effect on the power structure.

I think that many of the things that I've written and sung about, many people would find challenging and subversive. There's a well-established part of the world for that to exist in. It's not particularly revolutionary to make punk-rock songs, you know.

DB: There's a part of me that doesn't want to take any responsibility for helping to make the *Woodstock* movie. Because of what I think it enabled corporate America to do as a result of our grouping together a market, and putting it on a silver platter for "conglom-America" to feast upon for the next twenty, thirty, forty years. What it did to Warner Bros, was that it catapulted it into a lead position. And the youth market became easy prey for absolutely anybody who wanted to feast upon it and take advantage of it, and feed it, and glutton it. And corporate America, in various iterations, went out afterwards and kind of adopted an approach to this marketing that became a real global entity. *Woodstock* was the most successful — *is* the most successful documentary ever made in the world to date. It has been seen, and seen, and re-seen on television and expanded to a director's cut, beyond its original three-hour, four-minute length. And it's kind of fodder. We see it in all forms of media today. They've borrowed this kind of technique and that technique and they've made it part of feasting upon a whole new marketplace.

I mean even people like Steve Jobs were part and parcel of the feasters. I remember when the first iPod billboard went up, and it was exactly like the Hog Farm, of the people dancing in the dusk, and it was silhouetted, people dancing, women with their hair and skirts floating this way, hands in the air, sun going down behind them and becoming all dark — David Myers shooting this — it's like, they became symbols. And we created a batch of symbols for corporate America to feast upon. And I think that has led to a total dissatisfaction with where the aspirations of Woodstock could have propelled us, had we had the political mechanisms to be able to implement some of the concepts and values and the character that we all represented in those three days and in the movie.

And so today, when you see protestors, those people are in a way representing some of the values that we were trying to harness, corral, create, and digitize for posterity. Our legacy is the movie, our legacy is the music, our legacy is the lyrics. The John Sebastian, the Jimi Hendrix. Even the *Purple Haze*, let alone the *Star Spangled Banner*. It's been put on America's and the global palette. And I would love to think that the election of Obama represented perhaps a culmination, a second wave forty years later, of what happened at Woodstock. He could probably not have been elected had Woodstock not occurred, and had we not captured it in the way in which we captured it. There are accomplishments like that that I think we can be immensely proud of.

And then on the other side of the coin, for me personally — there is a whole lot of stuff for which I am not proud. That we were able to do it as well as we were able to do it. It was great that we were able to do it with the design that we had, but on the other hand it served a totally different purpose. Something we never could have imagined ourselves, way back then. So we're not — we're not to be blamed, but we're part of something, a movement, if you will — of this conglom-America movement — that is destructive.

* * *

The conglom-America movement is based in the systems of capitalism. It sees potential profit and exploits it until the resource is exhausted. Woodstock has plenty of economic life left in it. The re-releases of the albums and film and the debacle of the fiftieth anniversary concert have proven this. It is impossible to deny that this book itself is attaching itself to the very same movement. In a Jungian way, we all take part in things detestable. Our duality precedes us; we're all entitled to a little hypocrisy. In this way, the Woodstock generation emerged from the counterculture and went on to take their place in the establishment.

Co-founding Yippie Jerry Rubin was one of the early investors in Apple Computer. His image and politicism went through a complete transformation. In the 1980's he conducted a series of debates with Abbie Hoffman, called *Yippie vs. Yuppie*. Here, he stated that "wealth creation is the real American revolution. What we need is an infusion of capital into the depressed areas of our country." Rubin maintained this position until his death in 1994.

Abbie Hoffman had a difficult time adjusting to the societal changes on the seventies and eighties. In 1971 he released *Steal This Book*, which many people did. Bookstores gradually stopped carrying the title to prevent shoplifting. In 1973 he was arrested for intent to sell and distribute cocaine. He claimed entrapment, skipped bail, underwent cosmetic surgery, and lived on the run until 1980. He spent much of this time on Wellesley Island, New York, near the Canadian border. He surrendered to the authorities on September 4, 1980 and was sentenced to one year in prison, of which he served four months. During the 1980's he returned to the public eye and to protest movements, rallying largely against CIA collusion in South America.

By the time of his death in 1989, the FBI file on Hoffman was 13,262 pages long.

Chapter 26

Backstage Stories

Abbie Hoffman's status as a countercultural icon provided him with backstage access at Woodstock, even though he eventually squandered it during The Who's set and caught the business end of Pete Townshend's Gibson SG. After he knocks Hoffman off the stage, Townshend turns to the people standing in the wings. "The next fuckin' person that walks across this stage is gonna get fuckin' killed!"

There are always a few stories that you wish could have fit into a film. For this documentary, however, there were hundreds. All told, we had nearly forty hours of interview footage to sort through. We spent three days with Chip Monck; many of the stories in this chapter are his. I wish we'd had that much time with everybody else. Some of these stories are positively Dionysian.

Aidan Prewett: John, you were talking earlier about Jimi Hendrix, something with a Polaroid? I'd love to hear that.

John Morris: I met Jimi the beginning of the week after the Monterey Pop festival, which I didn't go to. But I was standing outside the Fillmore West with Bill Graham. And Jimi was coming down because he was going to play a concert on the back of a truck in Golden Gate Park. And he got out of the back of the van he was in and handed me a Polaroid, and said, "Somebody gave me this, can you show me how to make it work?" So that was my initial meeting, initial interaction with Jimi.

AP: A Polaroid camera?

JM: A Polaroid camera, one of the first Polaroid cameras. And it was just, somebody had given it to him. It mystified me too. Four of us ended up getting together, trying to figure out how to make it work.

John Binder: You should have handed him your guitar and said, "Can you show me how this works?"

AP: You mentioned you've had moments where an audience really takes over.

Chip Monck: It's interesting, the way that an audience will use a venue — depending on how important it is for them to get in, is normally the cause. It could come from counterfeit tickets, it could come from lack of security, it could come from too few entrance points, from a sold-out house where there should have been two shows and the second show should have been advertised before the first show. There should always be a gap either side of a show, so you can add another one if you're in a growth period.

One of the most intriguing — if not ingenious — methods of entering a stadium without a ticket was the Deustchlandhalle in Berlin, which the Stones played a couple of times. It usually has a bicycle racetrack in it. One of the crew pleasures that replaced the showers in this particular instance was trying to rush from the center of the floor up the curve of the bike track. Which is an impossible thing to do. It is impossible to run up the ass-end of a bike track. Yeah, the side — sure. Not the end. 'Cos it's almost a vertical elevation. I don't know how they make it. It's quite something. In the Deutschlandhalle, we were sold out completely for — I think — two nights. On the European 1970 tour.

All of a sudden, this myriad of sheets, like icicles, all tied together as though you were in prison and you were about to get out, started to drop — almost to the floor — from the roof. And I thought, *I didn't program this. Am I supposed to light them and douse them with Kerosene, or is there a reason they're hanging there?* And then all of a sudden, all of these people started to slide down it. The people who couldn't get in had managed to find their way to the roof, to slide down the sheets, and then — peculiarly enough — there must have been half a dozen people that had volunteered not to do so. These people either cut or untied the sheets, and let them drop.

Then there are the other occasions such a Stockholm. Now, Stockholm was on the same tour. Being European, of course, it's only sensible. It's basically a dome. It's not an air dome, so there are no pressure doors or things like that, to keep the dome inflated. But it's all glass and it's gorgeous. And the glass panes are maybe four-foot-wide, eight-foot-high. The whole building's glass, and it's got terraces around it with gardens, nicely planted and everything. I'd say after the first act was over, there wasn't a piece of glass to be found anywhere near the building. It must have been the same stuff they make telephone booths out of, that breaks into very small pieces so there aren't any shards or icicles of glass. There wasn't a glass piece left in the building. There must have been two dozen, three dozen cops standing around there with their riot gear on — shields, face shields, and things like that. Just kind of staring at the building, wondering *what happened to our building?*

Well, it appeared as though everybody that didn't have a ticket — did get in. I don't know where they sat, but they got in. So it's funny. The audience is an ever-changing, ever undulating — sometimes they're a teddy bear and other times they're a horrific monster. You never know what you're going to get. And it isn't necessarily the political climate of the country — or it isn't the way they grew up, or it isn't the — what they've been through. I don't know what hits, I don't know where it comes from, it just turns to — it can turn into something that's very pleasant, or it can turn into something that's absolute insanity.

AP: Could you tell us about Bob Dylan at the Village Gate?

CM: Certainly. I first met him at the Gaslight. We got to talking one evening, and Robert found out that I had a typewriter — one of those golf ball things. And he said, "I want to use your typewriter."

I said, "That's fine with me ... how, when?"

"Whenever I want to."

"Ah. Well I guess the only thing for me to do, since I work over here and my apartment is over there, and it's only about forty feet away — why don't you have a set of keys, and you come down the stairs in front of the Mills Hotel on Bleeker Street, and open the door and walk in. My office is over to the left, and the three walk-in freezers — that's my tool room, that's my closet, and that's my shower. So feel free. The typewriter's over there — you supply the ribbon and the correctatype, if you don't mind please. Here's a box of balls, I know you have trouble reading at times, so why don't you use Orator, which is the largest size for someone speaking in a lecture."

"Oh, wow, yeah that's great."

That's about the end of the conversation. Every now and then I'd find it missing, because he'd be gone for a couple of days and he needed my typewriter. It didn't make a difference that I cared about it or anything — he'd just take it, you know. So *Hollis*

Brown, Hard Rain, oodles of stuff was written at my desk. And he'd absolutely refuse any assistance whatsoever.

He said, "You can read the lyrics, but I don't need a fucking co-writer. And I'm not paying for one. So just read it, and shut up." "Okay...." Then I'd find in the wastebasket all of these crumpled up — not torn up — efforts at his writing. So I ironed them out on the ironing board, took them to Bridgehampton, my other place, which happened to be around the corner from Truman Capote — and stuck them in the barn, thinking they would be safe there. They weren't, unfortunately.

AP: What does the phrase "stick it to the man" mean to you?

CM: I don't even know what it means. See, this is the difference in our age.

AP: I thought that phrase came from your generation.

CM: No, I don't think so. *Stick it to the man* for all intents and purposes could only mean, to me, *give any authority at all a hard time*. Is that anywhere near it?

AP: If we look at Mick Jagger as an example of The Man — and you with the cream pies, and the cream pies *sticking to* Mick Jagger.

CM: But I missed him. It was 26th July, Madison Square Garden on the '72 tour — his birthday. And he's turned *something*. God knows what. We're not quite sure how old he is. It's not as though you can count the lines on the trunk. So a very good friend of mine decided that he would sponsor a pie fight. We had 250 12-inch paper plates with custard and meringue on them, as you would on a normal meringue pie. We had them shelved in appropriate cases from the bakery. We had to move them about every half-hour, because we were being sought after by security, by Allan Dunn who was Mick's right arm for years and years.

So these pies are being moved around from men's room to men's room and into closets and everything to make sure that they were still available for this gala event. There was a huge cake in the middle of it. And low and behold, underneath the skirt is an LP tank. This was connected to a huge balloon that was make to burst with the slightest bit more PSI being placed in it. And the balloon is basically supporting this make-believe cake. It was just *soupy* meringue — you might as well come out of a Campbell's soup can — that was the effect that I wanted.

I had a little squeeze trigger on the leg of the little catering cart as I was pushing it out. You can see in his eyes he knows something's going to happen. This sort of, "Oh, fuck. Here we go again." So I push this great cake out there. I'm just about ready to trigger it, and he gets it. He picks up a glass of champagne, downs the champagne and takes off. I pull the trigger just as he turns — and I end up with the entire contents of the cake on *me*. And all over all the amps. I mean, poor Rick Vandella from Ampeg was scraping meringue off amplifier grill sheets for days. Once it hardened it was like cement. And then the 250 came out, and all the crew and all the musicians, and even the people in the front row got into it, and everybody was throwing pies at everybody else. We had our day — but I missed the principal shot.

AP: Another example of — from what I've heard — you possibly "sticking it to the man," if that's even — let's throw that phrase out I won't use that anymore....

CM: Oh that's alright, I'll use it often.

AP: ... was leaving the Monterey Pop Festival with a joint behind your ear.

CM: Oh well, yes *that* was a good idea. Barbara Johnson, my first wife, and Peter Pilafian from the Mommas and the Papas and myself, decided that we'd go and have a look at a new housing development which was supposed to be as green as we are considering to be now. And I had a sidereal times shirt on, the one with the ribbons and all that. I thought I looked quite smart, and I had a joint behind my ear, that I'd forgotten I'd left there because my hair was considerably long at that time. But no mustache. That came later, after the police record stated that I had a cut on my upper left lip — I figured the best thing to do was cover it as quickly as possible.

I went through customs, and I got popped. Peter had a joint in his bag, and they attested it was mine as well. So I went through Bordeaux, which was a delightfully hard-core prison, and hung out in the corner. Didn't say much. And then Albert Grossman and Peter Yarrow were kind enough — Peter from Peter, Paul and Mary — and Albert Grossman who managed them — were kind enough as to find a solicitor, barrister, or an attorney that was particularly well-thought of in the community, and got me off. I had done about twelve days, in a quiet, rather unpleasant area.

AP: How did you come across Martin Luther King?

CM: Well, I was working with Kwarme Nkrumah, who was the Premier of Ghana. It was a strange way to meet. We'd done a performance at a very small theatre at the palace, and we'd borrowed everybody's stereo, everywhere — lining up all of these little speakers with name tags on the back so they would get back to the right people. After the performance I was taking everything down and putting it in an army truck. I had this little battery-powered 45-rpm record player that I carried with me just for the hell of it, and my two favorite singles at that time were *Turn, Turn, Turn* by the Byrds, and *Leader of the Pack*. I was playing *Turn, Turn, Turn* and this gentleman came down and sat in the back row, in a gorgeous white robe, with the beautiful golden scrambled eggs just in the right position. It was his Excellency — Mr. Nkrumah. And we got to talking.

Now there's a strange thing that happens in Africa, where if somebody complements something that you're wearing, like your belt or something like that — it would be practically expected that you would give it to them. I went through more pairs of Levis than you can imagine. So by the time I finished loading out, his Excellency said, "It's very nice music."

I said, "You like it? Oh, I thought you wouldn't, because it's so different from Miriam [Makeba]'s that you've just heard. I didn't think you'd…"

"It's very nice."

I said, "Well, the nice part about it is," taking one record and placing it atop the other, and closing the top, "it's yours." I bowed to him and left.

I'm driving out at about four o'clock in the morning, and — blaring out of this window of the palace — is *Turn, Turn, Turn.* He obviously had a brilliant stereo of his own, so he's just laid the battery one aside.

Then, at one time or another, I met Martin Luther King, because they were working together to establish the OAU, the Organization for African Unity. And I obviously knew more about Martin than I did about Kwame. I just kind of steered clear, because I didn't really know if I had anything of any value to say to him. What are you going to do, "Nice job?"

AP: Martin Luther King obviously commanded a vast audience….

CM: He knew exactly what he was doing, and he knew what needed to be done. I have a book from Coretta, his wife. When I did a performance with Stevie Wonder in Atlanta, which was a benefit for Martin. In fact, I think it was for a foundation of his, because I think he had passed by that time. So that's stuck in the bookshelf somewhere. He had a — what can you say — a dream.

AP: How did you get involved with JFK?

CM: I developed a club for a young lady in Hyannis, MA, and it was the evening of the opening. I finished ahead of schedule, and I got on my tanks a wetsuit and decided to take wander. I came up upon this netting — it was either a shark net or a sub net. There was a big hole in it, so I went through it, but I kicked it with one of my flippers. Very shortly thereafter, there was a Zodiac with the presidential seal on the underside and a bunch of .38-caliber hand weapons pointed down through the water. And a hand came up *like this* telling me it was time to come to the surface. So I did, and I was escorted to the beach and told to remove my mask and gear. I sat on a little cast-iron table of the outdoor furniture that you would have seen in that era. Somebody came out who looked very familiar, and asked if I would like something to drink. I said I'd have a beer, if I may.

"No you're not. You're swimming — you can have a cup of tea if you wish."

"*Yes ma'am, thank you.*"

The lady who was kind enough to serve me was Mrs. Kennedy. And then I met John. Shortly thereafter, it appears as though Kennedy was having a conversation with either Martin Luther King or Kwame Nkrumah. It appears as though Kwame and Kennedy were at one time talking — or it could have been Dr. King. And they said that they were having excellent presentations. So at that time I was given the chance to do a few of the presentations that Mr. Kennedy was doing.

AP: What were you going for, with that? What did he want?

CM: There wasn't much said — it usually came from a production, from camera, you know. I just liked the blue backing — I just wanted something that made you look really human — reasonably solid. It was almost going back to Broadway — it was certainly inoffensive.

AP: In your dealings with JFK — was there any moment that you recall as being particularly poignant?

CM: No, not really — I usually had my face glued to a monitor. And wasn't necessarily listening but was watching. I do remember driving from New Hampshire, late one evening, carrying a dead follow spot in a Ford car — we were doing the Ford Caravan of Music at that time — we were somewhere in New Hampshire, and I had to bring a Genarco follow spot back to Long Island to get it repaired. I heard of his death, and I just pulled over by the side of the road, and just — *what's the use?*

AP: One thing that we talked about with Pennebaker was the audience's change when Dylan went electric.

CM: Now that's a whole problem. There's two things that went on there. One of which is attributed to Bill Hanley, who was doing the audio — who also did the audio at Woodstock. There was a fault in the canon connector that was going into the back of Dylan's mic, and every time he touched it, it came looser. And it didn't appear as though there was anybody who thought it would be a good idea to interrupt the performance and change mics. Which was a big mistake.

So, number one, they couldn't hear the vocal. Number two, there was Bloomfield and Cooper backing him up, who were super, and there was nothing wrong with the experiment that he made. Half of the displeasure, I think, was the fact that the audio was shit. It wasn't the fact that he necessarily was changing from folk to something else. It's been blown slightly out of proportion. It was a number of circumstances that could have displeased the audience. The folk purist is a difficult soul.

AP: Am I right that you worked with John and Yoko on a performance at one point?

CM: Yeah I did one — the Geraldo Rivera "One to One" benefit at Madison Square Garden, where we also used the mirror as well. And Yoko came in and decided to change the whole set. Which endeared her to me *forever*. It was quite something to watch, and quite something to listen to. But — then again, I was there as a participant more than I was as a listening member. So I really had to be on my toes because she could do anything at any moment. If you thought Jagger was difficult at times! It was sprightly.

AP: What about the Pope?

CM: The Pope?

AP: The Pope. 'Cos you designed a show for him, yeah? I don't know if show is the right word....

CM: Yes, with all due respect to the Catholics — who may in fact be listening — yes, of course. The same thing with church. It is pomp and circumstance. That's what sucks you in. Because if God is not there to greet you — there better be something to keep your attention. I'm sure he drifts by every ceremony that's ever held, but the point is — he does have a little bit to do with the presentation, and how well the creases are in your robes. Or your cassocks.

AP: So what were your main considerations in staging that?

CM: It was a daytime service, so there was no need to light it — although it could have been great fun to light — there could have been pieces of steel in the structure, and scaffolding and things underneath, which would have gotten in the way of lighting a plane of fabric from below. Without any stripes, or shadows, or anything like that. So it was pretty big. And there were a lot of monks running around in cassocks, putting flowers in the right place. The Popemobile had to be able to be driven underneath the stage. The throne, which is the wrong word for it — was a beautifully etched piece of woodwork — and it was a pretty class performance. But they can afford it. It was fun doing it.

AP: What was the audience — or the congregation's — reaction in that space?

CM: It was fixed upon him — the Pontiff. Could not have been anything else. They weren't there for any interaction whatsoever except to listen to his holiness. I don't know. Not being a devout catholic, nor being *in the audience*, as it were — or the gathering, or the congregation — it would be very difficult to make an assessment for you. I can't do that. I know you want to get to the point of *how did the audience feel*, and *how did they react to each and every type of thing that we did*, but it's kinda hard, because there are departmental separations. And even though they're not written, they're definitely understood.

* * *

Chip Monck's experience in performance, politics, and even religious events highlight the artifices employed to create a feeling of reverence for the "principal." It becomes clear, then, that these propaganda techniques, employed so effectively by Albert Speer and Leni Riefenstahl, can be put to use in the services of something good. Music is another factor, a force of its own, that can manipulate emotion in a similar way.

Chapter 27

The Power of Music

Music, at Woodstock and elsewhere, is a chief magnet to draw the crowd. Carl Jung relates music directly to the collective unconscious, stating that music deals with very deep archetypal material: "Music expresses, in some way, the movement of the feelings that cling to the unconscious processes ... music represents the movement, development, and transformation of motifs of the collective unconscious."

Sigmund Freud is on record as stating his general disdain for most kinds of music. He was obsessed with understanding human responses; perhaps music presented too great a mystery. The following statement, then, is not altogether surprising: "With music, I am almost incapable of obtaining any pleasure. Some rationalistic, or perhaps analytic, turn of mind in me rebels against being moved by a thing without knowing why I am thus affected and what it is that affects me."

Neither Jung nor Freud counted themselves as musicians; their insight might be limited. Do performers have a separate insight that allows them to understand the power they wield?

Aidan Prewett: Do you feel a sense of power when performing your music?

Jann Klose: I don't know if power is the right word for it. I mean, it's an experience of drawing them into that — the emotion that I'm going through. And the more that happens, the more I feel like everything sort of becomes a channel. Like I become that — I become sort of just, a part of a bigger picture. Rather than just me on stage playing a song for somebody. I feel like I want to draw the audience in, and have them be just as much a part of it as the bass player is, in a sense — or the drummer, or other musicians on-stage. There's a feeling of satisfaction that comes out of that. A feeling of being really *in the moment*, and really experiencing every second. When you have that kind of connection with the audience — when you really feel like the room is listening — and you're listening to them — it's extraordinary. Nothing — nothing really feels better. It's a really great, great feeling.

Michael Shrieve: Music transports us and takes us to different places. I began thinking of the notes and the tones of music as invisible architecture. Literally. Because where else could you seemingly walk into different rooms that bring out different emotions, different feelings, tap into different sides of yourself or you know, heal you agitate you. Music is the most marvelous thing in the way that music takes you to different places. But you can't see it, you can't touch it, you can't taste it. It's invisible. But the notes and the tones, whether it's an orchestra, whether it's a band, a song — it creates an architecture and some kind of emotional space for us to be in.

Chip Monck: You can have a magic moment of movement on stage, and all of a sudden if you pull the right cue and everything changes to the precise color, and all of the focus is to this single entity, that's one of the nicest feelings there is. Sillily enough it can be as simple as *Midnight Rambler* when Jagger drops to his knees and takes his belt off and slaps the stage and every-fucking-thing goes red. And *only him* is seen. The belt hits the deck — and you hear this … *aahhh*. Then you know — "Got 'em."

AP: So music has its own energy and power?

Evan Gregory: Absolutely music has its own power. There's something very basic about how it affects people. And I don't think anyone would deny that there is just kind of an odd power that popular music and classical music has to kind of change peoples' emotion. So just on a very basic level, kind of taking that core principal of music, and applying it to existing material that's out there, was just really interesting to us.

Sarah Gregory: It's kind of interesting, when I read the few messages that we get, in criticism of — like our MLK videos — you have to remember that people are usually criticized when something is just different from their own spectrum of aesthetic preferences, really. I'm always curious of, if we had songified those speeches in a different genre, would those critics have then been able to receive it in a more open way. I think a lot of the time, pop music — current pop music of the day, gets kind of a bad rap from intellectuals, or academics, or whatever. In twenty years, if they looked back on that, would they then appreciate it, because it became "classic"? So for me, whenever I read criticism of any of our pieces, it doesn't really bother me. It's just interesting and curious to see — to sort of break down why people don't receive it in a positive way, because that's certainly our intention.

AP: Does music have some kind of unifying quality as well? Does it bring people together?

SG: There's such a shared culture of music. I mean, everybody knows *Mary Had a Little Lamb*, or —

EG: *I Kissed a Girl* by Katy Perry.

SG: *I Kissed a Girl* by Katy Perry. Whether they want to have that in their brain or not….

EG: For example.

SG: For example. So it's definitely unifying in that it *at least* provides a shared, like, media library in our brains.

Michael Gregory: The tough thing about music bringing people together today is that there are more and more niches of music. There are more and more categories, and when you think of everything splintering — like TV channels, for example — it's not like, just three basic cable channels, and it's not just everybody watching American Bandstand, and like, *everybody likes that new band.* Everybody loves music, but not necessarily everybody loves the same band, like they might have in the sixties.

EG: But music definitely does have that unifying power. When you think about how music is able to move your emotions when you're watching a film, or something like that. That's a very subtle way, where you're focused on this imagery, so maybe you're not quite as attached to the content or genre of the music, and it affects you on this very core level. That can change your emotions and unify the emotions of all the people that are having that experience at the same time and guide the way you're feeling. And most music is intended to bring people together. Whether it's to bring them emotionally together, or to bring their bodies together.

SG: *Boom chicka boom.*

MS: I think currently in the culture that we're in at this point in time, there are more defined tribes than ever before. In the history of the human race. What I mean by that is the concept of *it's global.* It's one world now. The internet and everybody being able to connect in different ways than ever before. It's the same with music. And so music fans of certain kinds of music, whether it's African music or electronica or classical music or jazz or singers, whatever it is, they can connect now. They can connect with other people who are not just in their home town or, they can connect globally and have places where they can share the music that they love together. And you see that in so many aspects of the music business where there are a lot of sub-genres available.

Like Metal for instance, I've been learning that it's got a hundred sub-genres. Speed Metal. Something that'll sound the same to me, I'll ask somebody who knows and they'll say, "No that's this, not that." And those people who like *that*, don't like *this* at all. So if you say Metal, you really don't know what you're talking about, because you don't know how many variations of the tribe there are. So I think those tribes are more defined than they ever have been.

Even in the business sense now. People like Seth Godin, people that talk about "You want to be successful, find your tribe." Find the people and the crowd who loves what you do. And just keep marketing to them, keep going to them. Give them plenty of water to drink and they'll be grateful, and they'll keep coming back. Now, *tribe* in the sense of what Santana did at Woodstock, we found our tribe. But remember this goes for Metallica as well, because any of those metal bands or any big group, they're the *tribe*. They're this person's tribe. If you go see Sting, everybody knows all the lyrics. People who last a long time like that bring an audience with them over many years, and they know the body of the work. But that holds true for so many different kinds of music and musicians.

If you were to make a map, a flowchart of tribes, it would be a big big task. Because there's so many sub-tribes. I think it's a valuable and valid thing to recognize. Before, in the hippie movement, that was all one tribe. Now I think there are many more tributaries to the river. That doesn't mean that it breaks it apart, it's still the river. It's very interesting that the genres become sub-genres, and the audience breaks off into their tribes.

Dale Bell: Woodstock was a whole group of people who managed miraculously — *really* miraculously — to come together at a place, at a time, to celebrate and wrestle peace from the music. And our film in its own way is an anthropological essay — representation — of how that can happen. Now, that we were peaceful, I think influenced governmental policy about an iota. But I think it demonstrated to the world that people could congregate, could become a unit, could communicate, could respect each other, and could go on with their normal lives after this movie. But everybody who was there became named as the Woodstock generation.

These people were individuals. I think part of what we tried to put into the movie to represent that was the stop motion animation that Hart Perry did from a tower. He was our youngest cameraman. On Saturday, maybe Sunday morning, he looked at the individual people who were getting up and down and moving around in the crowd — these were individuals. They were all off on little separate missions. They weren't big missions or anything else like that, but they were working together in order to step over somebody else or to move aside from somebody else, and to become part of this whole thing. Anthropologically I think it was as powerful as it could possibly be. I take great pride in being a part of all that.

* * *

Woodstock was a kind of revolution. The festival demonstrated the power and pervasiveness of the hippie counterculture, and helped define the end of the decade. The sixties themselves were filled with revolutionary moments. Many were deeply distressing. Others were truly hopeful.

Chapter 29

Hope for the Future

In the way that Woodstock was a mass demonstration of hope, Altamont was a mass demonstration of despair. This is the Jungian duality of the rock festival. The late 1960s was filled with horror, punctuated by brief moments of elation. Our own era is facing its own issues. In the political climate of 2019, we can look to other times for clues to what comes next.

Country Joe McDonald: All of those events of the sixties is the beginning of a *global* consciousness which seems such a stupid thing to say nowadays. But it did happen then. We began to think of each other as a species on a planet. It was really different than before. With my generation we grew up with people talking about heaven up there and hell down here, and whatever — and you had maps and things. But when somebody actually went to outer space, and took a photograph — you couldn't really argue about it. I mean, there it is. A globe, floating in space, with people living on it. It changed the way we thought. Everybody since then. For your generation, you've grown up with that as a given. It's not something you can — if somebody's arguing with you about that, they're clinically insane. It's a fact. And so that created a new spirit, you know. And everybody knows that, you know, we're not going to go anywhere else. So always in your mind is like — we're trapped here. I mean, the other mentality was "We can go over there and kill all those fuckers and we can take over." But that mentality doesn't make much sense anymore because we're all trapped here on the planet with oxygen — needing oxygen. So slowly it's changing. Makes everything else look ridiculous.

Paul Provenza: There is a growing audience that is more thoughtful, more interested, more willing to have a dialogue that's uncomfortable. Angry, and wants to see somebody else put it out there, that they can get behind and cheerlead. And because you no longer have to answer to the bookers at the *Tonight Show* to have a career — the variety and display of expressions of subversion are really fantastic. And so I think that's how you get into the consciousness, is just by putting it out there, and letting it spread. And we're in a position now where it can spread. I mean, Occupy Wall Street, it went global in a nanosecond. It's like, that stuff, those are *pffft!* Schools of fish. They're getting bigger and bigger and bigger, and they're getting more and more receptive to various stimuli.

So I think you can get into the consciousness now, by either conscious marketing, and manipulating, looking at what's popular and becoming the biggest fish in that school that's already turned. Or, you just put it out there and hope that those people who like that other person who you've connected with online, comes over to discover what you're about. And it becomes much more about a community. More about a community than a mass population. It becomes about community and mindsets and ideologies.

I would say that if you took all of these disparate ideas that are conflicting with the status quo, and you look at them in broad strokes, you essentially have what you see on the history channel all the time, where that big red sweep comes across Europe. You can kind of see it happen with metrics and stuff. It's fucking interesting. Did I answer your question at all?

Aidan Prewett: Yes! Absolutely. So do you see that there's some kind of hope for the future then, in terms of people being able to express... dissatisfaction with....

PP: There's absolutely no hope for the future. I've given up. I don't even have a dog in that fight anymore. I just want to see the good guys win. I'm only being marginally facetious. Hope for the future? I don't know. I think big-scale. I think Professor Brian Cox, Neil DeGrassi Tyson, Carl Sagen big scale. We're just going to be another species that comes and goes through the course of geologic time. I don't know why people give a shit about that. I really don't. But okay. So ultimately it's hopeless — it's ridiculous. We're just ants. Who cares. Let's just have as nice a life as we can, spread as much love and joy as we can, receive as much love and joy as we can, laugh as much as we can, and try and dodge the bullets, dodge the raindrops. And try not to get dirty. I think that's the best thing that we can do. Interestingly, while that sounds really nihilistic, I think that's how you change the world. It's by being the kind of person, choosing to live the kind of life that you would like the world to be like, and you manage that as best you can. And if enough people do that, most of the world is living like that. And that's really how you change the world — I think. And does comedy contribute to that? Does any sort of subversive art contribute to that? Absolutely. I think anything that subverts the status quo, anything that makes you question your assumptions, anything that challenges – anything that presents a challenge – a moral, ethical challenge that you just never really thought of before, all that stuff contributes to the need for the status quo to shift and grow and change.

* * *

The consciousness of a generation can shift at the behest of a host of varying forces. As we've seen throughout the examples of the twentieth century, the ideas that gain traction range from the most benign to the most nefarious. As Kurt Vonnegut tells us, the triumph of good or evil is largely a matter of organization: "There is no reason why good cannot triumph as often as evil. The triumph of anything is a matter of organization. If there are such things as angels, I hope that they are organized along the lines of the Mafia."

What is clear is that Woodstock was organized a little better than Altamont. But certain aspects of Woodstock were still handled poorly — the unfinished fences, the unfinished staging, the inability to rig Chip Monck's lights, food and water shortages, lack of amenities. The masses arrived, the rain hit, and everything was beautiful. What Woodstock did best was to handle each crisis in the spirit of its intended message: Three Days of Peace and Music.

After the festival, John Roberts and Joel Rosenman were no longer *Young Men With Unlimited Capital.* Their innocence and money was gone. As twenty-four and twenty-six-year-old rich kids, they had set out to use their money to fund an adventure. They ended up providing the party of the century. They played host to half a million people and sent a strong message to the rest of the world. They spent the rest of the 1970's paying off debts related to the festival. They both did so cheerfully — they had financed the adventure of a lifetime and left their mark on the post-war era.

Artie Kornfeld, having already been the youngest vice president in Capitol Records history, continued to work in the music industry. He didn't need to work too much; prior to Woodstock he had composed over sevemty-five Billboard-charted songs, including *The Pied Piper*, performed by Crispian St Peters, and *How Is The Air Up There* performed by the Bangles. In the 1980's he managed the band Survivor and helped push the song *Eye of the Tiger* into the stratosphere. Since then he has worked in a management/label capacity with artists like Sheryl Crow, Bruce

Springsteen, Tracy Chapman, Vanilla Ice, Depeche Mode, Billy Joel, and Neil Young.

Michael Lang's success at Woodstock gave him free reign across the music industry. He set up a record label and management service, continuing to deal with a variety of Woodstock alumni. By chance he was in Berlin with Joe Cocker in November 1989; they organized an impromptu concert at the newly reopened border. He has resurrected the Woodstock brand again for several important anniversaries. Interestingly, the 1999 Woodstock was marred by violence of a similar nature to Altamont. The 2019 festival has also had its share of controversy. I blame the poor timing of this controversy for Michael's inability to contribute to this book. But despite the near-constant organizational difficulties, Michael Lang still has the cherubic smile, the Theseus charm, and the iconic curly hair.

These four men laid the groundwork that allowed Woodstock to happen. They hired the best people in the business — people like Chip Monck and John Morris — and set about creating what they hoped would be the hottest concert ticket of the decade. They shattered all expectations. The organization of the festival was somewhat haphazard — it *had* to be, given the time constraints and venue changes — but it was the work ethic of this group that saw it through and made Woodstock the iconic, mythical beast that it is today. When the people started pouring in, it was the spirit of these professionals that held everything together, sometimes by a just a thread.

Outro

After spending so much time researching big crowds, I finally had the chance to speak to one myself. Melbourne's Hisense Arena, previously the venue of choice for The Who, Metallica, and One Direction, suddenly became my soap box. The reason: a teachers' strike. A packed house of ten thousand people, with maybe a thousand more spilling out onto the street. My teaching colleagues were opposing education cuts by the state government. I didn't know it at the time, but it became the largest industrial action in Victorian history. I saw a chance to stick it to the man.

As a member, I approached the leadership of the Australian Education Union and told them about the film. *Can I have five minutes of stage time?* They said yes. What happened next was one of the most terrifying and exhilarating moments of my life.

It started out terribly. I was welcomed to the stage by a silent crowd. I tried to speak, but my mic was off. Suddenly I was interrupted by a member of the crowd who approached the stage. He asked the union president whether there would still be time for debate if I was given my five minutes. "Yes," President Meredith Peace answered, "this is taking place while the media are leaving."

Then I was on — kind of. I tried to explain what we were doing — a documentary about crowds. This was immediately greeted with cries of "Too Long," "Hurry up," and even "Wanker!"

Meredith, the president, calls out: "Please let Aidan get through this. The yelling out only prolongs it."

My heart was beating out of control. I forgot what I was supposed to say next. I had some cue cards in my pocket but I found myself without the mental faculty to reach for them. They probably would have prompted ridicule anyway. I became acutely aware that every passing moment was an important opportunity to harness or maintain the crowd's attention. So far, missed opportunities.

Panicking, I tried to grasp at what we needed:

"We just need some sounds from you guys."

An implied instruction. The crowd settles momentarily. My first direction to the crowd comes straight from the Goebbels playbook: *Focus on a common enemy.*

"So, the first sound effect that we need is — I would like you all to react the way that you would if Premier Ted Baillieu came up on stage and said that he'll accept all of our demands effective immediately. What are you going to do?"

Immediately, the crowd goes nuts. Any previous dissent is washed away in a storm of jubilance from the crowd. This was the moment where everything turned — *I had them.*

"But what would you do if Premier Ted Baillieu came up on stage and said, Ladies and Gentlemen, we are going to implement performance pay. What would you say there?"

Boo. Hiss. And not just the usual stuff. There are some seriously angry people in this crowd — red faces, clawing gestures. This is a sore point. In the space of thirty seconds I've gone from a cowering heap at the mercy of the throng, to a de facto leader.

It's an incredible feeling. But in the back of my mind, I already know this power won't last. There's now a pressing urge to do everything I can to maintain it.

"Okay, two more things. Can we get a Mexican wave going from over here — here it comes!"

The wave was a killer. It traveled around the entirety of the stadium — and then straight up the middle of the floor seats. And the noise was tremendous — like a Dolby theatre mix broadcast over a thousand speakers. Truly surround sound. The terror of the prior moments was gone. The feeling had morphed into something like omnipotence.

"Okay. This is something that Mr. Baillieu needs to do with regard to public education in this state."

"Gimme an F!"

"Gimme a U!"

"Gimme an N!"

"Gimme a D!"

They roared in response. *Quit while you're ahead.* I thanked the crowd; it was over.

* * *

Dr. Justin Clemens: Was there a feeling of exhilaration?

Aidan Prewett: More like a post-traumatic kind of feeling, where I couldn't think about anything else for about three days afterward. It was constantly replaying in my mind. I was trying to make sense of it all. I'm still trying to make sense of it all.

JC: Was it a bit sublime, in that sense that it was very mixed — a bit of terror, a bit of shame, a bit totally high — ecstasy?

AP: Yes, absolutely. And coming off the stage was very enjoyable. Hearing the sound ... to know that I had prompted the creation of this cacophony, and to leave the stage with that sound still happening — that was a real thrill. And led to several minutes afterwards where I was very much in a euphoric kind of state.

JC: Wow. Yeah, *alright!* You can see how people get hooked on it, right?

* * *

Woodstock, the documentary that inspired me to pursue documentary filmmaking, gave me an excuse to test out the awesome power of an arena crowd. But Woodstock was forty-five times bigger than Hisense Arena. Imagine being in charge of *that.*

Ian Anderson had tried to warn me: *If you've ever seen ten thousand people rise to their feet as one and boo somebody — then you do sense this collective consciousness.* And so I found out exactly what he meant. It doesn't feel good. But when they're with you, it's another story.

I was very lucky to experience both extremes within my few minutes on stage. Jann Klose's utopian words come to mind: *A feeling of being really in the moment, and really experiencing every second. It's a really great, great feeling.* Like the juxtaposition of Woodstock and Altamont, this stage experience offered me some Jungian duality. Simultaneous crushing defeat and extreme euphoria.

A few months later I found myself facing yet another affront to my consciousness. This happened by complete chance — or perhaps Jungian *synchronicity* — on a plane.

* * *

Between Melbourne and my transfer at Abu Dhabi, I finally had the chance to speak to someone who attended a Hitler rally. I was seated next to an elderly woman who, it turned out, grew up in Berlin during the thirties and forties. Through the course of our conversation, she gave a human face to the throngs I've so often wondered about.

Her name is Walli. She's headed to Berlin. She's eighty-eight years old. We talk for hours. After a while I ask if I can start taking notes. I'm hooked.

In 1939, pre-war, Walli's father took her to see Hitler speak in Munich. It was a long speech, but her father had promised her Bratwurst afterwards, so she sat through it.

Walli: "He was absolutely engaging. Even as a ten-year-old I felt that. And the crowd was in his hand. But as a youngster I eventually became bored shitless. But I got my Bratwurst. Delicious."

Walli saw Hitler again in 1944, under very different circumstances. At age fourteen, she was working in a factory operating huge smelting pots to make V2 flying bombs.

One night the allies began a bombing raid that didn't let up for ten straight hours. On her way to the shelter, she heard a woman yelling *My baby!* and pointing at a building that was already on fire. Walli ran into the building and up to the baby's room. There was no baby there, but a nursery and supplies. Walli grabbed the folding cot, threw a few handfuls of supplies in, and tried to get out. The floor gave way and she landed on her feet on the floor below, still holding the folding cot. She made it out, barely, missing her eyebrows and some hair. The next day, Hitler toured the bombed area in an open topped car.

Walli: "The crowds this time were very different. They had just lost everything. But they didn't blame him — there was still a sense of excitement that he was there. The Führer really seemed to care. They were heartened by his presence and saluted. Just for those few moments, some may even have forgotten the horror of the previous night. He brought out such a feeling in everyone. But he drove right by me. I could have touched him."

What was the general feeling toward Hitler as the war progressed? "Hitler started out as our hero — the hero of the entire country. And he would have remained so if he hadn't gotten mixed up with Himmler and that maniac Goebbels. They were the real bad guys."

Walli has fond memories of the Hitler Youth. The girls' branch was known as the Bund Deutscher Mädel (League of German Girls). She became a Gruppenführerin — the highest level of youth leadership — and enjoyed activities that mirrored the Scouting movement in other countries. "I really saw it as a fun group. There wasn't too much about it that worshipped Hitler, other than the saluting." She later became a Cub Scout leader in Sydney.

She was outspoken — then as now. In 1940 she spoke back to her teacher: "If I was Fürher I wouldn't have got us into this war." The next day her parents were visited by the Gestapo, and had some explaining to do. They were let off with a warning.

> From *Prelude to War (1942)*:
>
> Voiceover: *Every day, in all German classrooms....*
>
> School Children Singing: *For Hitler we live, for Hitler we die. Our Hitler is our Lord, who rules a brave new world.*
>
> Voiceover: *Yes, take children from the faith of their fathers, and teach them that the state is the only church. And the head of the State is the voice of God.*
>
> Text on screen: *"I want to see again, in the eyes of the youth, the gleam of the beast of prey" — Adolf Hitler*

After the war, Walli married a Polish man who had spent four years between Buchwald and Auschwitz. He met General George S. Patton sometime after liberation. When they emigrated to Sydney in 1950, he quickly learnt to say, "Patton was a bonza bloke." They lived next door to Jørn Utzon during the Sydney Opera House architecture competition. They had no idea who he was until the competition winner was announced.

In 1965, Walli made her first return to Germany since 1950. She was very surprised to hear young black children speaking her hometown dialect. They were the children of American military officers.

By this time the division of Germany was in full effect. Walli's cousin had been a Messerschmitt pilot during the war. In 1961 he was lost behind the Berlin Wall. They reunited once in the early nineties, and again in the two-thousands. This final trip for Walli will be their last physical meeting.

The plane touches down. A smooth landing.

Walli bellows: "*The eagle has landed!*" She is triumphant, emphasizing her German accent. This elicits a few nervous laughs from the people seated nearby. I'm pretty sure I'll remember Walli every time I hit the tarmac.

* * *

Walli suffered through a world that was terrifying. She is an illustration of the kind of *Get On With It* attitude that is necessary to survive war. Antithetical to *Turn On, Tune In, Drop Out.* Walli's personal virtues are truly admirable, but we can hardly blame the next generation — the counterculture — for wanting to avoid a similar conflict in their time. You're not going to get through the Battle of the Bulge by listening to Peter, Paul and Mary. But don't you want to be able to prevent that in the first place?

The Woodstock generation saw what was happening around them and decided they had to stand up against it. They had to throw themselves upon the gears and levers of the machine. They did it with mass gatherings of their own design. And they did it with music.

It's now been several years since that first interview and I've found that in many ways, my own life has been shaped by *A Venue for the End of the World.* I've often found myself in strange and wonderful situations, which I'm sure is thanks to more than a little naïveté. This is probably the source of my curiosity; I want things explained until I feel like I've unpacked the concept. In some of the interviews in this book, I pushed a little too far with my questioning. But the responses I captured more than paid off. And all was forgiven, of course. This kid is curious — and fascinated.

I would like to suggest that Woodstock itself has entered not just the collective consciousness, but also the collective unconscious. It has become a part of the subconscious mythological world of labyrinths and minotaurs. The dove, the guitar, the peace sign; symbols of Woodstock. The staging systems, the iconic music, the crowd behavior — somewhere in the labyrinth of our mind, we've all been there. But if that's true, we've all been to Nüremburg too.

The modes and orders employed by the Nazis have been seen here to be carried on by others and used for benevolent purposes. Standing on the shoulders of giants like Speer and Riefenstahl, we're able to enjoy more effective, emotionally immersive concerts. But this is a Pandora's box — we continue to see the same tools used for nefarious political purposes. This will continue in perpetuity. The difference between good and evil is a question of intent. Which one triumphs is a question of organization. It brings to mind the words of Dr. Reverend Martin Luther King, Jr: "Those who love peace must learn to organize as effectively as those who love war."

Woodstock's mythology lives on. We've taken the advice of Timothy Leary; *Think For Yourself Question Authority*, and the festival has regained some of its initial sense of subversive danger. In doing so, our admiration for the participants can only increase. In the middle of a disaster area, these people created great music and formed a culture of their own. Over three days of peace and music they became a non-combatant army of half a million, and they stood up to be counted against the forces of war. The establishment was terrified.

Woodstock was dangerous. If such a gathering were to happen again outside the expected structures of society, it could be dangerous again.

Photography Credits

Cover foreground image: Jimmy Hendrix at Woodstock,
Arnold Doren ©1969
Cover background image: Balloon and Camp in the Distance,
James M. Shelly ©1969

Excerpt of Mario Savio's Berkeley Speech ©1964,
used by permission of Lynne Hollander Savio.

Acknowledgements

To my wife, Schy, who produces the film and works tirelessly to get so many projects off the ground.

To our little ones, Felix and Parker, who continue to inspire me every day. All of this is possible thanks to you.

For believing in the book, pushing for it, and working through many hours of edits, Lewis Slawsky and Alex Wall at Political Animal Press, who have rallied around this project to make it as groovy as possible.

For going out on a limb to represent me, giving me the confidence to push myself further, Debbie Golvan of Golvan Arts Management.

For their marketing prowess, Heidi Sander & Merle Clarkson.

For their generosity of spirit, Chip Monck, Ian Anderson, Paul Provenza, Joe McDonald, John Binder, Jeanne Field, Dale Bell, John Morris, Sarah Gregory, Evan Gregory, Michael Gregory, Michael Shrieve, Jann Klose, Chris Hegedus, D.A. Pennebaker, Ted Leo, Dick Cavett, Associate Professor Justin Clemens, Professor Louise Hitchcock, Professor Leon Mann, Professor John Frow.

For your invaluable feedback and assistance, thank you Belinda Peterson.

For their assistance with acquiring original photography: Chip Monck, Mark Goff, Richard O. Barry, Cherl Harrison, Patrick Dollar, Christopher Doren, Ric Manning, James M. Shelley.

For their assistance in accessing original film material, Franca Moretto, Vince Collins, Louis Mazzel, Lolio Peters, Drew Falconeer, Bill Marczak, Jay Colbe, Paul George, Bud Mitchell and Edward Folger.

For their work in capturing video & sound, Cameron McCulloch, Brice Varan, Marie Brandford, Mitchell Prewett, Amelia Peterson.

For their assistance in liaising with the artists: Anne Leighton, Stannie Ramsey, Bill Belmont, Lisa Troland, Molly Neuman, Peter Abernathy.

For their generous provision of accommodation: Sara Shein & Trine Ackelman at The Omni Berkshire, New York & Troy Pade at The Viceroy, Santa Monica.

For their outstanding hospitality in Tehran: Somayeh, Emad, Mahnaz, Elaheh and everyone at the Tehran International Urban Film Festival.

For their ongoing support throughout the film and the book: Anne Leighton, Stuart Coupe, Mick Wall, Jeff Apter, Durham Prewett, Vicki Prewett, Natasha Prewett, Mitchell Prewett, Simon Thomas, Nancye Thomas, Belinda Peterson, Rod Peterson, Amelia Peterson, Verity Edris-Peterson, Emran Edris, James Hallal, Marie Paterson, Ian Paterson, Arnold Prewett, Gwenda Prewett, Percy Prewett, Margaret Peterson, John Peterson, Gina Gallo, David Pike, BrinkVision, Helen Koziaris & all at South Oakleigh College, all at Rising Phoenix Entertainment,

Jan Wright, John Wright, the Summer family, the Oakes family, the Fordyce family, Emma Cavalier & family, Georgina Ward, Danny Simcic, the Australian Education Union, Mary Bluett, Meredith Peace, Erin Aulich, Justin Mullaly, Lyndon Stone & all at the Melbourne Documentary Film Festival, John Head and all at SheppShorts, Mark Atkin, Michael McMahon, Tony Ayres, Glenn Cochrane, Jarrett Gahan, Richard Leigh, Peter Krausz, Andrew Peirce, Glenn Evans, Lyndel Moore, Frazer Pennebaker, Glenn Nicholson, Marlies Dwyer, Seth Plunkett, Liz Pardue-Schultz, Greg Pardue-Schultz, Chloe Pardue-Schultz, Dr. Marty Singh, Dr. Jessica Welch, Denton Arthur, Steve Thomas, Stewart Carter, Miranda Worthington, Frank de la Rambelya, Peta Close, Tim Curtis, Nereda Terkuile, Rachel Sifris, Zoe Keystone, Renee Zylbersztajn, Michael Pittard, Toni Angelopoulos, Sara Downs, Meelee Chantherry, Ting Lo, Tim Carrol, Adam Plantenkamp, Michele Zeimer, Hatsuho Watanabe, Andrea Carmody, Renata Tilbey, Kay Wilson, Brian Beasley, Chris Grant, Andrew Chong, Helene Hiotis, Danny Meagher, Damien Bosworth, Jacinta Egan, David Tiley, John Davis, Stefan Engelhardt, Cameron McCulloch, Karl Siemon, Lily Rodgers, Emily Curtis, Hylton Brewer, Gilda Brewer, Renee Paxton, Ed Paxton, David Sacher, Zak Gottlieb, all at Midriff Explosion, James Watson, Sasha Mitchell, Aryou Taheri.

CPSIA information can be obtained
at www.ICGtesting.com
Printed in the USA
BVHW081121190819
556214BV00024B/2153/P

9 781895 131383